PARKER, JOHN
THE WALKING DEA
C000175182
C0000 00044 0904

The Walking Dead

The Walking Dead

A Woman's Brave Stand Against the Mafia

John Parker

S I M O N & S C H U S T E R

LONDON · SYDNEY · NEW YORK · TOKYO · SINGAPORE · TORONTO

First published in Great Britain by Simon & Schuster Ltd, 1995
A Paramount Communications Company

Simon & Schuster Ltd
West Garden Place
Kendal Street
London W2 2AQ

Simon & Schuster of Australia Pty Ltd
Sydney

A CIP catalogue record for this book is available
from the British Library

ISBN 0-671-71379-5

Typeset in Baskerville 11.5/13.5pt by
Palimpsest Book Production Limited, Polmont, Stirlingshire
Printed and bound in Great Britain by
Butler & Tanner, Frome & London

Contents

Book Three: Views from the Front Line

Acknowledgements

For decades now, the activities of the Mafia have been chronicled in a wide variety of books, movies and television series. By and large, they focus on the criminals themselves and often the Mafia Godfather has been given a misty, sentimental image, as much a part of folklore as Robin Hood, and dramatized by invented dialogue. A recent phenomenon is the outpourings of the supergrasses, whose confessions have led to a massive tally of arrests among leading mafiosi in Italy. They remain hidden away in their safe houses, and their stories have been turned into an industry.

But the Mafia goes on; it keeps acoming, controlled as ever from the beating heart of international crime in Sicily by the traditional families who still wield their power and gloat over their fortunes with the assistance of whizzkid aides with Harvard-style business degrees.

Beyond this modern, silk-suited criminal hierarchy is another group of people whose work is often anonymous, save for a few of the most famous among them. For the most part, they seldom receive the attention they deserve. This book is intended to redress the balance – by focusing on the heroes of the Italian fight against the Mafia.

Though this story must, by its very nature, be set against the backdrop of Mafia violence and global criminal activity that has dominated Italian life for a century, it delves more deeply into the experiences of some of those fighting that war; men and women who spend their lives surrounded by armed guards and seldom enjoy anything that approaches a 'normal' life. They are known in Italy as the Walking Dead and many of them later enter the gallery of the Illustrious Corpses.

I have centred the ensuing chapters around the career, recollections and observations of one of those fighters, Judge Liliana Ferraro, who has been in the thick of the judicial attack for more than two decades. Although not a front-line magistrate since her earliest days in law, she has operated largely from the Italian Ministry of Justice in Rome to which she was co-opted at the time when Italy was racked by the atrocities of the 1970s terrorist campaign, waged largely by the Red Brigades with background participation by the Mafia.

Later, she became a pivotal figure in a massive onslaught against the Mafia during the era of the notorious maxi-trials of the 1980s and as deputy and closest friend of Italy's legendary – and for once the word is not an understatement – Mafia hunter Giovanni Falcone. Eventually she inherited his job and mantle as Director of Penal Affairs for Italy.

Modestly, Ferraro declines the status of hero but her story, along with those of her colleagues or, as she puts it, 'the few of us who survive', provides a dramatic counterpoint to the recent history of the Italian Mafia, a period when it won world domination of the heroin market and became dangerously poised on the brink of new activity in the countries of the former Soviet bloc. These developments are forecast to have catastrophic effects in the explosion of cocaine sales throughout Europe and they present hair-raising possibilities in new areas of crime, notably in the arena of stolen nuclear material.

This book would not have been possible without the help and cooperation of Ferraro, and many others in public office in Italy who gave so freely of their time. It involved many interviews, on both sides of the Atlantic, the transcription of dozens of hours of tape-recorded conversations, and the scanning of more than 30,000 pages of documents of which more than 3,000 sheets were photocopied for fuller reference.

I am especially in the debt of Ms Valentine Costa, a school teacher from Palermo who apart from being my guide in her home city, helped with interviews which form part of the crucial summary of views from the island of Sicily where so much of this story is set. She kept me abreast of important developments which enabled this account to cover the most outstanding events in recent Italian history and spent many diligent hours transcribing and translating material from local archives.

While it is impossible to name all of those whose assistance was given so willingly, many of whom naturally wish to remain anonymous, I would like to record a special note of appreciation to Mrs Ferraro, Director of Penal Affairs at the Ministry of Justice in Rome (1992–1994); Dr Vittorio Mele, public prosecutor of Rome, former judge of the Supreme Court, Director of Penal Affairs from July 1994. Also in Rome, my thanks to the offices of former Prime Minister Silvio Berlusconi, Interior Minister Roberto Maroni and Justice Minister Alfredo Biondi. In Palermo, Leoluca Orlando, twice Mayor of Palermo and member of the national parliament, co-founder of the anti-Mafia La Rete party, provided a chilling account of his life, along with pertinent comments on the Mafia situation in Italy today. I am also grateful for the contributions of: Maria Falcone, sister of Giovanni Falcone and president of the Falcone Foundation; Umberto Santino and his wife Anna Puglisi, directors of the Giuseppe Impastato Documentation Centre of Sicily, a most extensive archive and source of much information; Franco Nicastro, former investigative journalist and now Presidente delle Regione Ufficio Stampa; Professor Padre Bartolomeo Sorge, director of the Pedro Arrupe Institute of Political Education, Palermo; Professor Francesco Renda, professor emeritus of history, University of Palermo and an expert on the Mafia in Sicilian culture; Professor Innocenzo Fiore, professor of social psychology at the University of Palermo; Professor Roberto Rovelli, professor of sociology, Palermo, for 'Mafia in politics'; Signor Marco Belli, at the Italian Ministry of Justice in Rome; Edda Mancini, also in Rome; Roberto Valero, in Milan, the United Nations Secretariat to the Commission on Organized Crime; and my translation team, Gaspari Domenico and Angela O'Connell.

Foreword
by
the Rt Hon. Betty Boothroyd MP
Speaker of the House of Commons

When the *Guardian* newspaper approached me in December 1994 to choose the woman I most admired, I had no hesitation in nominating Liliana Ferraro. She has been at the forefront of the Italian law enforcement effort against terrorism and organized crime for more than two decades. It was therefore a happy coincidence to discover that John Parker's book focused upon her career and the importance of her contribution to combating the Mafia, globally as well as nationally. Her name is rightly famous among international jurists and law agencies.

This was recognized when representatives of 187 nations gathered in Naples in November 1994 for what was the first United Nations Ministerial Conference on Transnational Organized Crime – an event which came about largely through her persistence and coordination.

Women in politics have a difficult enough job, even in this supposedly enlightened age. Mrs Ferraro's position as a civil servant is doubly difficult, lacking as she does the backing of an electorate. She herself has said that she started her career as a lawyer and then a magistrate in what was at the time one of the male-dominated bastions of Italian public office. That meant that she had to prove her competence by sheer endeavour and dedication – and to go on proving it.

Like myself, Mrs Ferraro had no qualms about tackling the vagaries of life at the hub of government, and she proceeded to demonstrate not merely her competence as a member of the judiciary but also her outstanding courage.

This was recognized from the very early stages of her career. She was brought to the Ministry of Justice in Rome at the time of the Red Brigades' atrocities in the early 1970s and beyond, when she began working the 14-hour days that have long since become her norm. She became associated with one of Italy's great heroes, General Carlo Alberto Dalla Chiesa, who successfully led the onslaught against terrorism and then took on the Mafia. He was promptly assassinated, and very soon afterwards Liliana Ferraro, after a spell as special advisor on terrorism to the EEC, joined the battle against organized crime, to which she has devoted her life ever since.

During this time some of her closest friends and colleagues have been murdered, first at the hands of terrorist killers and then by the Mafia. Most notable in recent times was the assassination of her dearest friend and boss, Dr Giovanni Falcone, Italy's most famous leader of the anti-Mafia crusade, whom she succeeded as Director of Penal Affairs for Italy in 1992.

It was, as John Parker demonstrates, a job which carried the most extreme risks in personal safety, and she had to live with that day and night. The murder of Falcone proved it is virtually impossible for security guards to offer absolute protection – the Mafia simply blew up a whole three-lane motorway to dispose of him. It is a burden which affects all in public life today, though none more so than those involved at the helm of the Italian experience against organized crime.

In the ensuing chapters Liliana Ferraro and, as she points out, all the others involved in the fight, are seen to live with a constant threat which would seem unbearable to those of us who are able to live a comparatively normal existence. Hers has been a life of quite incredible restrictions, away from the family, often sleeping in police barracks and working in bunkers, surrounded day and night by guards. She has known no other existence for many years now, though modestly dismisses the possibility she is some kind of a heroine. She invariably points to others as the heroes, especially those who have given their lives in support of what they all, as a collective against the Mafia, came to regard as their destiny regardless of the cost.

In portraying the lives of Mrs Ferraro and her colleagues in the judiciary and the security services, set against the backdrop of the appalling violence that has beset post-war Italy, John Parker's book is as much a tribute to them as it is a compelling account of what for so long has been regarded as an Italian phenomenon – but which today embraces us all, as the threat of organized crime goes on expanding each year with ever more frightening statistics.

Betty Boothroyd
London, 1995

Prologue

DATELINE, ROME 29 MARCH 1994

It is the day of the Italian general election. The Fiats and the Alfa Romeos are dashing around as best they can in the suicidal traffic, horns are hooting louder than ever and there is a general air of excitement because, whatever happens, politics here will never be the same again. Today, I am meeting Liliana Ferraro, the inheritor of a dramatic legacy, successor to Italy's most famous Mafia hunter and hero, Giovanni Falcone, and like most of the courageous anti-Mafia crusaders, she lives with the constant threat of assassination.

That threat has been with her for many years now and during that time she has lost some of her best friends and finest colleagues, shot or blown up in the bloodiest era of Mafia violence in Italian history.

As I stroll along the banks of the Tiber on my way to her office, a thought strikes me: How will the Mafia vote today? I ponder that question as I turn into Via Arenula, passing through a ring of Carabinieri in their bullet-proof vests, fingers on the triggers of their machine guns, to begin the security procedure to gain admission to the palatial building that houses the Ministry of Justice where Liliana Ferraro spends most of her waking hours.

At first glance, the voting intentions of a collection of hoods, extortionists, dope dealers and murderers might not seem important. In Italy it is, and for the last forty-five years the political colour of the nation and the balance of power in more than fifty tenuous administrations has been influenced by the support the Mafia has marshalled behind MPs from Sicily and southern Italy.

Tomorrow Italy's politics will have changed for good. Silvio Berlusconi, the media tycoon, is set to become the new Prime Minister. It is a miracle, everyone says, because five months ago he did not even have a political party. The Christian Democrats, who have dominated Italian politics since they took power with the clandestine backing of the CIA after the last war in a curious deal that gave the Mafia political legitimacy, are decimated.

One third of the members of the previous parliament have been caught up in the wave of corruption scandals which has hit the Italian political and business establishment. Hundreds have been arrested and there are those who will say that Liliana Ferraro must bear some of the responsibility for this. She was at the side of the investigative judge, Giovanni Falcone, when he started it all a decade earlier, delving deep into secret areas of Italian life that Mafia chieftains would murder to keep hidden.

I pass through the entrance to the Ministry of Justice, through a turnstile and then an X-ray machine like they have at airports. I am checked for weapons. My identity is verified by passport, driving licence and credit cards. Visitors who obtain a prearranged permit to see Liliana Ferraro must proceed through these checks and then pass through to a reception room to be met by a large bodyguard, six-foot-six at least. He indicates that I should follow him along the marble-floored corridors to the lift, and we proceed to the fourth floor.

Seated on a couch in an ante-room, I notice cameras positioned at both ends of the room peering down upon me and the significance of them becomes apparent when I am ushered into the inner sanctum, reached through double-locked doors and accessed by punching a special security code into the computerized system, which is changed frequently.

The visitor is announced by intercom and observed throughout on internal video monitors. Liliana Ferraro, looking at the security screen on her desk, must give final approval for the visitor to enter.

Finally I reach her, in the spacious office formerly occupied by Giovanni Falcone before she succeeded him in June 1992.

In this wide-ranging and high level position she is answerable directly to the Minister of Justice and has responsibility for liaison with the Supreme Court, the judiciary, the magistrature, the security services, the secret services and the police.

It was a job she accepted knowing full well her chances of surviving to die a natural death were not good. Virtually without exception, her predecessors who have occupied positions in the foreground of the fight against the Mafia have been assassinated.

She had been Falcone's deputy and they had spent many, many hours in that office discussing their work. The room is just as he left it, and she had permission from his family to leave his personal belongings, even down to a collection of ornamental porcelain ducks, set out on top of one of the bureaux.

Liliana Ferraro, an attractive woman in her late forties, operates in a very masculine world but her only apparent concessions to it are her toughness and her smoking habits; she incessantly draws on pungent Italian cheroots. She is a woman of courage, a civil servant whose dedication to her job goes well beyond the call of duty. She sees it not as a job but as her destiny. It becomes very clear that no woman, no man, would put themselves at such risk for the sake of a mere career.

Her face beamed a large smile as I walked into her office, warm and welcoming. She stubbed the remains of a cheroot into the ashtray on her modest desk and fumbled for a replacement which she lit immediately. She coughed loudly and the light on my tape recorder which I had just switched on flickered. She apologized and began talking, about herself, her job, the Mafia, corruption and Italy itself, on the brink of political upheaval.

She speaks very good English which is not an especially common attribute in Italy, but then neither is the speaking of Italian especially common in Britain. She laughed out loud when I mentioned it and seemed to enjoy any opportunity to relax from seriousness, however briefly.

I asked her about fear and she turned her head to one side for a moment, as if taking a gentle blow to the chin, paused to blow the smoke from another inhalation into the air, then waved her hand dismissively: 'If you thought about it, it would grip your thoughts permanently until it took control and you could never do the job. No human being can say they are without fear, but what I do is like a habit. It is something that I believe in, and so I must go on. And when I think about the risks, the possibility that I might be shot or blown up, I then think of others in the front line of war who are in greater danger than myself. I am not a hero; others and my dead colleagues are the heroes.'

She tries not to dwell upon the threat to her life. It is there not simply because she is in the command centre of the battle against crime. She is part of a significant chapter in Italian history which is as much about the culture of the Mafia and its deep-seated position in Italian society as it is about crime itself.

We sat discussing recent events in Italy during the first of our meetings in the late afternoon, and on into the evening. She told me that she knew personally many of the magistrates, judges, policemen and politicians who were murdered in recent times. For her, and those many others who courageously take up their positions in the war against the Mafia, any vestige of normal life is sacrificed to an existence spent in bunker-like conditions sleeping in police barracks with round-the-clock protection, in which few social pleasures can be enjoyed.

That is the irony of Ferraro's life. In a supermarket no one would give her a second glance. She is an elegant woman, gregarious, and enjoys entertaining but has few opportunities to do so. Who wants to take the risk of sitting down to dinner with Liliana Ferraro?

Certainly, you would never see her in a supermarket, or catch sight of her on the streets of Rome. She can never set foot outside her office or apartment without her heavily armed bodyguards. The normal pleasures of life that other women like her take for granted – dining out, going to the theatre or just for a casual stroll – are luxuries seldom enjoyed.

When she does go out, she is bustled quickly into her waiting armour-plated car to avoid possible snipers and her motorcade races through traffic with sirens blaring. When she takes a break, it is far away, with advance security arrangements. She was married once, to another magistrate, and the life they led contributed to their eventual parting. She is glad now that she did not have children, because they too would be in mortal danger.

Like other judges involved in this work, when she travels in Italy she often stays in the deep confines of a military compound. Nerves of steel are an absolute requirement, although beneath the strong facade of this woman, the worry lines show. Though she dismisses fear as a preoccupation, the knowledge that her predecessors have been savagely murdered by the Mafia hangs like a great, dark cloud over her.

Though traditionally women have not been direct targets of the Mafia, because they are put on a pedestal in the framework of family values, it will not deter them in her case. 'Yes, I have fear,' she tells me. 'Who could not have fear when they have witnessed, as I have done, the terrible carnage inflicted upon so many of my colleagues these past two decades? I try to keep it in perspective, retaining a balance between fear and conviction. I have to believe in the job, otherwise I could not live in this situation. My fear is like a film where the camera gives a faded shot. It's not immediately present, but always there, in the background.'

Her responsibilities cover management and strategy in the war against organized crime. Her office is the link between government and the judiciary. She is involved in the creation and the interpretation of new laws, and in liaison with international groups, the European Community, the United Nations and with the governments of countries where criminal activities and money laundering may be linked to the Italian Mafia.

She is concerned with laws governing civil rights and was a key figure in the preparation of Italy's proposals for a United Nations War Crimes tribunal in the former Yugoslavia. She has been involved in the legal discussions concerning the recent attack on corruption in Italian public life and when I met her she was in the middle of arranging an international conference on organized crime, under the auspices of the United Nations.

It is a substantial role, controlling a Civil Service department of diverse interests. But the fight against the Mafia remains an overriding preoccupation, a seemingly impossible task, battling against a criminal influence embedded in Italian society and whose tentacles – the word is right because the Italians call the Mafia the Octopus – spread world-wide and whose complexities are far, far greater than the popular image gained from fiction and Hollywood myth.

Liliana Ferraro is not dealing with folk heroes. The men she chases are vicious, foul gangsters who also happen to be multi-billionaires and have bought, blackmailed and murdered their way into the highest levels of political and commercial influence. For this reason, no one in the international fight against organized crime, from Scotland Yard to the FBI, doubts the courage of Ferraro. She was given a hero's welcome, loud cheers and applause, when in 1993 she attended an anti-Mafia summit meeting of European and US enforcement officers at Arles, France.

She has tasted success and saw the arrests of several big Mafia chieftains not long before I visited her, but she has no illusions about the job at hand. In fact, she is fearful that the success itself leads politicians and people to believe that the Mafia is beaten. It is not. She is convinced that despite the recent campaigns against it, the Mafia has already regrouped. It recovers quickly, just as it always has, and even those Mafia chiefs in prison continue to run their empires with impressive continuity.

Today, they are not merely criminals. They control a financial might that world banking officials secretly fear because of the power that lies behind such incalcuable amounts of dollars.

Ferraro also expects the Mafia to try to take advantage of the political upheaval in Italy. They are past masters at using the cover of national diversion to bolster their own position. This has happened before, during the seventies when the Red Brigades were the scourge of Italian life and locked up the attentions of the military and the police, the Mafia acquired new strengths which were soon to become apparent in the explosion of the international trade in heroin which it dominated.

As we talked, the result of the election was unknown and the nature of the new political alliance about to gain power obviously caused her some personal concern. She waved it aside. She could not, or would not guess at what might happen to her personally in the new administration. It would obviously be immersed in attempting to live up to election promises and tackling the desperate state of the Italian economy. The war on the Mafia might be destined to drop down the list of priorities for some time to come.

The fact remains that nearly 1,500 businessmen, politicians and civil servants had been arrested in the previous nine months and another 3,000 had received warrants calling them in for questioning. Five former prime ministers including the longest serving of all, Giulio Andreotti, were interviewed. Andreotti, Italy's most prominent politician of the last half century, himself faced accusations of having Mafia connections.

To the exasperated Italian public, the sight of ministers and MPs being accused of graft at a time when so many were being thrown out of work or forced to accept lower pay for longer hours, was simply too much. A change was certain on that day. And perhaps it would hold implications for Liliana Ferraro, too . . .

BOOK ONE

The History

The Mafia grew out of Sicilian culture during past eras of oppression and neglect . . . it came from the middle classes faced with the duality of tyrannical landlords and poverty among our communities. Once the Mafia meant protection and a certain kind of justice. Then the rules changed and it degenerated into outright criminality.

Professor Francesco Renda, emeritus professor of history, University of Palermo, to author, 1994

CHAPTER ONE

Corruption and Violence Grew Out of a Culture of Consent

Like many of Italy's most famous Mafia fighters, Liliana Ferraro hails from a region which was one of the traditional strongholds of the criminal organizations which have perpetrated such violence and social disruption upon her nation. 'I was born in Salerno, which was then an absolute jewel of the Campania coastline which has always been so popular with visitors,' she told me. 'When I was a young girl it was a beautiful little town, very clean and whimsical. The sun was always shining, the people friendly and it was in that era when crime and the Mafia were still a distant vision for local families, something we knew existed but seldom touched us.'

Today, as visitors to that most popular of holiday resorts along the spectacular coastline between Naples and Salerno will know, the demands of modern tourism and housing needs have brought heavy development. Naples and Salerno are virtually linked by endless lines of white painted houses clinging precariously to the rocky facades of the deep gorges of the Neapolitan coast. It is a region, like Sicily, that is steeped in dramatic criminal tradition. 'We always knew there was this criminal organization, known as the Camorra, one of the major Mafia groups, in the background of our lives,' said Ferraro. 'But at the time, it did not confront us on a daily basis. My grandfather who was a pharmacist and my father who was in commercial activity used to speak of it. But by and large we were untouched by it. Mainly, the communities around the trading centres, like the food markets and the ports of Naples, were most affected. These were the areas controlled by the Mafia and we knew that certain towns, certain areas were in the total grip of the criminals but it was not so open and widespread as it is today. These were the traditional heartlands from which today's Mafia grew, although of course we have to go back much further in history to discover the origins.'

The Mafia's infiltrations into Italian life go back centuries and grew from a curious paradox of fear and consent. The criminals were protected by the age-old tradition that exists in Mafia-controlled communities – *omertà*, the code of silence, bought by patronage and maintained by ruthless violence and vendetta killings. No one sees anything. No one hears anything. No one tells anything. And only in comparatively recent times, in the past few years, has this attitude begun to change.

'It is in our distant past that any account of the activities of the modern Mafia must begin,' said Professor Francesco Renda, professor emeritus of history at the University of Palermo. 'The attitude that has fostered the Mafia for more than a century is buried in our history, but more precisely, in our culture.'

Professor Renda was one of the speakers at a conference on the subject of the Mafia in Sicilian culture which I attended in Palermo, in April 1994. The hall was packed to overflowing. People from all walks of life and age groups came to listen and contribute their views. The event fell almost exactly 100 years after the first mass trials of Mafia criminals occurred, and with all their personal experiences of the killings and the rackets that go on to this day in their midst, it seemed curious that so many people should gather in a communal contemplation of their troubles.

It was a kind of mass wringing of hands: they know what the problem is, they know what is needed, but they do not know how it can be solved, because still there are sections of the community – and politics – which continue to foster the Mafia. And as a young girl student said from the floor, 'It is all very well to say we can fight them. En masse, in demonstrations, we can vent our feelings. But as individuals when we are looking for work, or voting, or running a business, it is impossible and dangerous. We are likely to be killed.'

And so, Professor Renda insists that we must travel back through time to discover the roots of the Mafia, and to understand how an organization such as this, which grew into a clinical killing machine and a huge financial conglomerate, can flourish and operate in a modern society.

The 'history' goes back to the Middle Ages when the brigands who were the modern Mafia's ancestors had a reputation among the masses that, in fact, could be compared then to the legend of Robin Hood. Emotional Italian artists of the fifteenth and sixteenth centuries and beyond portrayed the *banditti* as heroes, fighting for the oppressed peasantry, though the reality was rather different.

Unlike Professor Renda, many eminent chroniclers of the Mafia insist that it is too contrived to seek explanations in history for the Mafia's grip on Italian life and yet it is also far too simplistic to dismiss its members as a huge gang of sadistic, violent, feuding, cut-throats. They are all of that, and more, yet they are treated with subservience by large sections of the community. Deference to the Mafia became, through decades of weak government and complicity from politicians, a way of life. The Mafia is feudal, and its leaders come from the middle and upper classes.

Who are they? The question has been asked time and time again down the ages. As one Italian historian enigmatically wrote some years ago, 'The Mafia is everywhere and nowhere.'

He did not mean they were an elusive, anonymous, secretive bunch of crooks who hid from the law, dodged officialdom and kept out of sight. That has never been true of the Mafia. Everything they do is well known. They are bold and upfront and the activities of their leaders have been obsessively chronicled down the ages like no other group of people in history, with the exception of European royalty.

The Mafia has always been in league with its nation's rulers but the only promise it will make is that if things do not go its way, someone will end up dead. It is involved in big business but never signs a contract. It has bank accounts and sleeping-partner investments in major cities and financial centres around the world containing so much money that it is no exaggeration to say that it could manipulate an international currency crisis.

The law enforcers and the politicians even know who 'they' are: a remarkably small number of people at the core who rule by their own traditions and rituals and an army of perhaps 100,000 men operating on a strictly territorial basis.

The Neapolitan Mafia, the Camorra, is the one which operates in Liliano Ferraro's region. 'My modest upbringing was quite typical of life in provincial Italy of the south, where religion and family values were overbearingly important. I suppose we were edging towards a post-war middle class which provided us with a comparatively decent standard of living and education,' she said.

In her childhood, the Salerno area was a fairly law-abiding place and did not have the reputation the Neapolitan region has today as one of the worst centres of criminality. As Ferraro acknowledges, the criminals were always present and anyone in business in the Camorra territory then, as now, was faced with not just the taxes of local and state government, but the unofficial tax paid for so-called protection.

The system which became embedded in Italy's culture and exploded into the political fiasco that sparked the 1994 general election is perhaps no better described than in a passage from an essay by Mr S. Merlino in the *Political Science Quarterly* published in September 1894. It provides an easy insight into what was to become the launch pad for modern-day Mafia activities:

> A traveller landing in Naples might see, as soon as he stepped ashore, a mysterious personage approach the boatman and quietly receive from him a copper coin. Who was this man, comparatively well dressed, adorned with jewellery, who came forward with the air of a master, claimed his due and received it without uttering a single word? If the traveller should have put the question to the boatman, he would have been told, the man was 'the Camorrist'. On arriving at the hotel, preceded by the porter with his luggage, the traveller would notice a second individual, equally mysterious and taciturn to whom the porter – or, if there were two, each of them – handed with

> evident submissiveness again, a coin. On further inquiry, the traveller would be given the same unsatisfactory answer: 'It is the Camorrist.' On taking a cab, a similar incident would occur and so on through a tour of the town. At railway stations, at custom houses, at street corners, in coffee houses and taverns, in gambling dens, the Camorrist levied taxes on the business and pleasures, even of the poor. His functions might appear successively as those of the policeman, the justice of the peace, the broker and the money changer and many others. Who, then, was the Camorrist? And who gave him the authority for his acts? The answer is that he is a member of a secret association and that the power he wields was conferred by nobody, merely assumed. Whatever illegality there was in the fact of the existence of the Camorra was practically obviated by custom and the acquiescence of the government. The Camorra, indeed, was almost a branch of government . . . though it acted quite independently of government and rather as its rival . . .

The Camorra, as Mr Merlino pointed out back in 1894, was a localized grouping under the umbrella of the wider organization known as the Mafia (then spelled as Maffia). And by the middle of the nineteenth century it was being described as a secret society and already being exported to the United States with the mass immigration of Italians, Sicilians and other Europeans, where it became known as the Black Hand.

The regional geography of the Mafia in Italy itself has altered little since then and an explanation is perhaps necessary for those not familiar with the Mafia's structure to clear up the often mistaken interpretation of Mafia and Cosa Nostra as being one and the same, an all-embracing entity.

Although the term Mafia is widely applied to criminal and even social groups – the Russian Mafia, the Fashion Mafia or the Cambridge Mafia – in Italy it is a term which describes a cartel of four groups and Ferraro can quote the modern statistics which demonstrate the power they wield.

The Cosa Nostra, based in Sicily, is by far the most important, powerful and ruthless. It grew on a island which today has a population of just over 5 million, with 390 municipalities, though the Cosa Nostra more than any other Mafia group has spread its representation right across Italy and throughout the world, often in league with local criminal organizations. Its structure is pyramidal and today consists of 180 principal families with 5,000 members at its core, controlling an estimated army of perhaps 15,000 'soldiers' and an unknown number of clandestine figures embedded in Italian life. Membership is by invitation only!

The Cosa Nostra moves with the market, trades in everything that it can earn from, ranging from drugs to arms, and controls a dangerously large amount of money circulating in the international banking system.

The Camorra, next in the order of importance to the Sicilians, was established in and around Naples. It was born out of a collection of gangs who by the middle of the nineteenth century openly involved themselves in local protection rackets, smuggling, building work and parts of the farming industry and, more recently, became involved in international organized crime as their affiliation with the Cosa Nostra grew stronger. Today, there are 100 Camorra clans, with approximately 7,000 core members and many thousands of affiliates operating in the Campania region, with its population of 5.7 million and 549 municipalities. The Camorra structure is less regimented than the Cosa Nostra although it has long since extended its activities far beyond regional or national borders.

Next is the group known as the 'Ndrangheta, which sprung initially from the bandits who used to roam the mountainous villages of Calabria at the very toe of the Italian boot. In modern times, the 'Ndrangheta became best known for kidnappings – one of its victims was the grandson of the oil magnate John Paul Getty – an enterprise so successful and lucrative that the Calabrian Mafia established a base in Milan where many abductions occurred, providing huge ransoms which funded other criminal activities.

The fortune it derived from kidnapping helped establish the 'Ndrangheta among the Mafia's leading arms dealers and today they are firmly entrenched in that business, along with other major interests, especially money laundering. Of all the Mafia groups, it is the one which is often in closest alliance with the Cosa Nostra.

The fourth band, the newest and least known, has provided some of the Mafia's most violent men. Centred on the region of Puglia towards the heel of the boot, notably in the towns of Bari, Brindisi and Lecce, they are known as the United Holy Crown (*Sacra Corona Unita*) and because of the remoteness of the south-eastern coastline, secured their fortune largely from contraband, cigarette smuggling and lately the international arms trade.

Each group has its own provincial 'commission', a council of Mafia chieftains whose basic role is to divide up the areas of operation and take major decisions such as the elimination of those who step out of line.

The more romantic images of the Mafia come from the past. On mainland Italy, in the Neapolitan kingdoms, the largely oppressed, impoverished peasantry came to rely on the protection and help of the *banditti*, which is recorded in contemporary accounts.

The Sicilian Mafia could go back further in an appalling historical catalogue of oppression by barbaric invaders. The island has been sacked and possessed by just about every nation that had access to the Mediterranean since pre-Roman times and its fine, if crumbling architecture and superb archaeological sites reveal many clues to its colourful past.

The Phoenicians, the Greeks, Carthaginians, Romans, Normans, Vandals, Arabs, Germans and Spanish all left their mark. For two millennia the island remained under the boot of devastating foreign rulers until Giuseppe Garibaldi and his army of Red Shirts conquered Sicily and Naples for the new unified kingdom of Italy in 1860. It was the probable starting point for the Mafia as we know it today, Garibaldi having gained the support of local brigands by authorizing 'robberies, arson and poisoning' to fight the remaining Bourbon kings.

Some writers have put the starting point even earlier, claiming that the Sicilian Cosa Nostra began as a resistance force against invaders as early as the ninth century, a theory which had been dismissed by modern Italian historians who say this was merely an attempt to give the traditions of Cosa Nostra some credence and respectability.

But there is little doubt that the forefathers of the present-day Cosa Nostra were the tribal leaders who were given unofficial control of the island provinces by a succession of absentee rulers. As the rest of Europe and the Italian mainland prospered through the Renaissance, Reformation, colonialism and capitalism, Sicily remained a backwater of oppression of a unique kind, with its various invaders happy to leave control in local hands provided the supplies of sulphur, rock salt and grain from the fertile Sicilian soil continued to be shipped regularly from the port of Palermo.

The word 'maffia' has been variously traced to a number of origins but the most likely is its use in 1799 in connection with a group of Freemasons in a Sicilian village. Certainly, there is ritual and masonic-like initiation ceremonies attached to the Mafia as it exists today.

The first recorded use of the word to describe a collective is in reports of Garibaldi's invasion, when he was supported by a local force of 2,000 peasants who were described as '*squadri della maffia*'. Garibaldi promised them that their years of enslavement were at an end. Unification would bring great social change to Sicily; life would be at last tolerable. But nothing happened.

Sicily was ignored and left to its own devices for years and the attitudes of the mainland rulers were initially no different from conquerors of the past. They saw the island people as a separate race, an attitude still prevalent in the north of Italy today.

One other clue to the emergence of the term Mafia appeared in 1863, when a celebrated play entitled *I Mafisusi della Vicaria* was performed. It described the life in Palermo prison in which there existed a '*consorteria mafiusa*' – a secret society of criminals, with a hierarchy which had its own rules, ran the prison by bribing or scaring the guards into submission, and allowed prisoners to receive its benefits only after an initiation ritual in which they had to swear an oath of allegiance.

Outside, that same hierarchy eventually took control. The Mafia quickly grew rich and powerful, and was used by land barons and the Catholic Church to keep control over the peasants and protect their interests. Gradually, politicians, too, began to court their support.

The condition of Sicilian people and those in the south of Italy barely improved and so the people, too, began to look to the Mafia for leadership and protection. The social attitude which had shown itself over the years as a general distrust and disrespect for outside authority became one of the basic elements of the present situation.

This was made quite clear at the debate I attended in 1994. Speakers acknowledged that even today, villages and towns are still dominated by Cosa Nostra families whose influence is even greater than the church and certainly greater that the state. 'Who will look after us now?' asked the educated young woman with true apprehension when the Madonia chieftain was arrested. 'When he was around, we did not lack anything.'

It was, said Professor Bartolomeo Sorge, director of the Institute of Political Education which organized the Palermo conference, an illuminating comment and one that highlighted not only feelings that were common in Sicily but the inherent problem facing those fighting the Mafia. 'These peculiarities of the Sicilian character, and to a lesser degree in the south of Italy, are linked inextricably to the complexities which embrace our culture, our economic well-being and our politics. The people know that these men are today connected with criminal activity, drugs, murder . . . yet the Mafia has for years been fostered and protected by Sicily, its people and its politicians and only now is that attitude slowly beginning to change and becoming more aligned to the national Italian trend of abhorrence.'

There are those who believe the modern Mafia has already broken that bond with the people by its very actions. In the era of collaboration with the State, which began in the 1980s, some of the secrets of Mafia tradition emerged for the first time. Families who belonged to the Mafia were considered to be distinguished members of the community. Members of the Cosa Nostra had to be Sicilian born and bred. They had to conform to the accepted political affiliations of the day, and could not support or have contact with any political group without the permission of the ruling commission, known as the *cupola*, which would only be granted for a specific purpose, such as commerce. Cosa Nostra members supposedly had to conform to a high moral code, based upon a strong family life, with no illegitimate children. Homosexuality was banned, and those who were found to indulge would be killed. Women in the family were placed upon a pedestal and treated with respect and honour, and husbands should not degrade themselves or their wives by associating with prostitutes. Killings and vendettas were an accepted part of the system of justice and the old Robin Hood image was further promoted by the ruling that Mafia chieftains had to 'look after' the local community of which they were head, or Godfather.

These warped values of Cosa Nostra life, which it appeared mafiosi adhered to only when it suited them, none the less contained built-in social structures which went far deeper than sociologists had previously imagined. By then, according to the new breed of Mafia collaborators with the law, the way of life had already been overtaken. Modern Mafia people subverted these 'ideals' by their violence, drug dealing and killings which no longer precluded women and children as victims.

Liliana Ferraro believes that therein lies the key to success in arresting Mafia bosses. 'We are seeing an inversion of these traditions which have passed through generations. The people, the communities themselves, are at last beginning to reject the Mafia, to stand up and be counted, to inform upon the criminals and cooperate with the law. It requires considerable courage. Many people who have done such things in the past have simply been murdered, wiped out. That is the difficulty, always, that we have faced: our communities have been held to Mafia traditions of *omertà* and consent first by fear and secondly a deliberate, yet often quite false, feeling of well-being that Mafia chiefs manage to instil upon small communities.'

The wind of revolution may well have been stirring when I had those conversations with Ferraro at various stages during 1994, but in truth the collapse of the Mafia is not even in view, and she knows it better that anyone.

The phrase 'The Mafia is beaten' has been spoken with incredible regularity for decades. Ferraro and her present-day colleagues know that it is a dangerous illusion, a mirage that has appeared frequently since the turn of the century. Exactly those words have been used in newspaper headlines since the late 1800s, and it still isn't true.

Seldom has history repeated itself so often as it does in Sicily. In 1867, the Mafia had become so powerful that when a parliamentary commission was set up to examine the Sicilian phenomenon, the result was a whitewash. The same thing happened again a century later. By 1874, Prefect Rasponi of Palermo complained to the Ministry of Justice in Rome, giving an assessment that could easily have been written a hundred years later:

> The Maffia has invaded all classes of society. The rich use it to safeguard their person and property, or as an instrument to maintain that oppressive influence and weight they see coming to an end . . . the middle class embraces it and uses it, because it judges it a powerful means to acquire popularity or to obtain wealth. Lastly, the proletariat more easily becomes mafioso through a natural hatred of public authorities and their laws.
>
> 'By secret contrivance, the Maffia simultaneously gives and receives protection and it acquires strength as more and more often it sees people asking for its help instead of the local authorities'. It has grown as powerful in the cities as in the countryside . . . a hidden power which has instilled silence where there is crime, rendered witnesses dumb, frightened jurymen and ensured immunity from misdeeds, convincing themselves that the law cannot touch them.

The parallels between then and now are incredible and what became a Mafia tradition of corrupting those in power and eliminating all who stood in its path was established in that era, in the 1880s, and particularly during the administration of Francesco Crispi, prime minister of Italy from 1887 to 1896 who was dubbed 'the worst mafioso of all'.

The first of many who became known as the Illustrious Corpses, Marquis Commendatore Emanuele Notarbartolo was murdered during Crispi's time, and today the murder is being re-examined by university students in Palermo as they seek the origins of the atrocities that have occurred in recent times.

It is an interesting case which has modern parallels. Notarbartolo, head of the Bank of Sicily, became increasingly alarmed that fortunes were being made by Cosa Nostra leaders by the illegal manipulation of credit.

Some of these funds had been used to support Crispi's so-called Social party and ensure its electoral success in the

Sicilian provinces. Notarbartolo wrote a long and confidential report of his findings to the Minister of Finance in Rome who passed it directly to Crispi, who in turn sent it on to a well-known mafioso MP from Palermo.

Notarbartolo, however, quickly found the tables turned on himself. He was accused of fraud and dismissed from office in disgrace. Later, during a period when Crispi was out of office, it was recognized that he was the victim and at the beginning of February 1893, he was given his old job back at the bank. He set off to return to Palermo but was stabbed to death on a rail journey through Sicily. His body was cut up and thrown on the tracks.

A number of minor mafiosi were rounded up and one was charged with Notarbartolo's murder. He was acquitted through 'lack of evidence'. The Cosa Nostra rejoiced at their man's freedom, he was given a hero's welcome and the judge who had proclaimed him innocent was made an honorary citizen of Palermo.

Notarbartolo was written off as a dangerous lunatic and it would be many years before his true courage was recognized. Though his death was simply one of hundreds of murders committed by the Mafia during this period, it may be regarded for the purposes of this book as a starting point: the man who spoke up and began a personal fight against the mafiosi, for which he paid the ultimate price.

In Palermo, years later, they named a street after him, the very street where Giovanni Falcone came to live when he moved back to Palermo to begin his own personal and most famous crusade against the Mafia in 1979. And it is there, today, that tourists can still see the shrine outside his home.

CHAPTER TWO

The Model Godfather and the First Illustrious Corpse

When I first met Liliana Ferraro she was already engaged in a landmark operation aimed at achieving global action against organized crime under the auspices of the United Nations. It was important, because the Italian Mafia had dominated the international crime scene for decades, had launched the drugging of America with its own-brand heroin in the 1970s, and in the 1990s was delivering Columbian cocaine to the doorstep of every European nation – yet there was no international strategy to fight them.

'It was Giovanni Falcone's idea and as successor to his office, I inherited that dream,' she told me. 'Falcone used to travel the world attempting to stir up international co-operation. He believed strongly that the war against the Mafia and organized crime as a whole could only be won with global co-operation. I share that vision as the only way forward and it was fitting that Italy, which has experienced such shocking and barbaric carnage, should formulate and promote such an idea.'

But it took years to achieve. Serious dialogue between Italy and America – the two nations most affected – did not even exist before 1982 and there were, as Ferraro pointed out, historical facts which had prevented it. 'If you have a problem,' she said, 'you can find a solution only if you recognize the existence and nature of that problem. If you deny there is a problem, then it is impossible to solve.'

That, basically, was the crux of the scandalous inability of successive administrations on both sides of the Atlantic to take on the Mafia and one which fostered attitudes which in the end allowed the Mafia to flourish.

Italy itself, and even the Roman Catholic Church, did not formally recognize the existence of the Mafia until the 1970s when association with it became a crime. At the same time, contact between Italian and US law enforcers was always haphazard and blurred by US intervention in Italy at a time when a strong and clandestine presence of CIA agents were more concerned with defeating Communism than the Mafia.

The lack of contact between the two nations so inextricably linked by Mafia families was also a product of the long-standing attitude of J Edgar Hoover, tyrannical director of the FBI. He persistently and adamantly rejected the theory that 'the Mafia' even existed, a view he rammed down the throats of successive American presidents from his appointment to the job in 1924 until his death forty-eight years later.

It was his rejection of the very idea of a Mafia hierarchy that permitted the organization to prosper in the US, and eventually Mafia figures who had emigrated to America acquired the sophistications of the free-range criminality of the Prohibition era and exported it back to Italy. The American connection is a crucial element in every stage of the progression of the Mafia from the turn of the century to the present day.

And it was fitting, in Ferraro's view, that among personalities whose history would be featured in the 1994 UN conference on organized crime, was an American detective named Joe Petrosino who became the first man in Italo-American history who attempted to expose the link.

The story of Joe Petrosino was buried in history but has been revived by local historians as the rediscovery of the Mafia in Italy goes ahead. He came to prominence in the New York police force investigating the activities of criminals of Italian origin, and especially the case of a Sicilian emigre named Vito Cascioferro who is today recognized as the Mafia's very first *capo di tutti capi* – the boss of bosses.

Don Vito's story bears striking similarities to the fictional account of the origins of Vito Corleone, romantically portrayed in flashback sequences in the second of the *Godfather* movies by

Robert de Niro. Vito Corleone, as fans of the *Godfather* trilogy will be aware, came from Sicily as a boy, from the village of Corleone from which he took his name, and established himself as the Godfather among New York's poverty stricken Italian immigrants.

The official history of Vito Cascioferro can be culled from the archieves of the Italian Carabinieri and the New York police department. Born in Palermo in 1862, Cascioferro grew up a young hothead in traditional peasant surroundings, illiterate and rebellious. He was a natural candidate for the Cosa Nostra and in his early twenties had been ritually enrolled in the organization as a Man of Honour – the term used by the Mafia for all its recruits.

Cascioferro was among the hundreds of thousands of Italian immigrants who got into the United States in the period before strict quotas were introduced in the twenties. In the late 1890s emigration from Italy was a trickle of less than 1,000, but had hit almost 150,000 a year by 1913. Italians, unable to speak English and whose work experience had largely been in farming, stuck together and formed their own communities. Close on 600,000 Italians decided to stay in New York, where they had landed.

They crowded ramshackle homes in the Lower East Side. The majority were god-fearing people predominantly from southern Italy and Sicily, struggling to survive the city life in sweatshops and slums. Among them, and preying on them, were men of the so-called Black Hand, a name given to early Mafia-style gangsters in New York, though it was erroneously taken from Corsican bandit origins. They were Sicilian Cosa Nostra people who had fled the crackdown on criminality in the south of Italy in the 1890s.

Vito Cascioferro moved in with his sister over a shop on 103rd Street. He had skilfully hidden his criminal record which began in 1894 with a charge of assault and extended through to 1899 when he was accused of kidnapping Baroness di Valpetrosa, and fled to America to escape trial.

True enough, pretty well every murder, robbery, protection racket or crime that had even a remote Italian connection was being blamed on the Black Hand, whose activities attracted international attention.

New York detective Lieutenant Joe Petrosino himself dismissed its existence as an organization at first. However, Petrosino became convinced of the importance of Cascioferro in the New York community, and discovered that his quarry was known throughout as Don Vito, the man to whom all others turned to for decisions and at times of trouble and whose services were paid for by local Italian traders and businessmen.

Don Vito is credited with establishing a sliding scale of local tax – 'protection' – which were to be paid to him and other lesser bosses, exactly conforming to the time-honoured traditions which could be traced to the whole of southern Italy in the eighteenth century. Within three years, Don Vito had perfected his system, and no businessman in his area of operation could escape his tax.

Petrosino began to take a particular interest in Don Vito and in 1904, the New York police had linked him to many crimes, and wanted him for the murder of an Italian who was stabbed to death, cut in pieces and stuffed inside a barrel. Don Vito was tipped off that he was about to be arrested, and fled first to New Orleans and then back to Palermo.

Petrosino was sent to Sicily to trace Don Vito and to check the names of illegal immigrants who might be resident in New York. His visit was supposed to be secret but by the time his ship sailed into Palermo, Don Vito's men were waiting at the dock to keep watch for his arrival. The detective went first to meet the American consul in Palermo, James Bishop, who warned him to trust no one, and especially not the police. 'I will tell you stories that will make your hair stand on end,' Bishop warned.

Then Petrosino was set up by a man who said he would introduce him to two informers. It was arranged that they should meet in the Piazza Marina, in the centre of Palermo. The detective arrived early, and was seen pacing up and down. A police account of his killing records that he was taken by the needs of nature to relieve himself beside a fence. At that moment, two shots rang out and the detective fell dead with his privates exposed, a classic Mafia humiliation of a victim.

It is still a common feature of Mafia killings to involve the genitalia; numerous victims in later years were shot or strangled and had their genitals cut off and stuffed in their mouths.

Don Vito was arrested on 3 April 1909 but he could state

exactly where he was at the time of the murder – at the house of a local VIP who confirmed his story. The murder was carried out on Don Vito's orders by three men who included Giuseppe Fontana, who had previously been acquitted of the murder of the bank president, Notarbartolo. Don Vito, imprisoned temporarily in Palermo during the investigation, eventually walked free.

Through the remaining years of the pre-Mussolini era of Italian politics, Don Vito built up a criminal network, remaining always in contact with his old friends in New York. Murders, extortion, kidnapping, smuggling all leapt in the statistical charts. In the province of Palermo alone, the murder rate between 1921 and 1925 ran at an average of 250 killings a year, with almost as many attempted murders and 12,000 other major crimes annually involving kidnap, theft and extortion.

A contemporary report summed up the chaos: 'Total lawlessness prevails, unchecked . . . through every aspect of Sicilian life and rampant over the entire island . . . and the scum who perpetrate it are protected by politicians anxious to secure their votes.'

The interchange between the Italian and American gangsters also continued, to the extent that the Italian economy was boosted substantially by literally millions of lire coming in from immigrants in the US who were sending funds back to their native home.

It took the dictatorial powers of Mussolini to enforce the first major attack on the Italian Mafia after he took power in Italy in January 1925. He abolished democratic elections that year and cut off the Mafia's political arm, which had reached Rome through corrupt elections in the previous decade.

Mussolini promised action against the criminals and in 1926 appointed Police Prefect Cesare Mori, known as the Iron Man after his attack on peasant agitators after World War I, to go down to Sicily and clean out the Mafia once and for all. He took a heavy band of armed men and equipped himself with a new law which he invented himself, outlawing sympathizers 'to associations which have a criminal character' but did not name the Mafia specifically, and for good reason.

When Mori began what was a most savage attack on the

minor mafiosi in which thousands were rounded up, tortured, killed and imprisoned, the net was indiscriminate. Dozens of left-wing activists and peasant agitators who were no more Mafia than Mori himself were among those he arrested. Landowners and the elite turned informers and they got rid of all their undesirables in one fell swoop. Grave injustices went unchallenged. But Mori became Mussolini's much-hyped hero.

In 1927, Mori built a huge cage at the courthouse to try the first 154 accused. Fifteen other such trials took place in the next three years. By the end of the decade, the Iron Man announced that the Mafia was finished, wiped out. The headline 'The last of the Mafia' appeared again as writers and journalists, especially from Britain and America, swallowed the propaganda. 'Mussolini has strangled the monster in its lair' said *The Times* in London while the *New York Times* proclaimed: 'The Mafia is dead – a new Sicily is born.'

Mussolini himself declared: 'Prefect Mori has acted like a surgeon and cut out an odious growth. Five million hard-working patriotic Sicilians will no longer be harassed, taxed, robbed or dishonoured by a few hundred malefactors.' It was simply not true. A large number of major Mafia figures were by then languishing in jails, including Vito Cascioferro. He was an early target. The boss of bosses who lived a life of luxury with no visible means of income could not be allowed to remain free. Mussolini himself decreed it.

Don Vito was quite familiar with the experience of being arrested. He had been taken into custody many times. In his lifetime he had been accused of committing sixty-nine murders but was never found guilty of any charge. This time Mori, determined to make him an example, put up charges relating to two murders which, in reality, Don Vito did not commit, and the evidence was fixed. He was imprisoned for life though continued to run his empire from a luxuriously equipped prison cell. He died there in 1945, and the cell thereafter became 'reserved' for VIP prisoners.

Though the Fascist regime had cleared out hundreds of bandits, there were still many who represented the high Mafia elite, largely in the Sicilian middle class, who remained largely untouched and so gradually the Mafia began to re-emerge, quietly infiltrating itself back into a position of power in Sicily and aided particularly by developments in America.

In parallel to the Sicilian experience, the organization set up by Don Vito Cascioferro had been expanded through every major American city. Names began to appear that would become infamously connected with every Mafia tale this century, men who became household names: Alphonso Capone, from a Neapolitan Camorra family, the ruthless Vito Genovese, and others like Salvatore 'Lucky' Luciano, Frank Costello, Joseph Bonnano and Joe Adonis who all jostled into the Mafia power play that emerged with the introduction of Prohibition.

The exploits of the Prohibition gangsters are now so well known they do not need repetition here, except to record that wave after wave of attacks on Mafia-linked crime bosses throughout the 1920s failed to stem their march forward. The slaughter, the gang wars, that whole period of American criminal history of the 1920s and 1930s and then on into the trials of the early 1940s, was spectacular for one particular reason: the mortality rate from battles among themselves, as ever, achieved a far greater elimination of Mafia personnel than J Edgar Hoover's FBI ever managed, and there were always plenty of replacements: illegal immigrants from Sicily.

The American-Italian connection was also strengthened by a number of developments before and during World War II. As Mussolini himself well knew, the claim that the Mafia had been defeated was illusory. Mori's attack on the Mafia soldiers turned them into local heroes; no long-term damage was done. And it is worth recording that Cesare Mori was one of the few men in Italian history who wreaked havoc on the Mafia and was not assassinated by them.

Another important factor was the importation of US gangsters back into Italy, notably in 1938 when Vito Genovese fled to his native Naples ahead of an arrest warrant for murder in New York and took with him almost $1 million in cash, part of which he donated to the Fascist party to secure his trouble-free existence in his temporary new home. In return, he slid effortlessly into Neapolitan life, entered the political circle on the very edge of Mussolini's entourage and continued his association with the rackets from his Naples base without hindrance from Mori or any other Italian law officers.

Genovese donated $250,000 to Mussolini to build a new Fascist party headquarters, and then when war broke out partially financed and supervised the construction of a new munitions factory. He was also suspected by American intelligence of working for Mussolini's secret service.

Mussolini personally awarded him the title of commendatore. Genovese garnered friends in high places and not least among them was Mussolini's son-in-law, Count Galeazzo Ciano, to whom he supplied cocaine. With protection in the highest quarter Genovese had, by the early part of the war, established a narcotics trade that would be the foundation for great post-war expansion.

In Sicily, there was one other constant factor which, over the years, has allowed the Mafia to flourish: neglect of the social structure and mounting poverty. It ensured that the Mafia would be fostered by the ordinary people, the common working man. No one else cared. As World War II progressed, discontent was already rife in the south and in Sicily and it provided fertile ground for the Mafia's revival process, aided of course by the war which brought many more opportunities in the way of smuggling and black market trading.

It is an intriguing possibility, however, that the Mafia would have remained a fairly modest influence in post-war Sicily had it not been for a most staggering development which would ensure its total reincarnation. That development came from the least expected quarter: the American war department whose intervention through the American Office of Strategic Services (OSS) Special Operations branch promoted the Mafia right back into the mainstream of Sicilian life, and international expansion.

CHAPTER THREE

US Intelligence Makes a Pact with The Mafia: Help Us and We'll Help You

In spite of a hefty weight of unpalatable evidence, Liliana Ferraro refuses to join the chorus of critics in her own country and in America itself who blame the US for putting the Mafia back in business at the end of World War II. In a nutshell American Intelligence, directed from the highest level, made pacts with Mafia chieftains during and after the war aimed first at ousting Mussolini and the Nazis, then at subduing Communists in the post-war political power play. The deal wallowed in murky waters and truth became barely visible due to later CIA activity in which links with the Mafia were clearly present.

It is one reason why any kind of working relationship between the law agencies of the two countries took so long to establish despite the importance of the drugs traffic which came to haunt the US and eventually the rest of the world, with a flood of heroin emanating principally from Sicily.

The story really began in the dying days of the war. Liliana Ferraro, a mere babe in arms when the Allied Forces finally booted the Nazis from her country, learned from her student days the edited version of that part of Italian history. Later she would be able to secure a more accurate picture. Further pieces of the jigsaw became apparent from her experiences as a young magistrate during the terrorist era when America took what many historians and politicans came to regard as a totally unacceptable interventionist role in the post-war reformation of Italian politics, and as a byproduct, gave new life to the Mafia.

Ferraro, who gained her law degree from the University of Naples in the sixties and then immediately began studying to become a magistrate, was in a key station of the Italian judiciary system by the time the results of the US post-war actions eventually came home to roost, but today she takes a sanguine view of those developments.

'We cannot apply our modern criteria in our judgment of events in the past,' she told me. 'Nor do I believe that there is great antagonism in my country against America for what happened. The Mafia would have risen again, with or without help from the American secret service. It is a piece of history, a part of the political history of the world, that we must accept and place in context. There was a political attitude that existed in the US at the time in regard to the rise of Communism in Europe and that had a bearing on what happened in the last days of the war and beyond but we must place it in its historical setting, of wartime and post-war chaos, when the Cold War was at its very beginnings.'

It is in Ferraro's nature to be so forgiving. In the conversations I had with her, she displayed a remarkable ability to accept and explain the failings of others and not to allow the past and a particular period of her nation's history to get in the way of the new spirit of 1990s' harmony and co-operation which she has been promoting so wholeheartedly with her counterparts across the Atlantic.

Like many Italians from those areas where passionate politics and local customs emerged from the turbulence of the colourful era of Italian kingdoms, she is able to draw on an overview of that history with a resigned acceptance of trauma inflicted by foreign invaders.

Recrimination is not part of her vocabulary and in spite of the horrors and murders she has witnessed among her colleagues, she looks ahead, taking the memory of those who have died – 'so many deaths among close friends' – as the inspiration for her own work and for the future. Others have been, and still are, far less able to assign those post-war events to history and are quite vociferous in their attacks on the US for actions which would reverberate down the century.

Not least among them was US Attorney Michael Kennedy, who was defending a Sicilian Godfather at the famous Pizza Connection trial in New York in 1986. He declared frankly: 'Mussolini had clipped their wings. But after World War II, the Harvard liberal types in the OSS put the Mafia back in power because they sought indigenous leaders. We [America] backed the wrong people in South-East Asia for the same reason. It is a policy that has consistently put us on the wrong side.'

How right he was.

There have been many fanciful stories about how the Mafia gained power after it smoothed the way for the Allied landing in Sicily in 1943. It is now possible to be specific, with the help of new information from interviews and archive material which provide a clear picture of how American intelligence targeted the Mafia's supreme boss in the US, Lucky Luciano, to enlist the aid of the Sicilians, and why the Americans, in their wisdom, deliberately installed the Mafia to run Sicily and parts of the south of Italy after the War.

For years, the Americans denied that Luciano, or any other Mafia gangster for that matter, made any significant contribution to the war effort, though later conceded that he had assisted in a limited way on the question of sabotage.

So let us get immediately to the truth, culled from previously classified documents. The story actually began in 1942 when Luciano was in the sixth year of a 30–50 year sentence for prostitution and racketeering at the Dannemora Penitentiary, located on the furthest tip of New York State, close to the Canadian border.

At the beginning of 1942 Lieutenant Commander Charles Haffenden, head of the US Naval Intelligence unit B-3, controlling 150 anti-subversion agents around New York, had been hitting a brick wall in attempts to curb sabotage in the east coast dockyards, heavily populated by American-Italians.

Haffenden was attempting to halt the many incidents of Nazi sabotage. One of the most spectacular was the sinking of the French liner *Normandie* which caught fire and overturned in New York Harbour in February 1942 while it was being converted into a troop carrier.

Haffenden was advised that if there was one man who had particular influence on the labour unions in the dockyards, it was Lucky Luciano since the Mafia controlled the docks. The lieutenant commander sought approval from his superiors and in April 1942 made contact with Luciano's lawyer, Moses Polakoff, who in turn had a conversation with Luciano's closest associate, Meyer Lansky. Polakoff replied that Luciano would be pleased to co-operate with the war effort, provided he was moved to a more convenient location.

On 12 May 1942, Luciano was transferred to the comfortable Great Meadows Open Prison, sixty miles from Albany where, three days later, a letter arrived, special delivery from the head of the New York State Commission of Corrections, to Vernon A. Morhous, warden of Great Meadows: 'This is to advise you that I have granted permission to Mr Meyer Lansky to visit and interview Inmate Charles Luciano in your institution when accompanied by Mr Polakoff, the inmate's attorney. You are authorized to waive the usual fingerprint requirements.'

The upshot was that Haffenden made several visits and Luciano agreed to send word to the dockyards to assist if his application for clemency after the war would be favourably reviewed. His edict to the docks had an immediate effect. Sabotage decreased almost overnight and by the end of June, eight German secret agents had been arrested in New York and Chicago. It was a major coup for which the FBI wrongly claimed credit.

Having successfully made use of Luciano, US intelligence contact was continued by another department of American intelligence, the Special Operations Unit of the Office of Strategic Services. In February 1943, the question of an Allied landing in Italy was already being discussed and there were a number of options for a coastline that would provide potentially the best point of entry.

Lieutenant Haffenden was once again called in to resume his contact with Luciano. Haffenden's initial task was to discuss the landing sites of Sicily and southern Italy and it was agreed with Luciano that Meyer Lansky would set up a meeting with Sicilians living in New York who could give guidance as to the most suitable points of entry for an Allied invasion force when the time came.

It was a remarkable meeting in which American intelligence clearly had to take on trust the word of Luciano and Lansky that everything discussed would be classified as top secret since it involved plans for what was a most vital expedition, a turning point in World War II.

Haffenden was amused and surprised at the result. Lansky and Joe Adonis, another key Mafia figure, arrived at his offices at 90 Church Street, New York, with a score of native Italians and Sicilians with handle-bar moustaches, many of whom could not or would not speak English.

The Italians pinpointed easy landing sites which many had known well in their youthful days as smugglers on a map of Italy. Using that information, naval cartographers compiled an overlay. Later, Luciano and other US Mafia figures compiled lists of names of their Sicilian and Neapolitan brethren who would be contacted in due course to assist. Eventually, an OSS Special Operations Unit compiled a list of more than 100 names – and almost without exception, they were Mafia people.

By early April 1943, plans were already well advanced for the Allied invasion and there was a general agreement between Winston Churchill and the war commanders Montgomery and Eisenhower that the Allied forces should land in Italy as soon possible, and with the minimum loss of life.

By early June, British agents, in contact with the resistance movement of Sicilian left-wing groups and separatists, were plotting the landing sites. The Americans, with the OSS now engaged upon one of its first major field operations of the war, was largely using its contacts with the Mafia.

Between February and April 1943, a number of American agents were flown from Africa and parachuted into Sicily to be hurried away into hiding by the local collaborators. They were the advance party for the invasion, and one at least was to make contact with the then head of the Sicilian Cosa Nostra, Don Calogero Vizzini.

Eisenhower had already made it clear to Churchill he was prepared to do business with anyone who could ensure Italian co-operation and Churchill supported his view in a memo to Roosevelt in July, 1943: 'My position is that once Mussolini and the Fascists are gone, I will deal with any Italian authority which can deliver the goods . . . provided they are the ones who can make the Italians do what we need for our war purposes. Those purposes would certainly be hindered by chaos . . . we have no right to lay undue burdens on our troops.' Churchill was obviously thinking more in terms of political groups, rather than criminal.

However, ideas over who should take over as military governor in Sicily had been the subject of discussion between London and Washington since the end of April, as the invasion of Sicily drew near. The British had suggested several names for the appointment but at this point American intelligence became involved and made its own suggestions as to who should take over the administration of the island after the invasion.

On 1 May 1943, the office of the Joint Staff Mission in Washington sent a cipher telegram marked most secret and addressed to the War Cabinet Office, London:

> Position here in regard to planning organization of Civil Administration . . . is becoming complicated . . . the Secretariat of War and Navy recently agreed that US War department be designated to plan handling of Civic affairs in the territory about to be occupied and co-ordinate activities of civilian agencies . . . during period of military occupation.

Whatever 'complicated' discussions were taking place in the background, they were not made known to the British Foreign Office. After further exchanges over who should take the role of military governor, the Americans telegraphed the Foreign Office in London on 9 July: 'Someone is found . . . who has superior experience and knowledge of country and language. The latter would make a special appeal.'

That man was Colonel Charles Poletti who was, before military service, lieutenant governor of New York City. He was familiar with all matters Mafia and, according to Luciano himself, 'was a very good friend of ours'. We must always treat with caution these allegations by gangsters of their 'friendships' but true or not, Poletti found himself being parachuted into Sicily on 13 July.

He was met by the 'local resistance' people and hidden away in a house in Palermo where he began to have clandestine meetings with local VIPs. He had a list of names supplied by the OSS who were to be contacted to secure the co-operation of the civilian leaders, led by Mafia boss Don Calo Vizzini himself. He, in turn, had earmarked several hundred 'trustworthy' people who would smooth a path for the invading armies – a task which, as Churchill had outlined, principally involved averting all possibility of chaos which would keep the troops tied up in Sicily for far longer than was necessary.

When the Allied forces landed, the British Eighth Army combined with the Canadians advanced along the east coast of Sicily. It took the full five weeks to secure their positions and defeat the resistance of German and Italian troops, and this part of the operation cost the most lives.

The Americans took the west coast and the route had been carefully prepared to make the most of Mafia help. Don Calo Vizzini whose home town of Villalba was the first major objective of the US forces came into the town square as the troops arrived.

Strong rumours at the time of the invasion suggested that Lucky Luciano had been flown into the island by the Americans and was with the US troops as they moved into Villalba. One report claimed that Luciano climbed from the lead American tank in the centre of the town and openly embraced Don Calo. Historians have always treated the story with suspicion but it is perhaps unimportant whether Luciano was there or not.

After arriving in Villalba the Americans prepared for a heavy battle as they pressed on to the Cammarata heights where a large force of Italians was known to be entrenched. Overnight, however, Giuseppe Genco Russo, Don Calo's number two in the Cosa Nostra who lived in the neighbouring town of Mussomeli, kidnapped the Italian commander as he passed nearby and two thirds of his troops deserted, and ran off into the hills.

And so the battle of Cammarata was won without a drop of blood being spilt and the Americans completed their move through the west coast in just over ten days. The British and the Canadians, meanwhile, pressed on along the east flank and experienced some strong pockets of resistance from sections of the three divisions of German troops still fighting.

On 17 August, Churchill jubilantly waved a telegraph from General Alexander announcing the Anglo-American victory in Sicily: 'At 10 a.m. this morning, the last German soldier was flung out and the whole island is now in our hands.'

By then, Colonel Poletti had been in Sicily for thirty-one days and as the designated head of Allied Military Government (AMGOT) in Sicily, he was instructed to ensure that anti-Fascist people were placed in charge. Mussolini was finished and the whole of southern Italy was waiting for liberation. Poletti, since his arrival on 13 July, had established 'acceptable' administrations in most of the key towns of Sicily so that he could move on as quickly as possible to take his AMGOT command through southern Italy and on into Rome.

Many of the new mayors appointed by Poletti were, whether he appreciated it or not, mafiosi and contemporary reports from British officers arriving on the island after the invasion recall their surprise at being confronted by small men in American military uniforms who spoke no English but were running the show.

The most senior of the new appointees was the rotund little man from Villalba, Don Calo Vizzini, who was made an honorary colonel in the US Army and Mayor of Villalba. Don Calo spent seven days at Poletti's headquarters and guided his hand as he appointed the mayors of the Sicilian towns.

If anyone had bothered to check, they would have discovered that Don Calo himself had a long criminal record. As for the exiled Vito Genovese, he immediately saw in the chaos of post-Mussolini Italy a route to massive wealth in the burgeoning black market which, as everywhere, became a major problem, highlighted in another British Foreign Office memo which recorded: 'Black Market: this is rampant throughout the island. All steps being taken to curb it.'

Other Foreign Office documents containing reports from the scene by British officers actually forecast the resurgence of Mafia power in the wake of Poletti's appointments for the civil administration: 'The aftermath of war and the breakdown of central and provincial authority provide a good culture ground for the virus' – the virus in this case meaning the Mafia.

Vito Genovese resurfaced soon after Colonel Poletti's arrival in Sicily and offered his services. Poletti certainly knew that the gangster was a fugitive from US justice. Even so, he accepted Genovese 'in good faith' and at a very difficult time – in spite of the reservations of the OSS. They considered him a possible Fascist spy. He became Poletti's aide and later acted as an interpreter at military courts and tribunals in Naples.

While apparently assisting the Allies, he was also looking after his own business and that of the Mafia and very quickly set up a massive black market operation. Genovese travelled back and forth, moving freely around the liberated south with the benefit of a clutch of travel documents and passes to the American PX stores.

With the help of the Sicilians and the Camorra in Naples, the black market enterprise flourished, dealing in everything from cigarettes to lorry loads of grain and olive oil and citrus fruit from Sicilian farms. Before long, the Americans ordered their own clamp-down on black market activity. One diligent officer, Sergeant Orange C. Dickey, of the US Army Criminal Investigations Division, discovered that Genovese – then assigned to a military court in Naples – was at the heart of the ring operating along the Neapolitan coast.

Dickey told a superior officer and was ordered 'to drop it'. He didn't and travelled to see Poletti who refused point blank to discuss Genovese. Dickey would not be put off. He telegraphed the FBI for information on Genovese and eventually obtained authority to arrest Genovese for murder and have him sent back to the US immediately. When confronted, Genovese took the sergeant to one side and offered an immediate cash payment of $250,000 if he would walk away and forget he had ever seen him, make up some story that he had escaped. Dickey refused this and all other offers which Genovese made, including that of a gift of a superb coffin which he would undoubtedly be needing if he persisted.

Dickey personally accompanied Genovese back to New York in August 1944 where he was taken into police custody to stand trial for the murder.

Lucky Luciano, meanwhile, was standing by to re-enter the fray. On 7 May 1945, the very day the war in Europe ended, Luciano's lawyer filed a plea for clemency to Thomas Dewey, Governor of New York, who in turn sent it to the state parole board, all of whom were his own appointees. Dewey, who always denied allegations that he had accepted a $250,000 donation towards his election campaign funds from the Mafia, made a personal recommendation for Luciano's release on the grounds that he had 'performed noble and, because of security, necessarily secret labors for the Allied cause.'

On 3 January 1946, Dewey announced the parole board's agreement that Luciano should be released, having served less than a third of the minimum designated sentence. Luciano, however, was furious when he discovered a proviso – that he would only be released on condition that he left the country immediately, Luciano having overlooked the fact that he had never bothered to become a naturalized citizen of the United States.

He was deported to Italy, where he went straight into business, taking over the black market operation left by his former lieutenant from the 1930s, Vito Genovese. It was the platform for the creation of a new Mafia empire, based in Italy but with very considerable contact with the US.

Meanwhile, Vito Genovese was also preparing his own route to freedom from the confines of Brooklyn jail, where he had a succession of well-known visitors. The case against him rested on the evidence of two key witnesses. One of them, Peter La Tempa, was taken into protective custody at his own request. Four days later, he was taken ill and died. An autopsy showed he had been given enough poison 'to kill eight horses'. The only other witness, Ernest 'the Hawk' Rupolo, disappeared. A few years later, his body, full off bullet holes and stab wounds from an ice pick, broke free from the concrete weights which had been tied around his ankles and floated to the surface in Jamaica Bay. The case could not proceed, and in June 1946, the New York district attorney's office had to order Genovese's release.

The underworld celebrations on his return ran for days and Genovese, using Luciano's name and claiming to be his rightful heir, announced his intention of taking control of the New York families and simultaneously decreed that in future, their business would include narcotics.

The scene was set for violence and retribution among the warring factions as the US people fought among themselves.

The Sicilians, with key people in every major town on the island and already making fortunes out of the black market, were ready and only too willing to join the narcotics business that Genovese was promoting in New York, and which Luciano had inherited in Italy.

Ahead lay a decade of consolidation by the Sicilians and a period of infighting among the American families which ended with Genovese as the undisputed boss in New York in consort with five families in Sicily. This would ultimately lead to the Italian Mafia's world domination of the drugs trade from which untold billions would flow.

This prospect – already in view at the end of the War – did not stop American Intelligence bypassing the criminal implications and heading directly for the political jugular of Italian politics. US Central Intelligence was already heavily involved in ensuring that the new political colours of Italy were in accord with American interests, having warned that Italy was an area in which Communism might flourish. This was confirmed in the Italian elections in 1946, when the Christian Democrats, whom the Americans wanted to see in power, polled only 20 per cent of the vote.

With the approval of President Truman, the US Central Intelligence Agency was given a multi-million purse for 'covert' action in Italy, specifically earmarked to give 'support through the CIA to the democratic centre-left and centre-right parties'.

Truman set aside upwards of $80 million to ensure that the Christian Democrats were installed into power without delay and even that was insufficient to satisfy the hawks in the intelligence community who considered that Italy should be a major priority for America's post-war intelligence network. It was the first item on the agenda at the very first meeting of the US National Security Council on 19 December 1947.

Following this meeting, the American Secretary of State was instructed to co-ordinate anti-Communist propaganda activity. A specific and 'top secret' directive written by James Forestal, later US Defence Secretary, instructed the Director of Central Intelligence to supplement the propaganda mandate with immediate plans for 'covert psychological warfare' to begin in Italy.

It would require the entry of an unspecified number of agents whose task would be broadly to inspire anti-Communist propaganda, promote the Christian Democrats as the most electable Italian party, and make secret contact with all other groups and affiliates who could ensure these objectives were met. Tacit approval was also given by CIA chiefs for agents to make direct contact with the Mafia in their strongholds in Sicily and southern Italy, where they could sway the electorate.

The result is now recorded in the archives of the CIA as one of its first major successes in overt political action in any foreign territory. When a new election was called in Italy for May 1948, the Christian Democrats polled 48 per cent of the vote, more than double their representation in 1946. The vote from Sicilian provinces sent a crucial number of Christian Democrat MPs to the national parliament and for years to come, represented the pivotal power-base on which successive Christian Democrat administrations came to rely.

The Mafia, in this way, held considerable sway over its politicians because of its ability to deliver huge votes, ensured by the simple volume of Mafia membership and by shotgun diplomacy at the ballot stations. From that base, established first by AMGOT when it appointed the Mafia mayors in 1943 and then by the CIA seeking to put a permanent seal of anti-Communism on the Italian election in 1948, the Mafia went on to form clandestine relationships which would extend to the highest level of Italian political life.

This was already feared in 1948, when political analysts recorded their surprise at the extent of support for the DC (Christian Democrats). Soon after the elections, a group of opposition MPs supported a move to call for a Parliamentary Commission of Inquiry into operations of the Mafia in Sicily.

The Christian Democrats reacted angrily against the proposal and quashed it. Minister of the Interior Mario Scelba, himself a Sicilian and whose name would later be mentioned in a trial of Mafia killers, called it a 'shameful and insulting' slur on the people of that island community.

Another senator from the Mafia stronghold of Partinico would admit that he had mafiosi among his electorate. He had received – whether he wanted it or not – electoral support from a silent but powerful figure in the Mafia. His name is seldom mentioned today, but Frank 'Three Fingers' Coppola had become, with Lucky Luciano, a man who would wield great influence on the future of the Mafia. While Don Calo remained boss of bosses, and in each town there were men of similar importance, Coppola brought these strands of local power together and can now be identified as one of the engineers of the new Mafia in Sicily, the man who set out the ground rules for the organization that exists today.

And when the CIA moved in during the autumn of 1947 with their bountiful supply of American dollars, courtesy of President Truman, Coppola and Don Calo were among those sought out for 'advice'. As would be shown on many future occasions, the CIA had no qualms about using criminals in the furtherence of its aims and to them Coppola, whose file in the United States demonstrated his political contacts of the 1930s, was a ready affiliate to the CIA's covert manipulation of the voting intentions of the Italian electorate.

Coppola, a thick-set, dynamic man, was a native of Sicily but had emigrated to America during Mussolini's purges. He rose in the American ranks, but fled back to Sicily after the war as the net began to close on him. He was joined by several other recent escapees from American justice and quickly established himself as a formidable and influential figure as the Italian Mafia developed. Coppola brought the Sicilian Mafia along the road to internationalism and the drugs trade, with the timely intervention – courtesy once again of the American authorities – of Lucky Luciano himself.

As one veteran left-wing politician told me in Sicily in 1994, when we were discussing the history of the Mafia:

> The Cosa Nostra on the one hand came out of our culture, and our history. But we had an another enemy we did not even know we were fighting – the secret hand of the CIA. Not content with re-inventing the Mafia, the CIA paid out millions to buy power for the DC [Christian Democrats], and gave the Mafia political legitimacy at the same time. The repercussions would be immense, far greater than anyone could have imagined at the time, and I doubt whether the CIA even considered the future possibilities.

Luciano, the most influential figure of all, took up residence in Naples but towards the end of 1946 was to be found in Palermo where two adjoining suites had been booked at a hotel, one for himself and one for Don Calo Vizzini.

The topic was narcotics and Mafia business in general and it marked the formation of contact between the Sicilian Cosa Nostra and the American in the exportation of drugs, a trickle at first but mounting steadily through the next two decades to quite terrifying levels.

In New York, Vito Genovese had assumed control of the Luciano family and had aspirations to become the supreme head, in succession to Lucky Luciano himself. Genovese's ambitions split the Mafia, though the alleged reluctance of the American crime families to deal in drugs has always been overstated.

They weren't that fussy and on 21 November 1946, after a meeting in Palermo with Don Calo, Luciano took a boat to Cuba and checked in at the Hotel Nacionale. Luciano had, in advance, summoned every major Mafia chieftain from the US to attend his little get-together in the sunshine and a score of America's most famous mobsters turned up to give Luciano a Christmas party – Costello, Lansky, Vito Genovese, Joe Adonis, Joe Bonanno, Joe Profaci, Santos Trafficante, Albert Anastasia: they were all there, and virtually to a man had relatives back in Sicily.

Luciano had, in the short time he had been back in Italy, established connections with a major drugs company in the north whose wartime production of morphine base could now be diverted and reprocessed for the heroin market. He had already set up a small processing factory outside Milan.

Luciano himself had planned to stay in Havana and supervise the operations on two fronts: the Mob gambling interests in Cuba and the reception and onwards transmission into America of narcotics shipped from Europe by the Sicilians. He had reckoned without the intervention of the US head of the Bureau of Narcotics, Harry Anslinger, who reported to President Truman direct that the Italian Mafia was – even then – responsible for a sharp increase in the flow of narcotics into the US.

The US made a formal demand for Cuba to have Luciano deported to Italy and, with some reluctance, the Cubans eventually agreed.

The efforts of Anslinger, however, were ultimately thwarted. With the willing cooperation of the Sicilian Cosa Nostra, Luciano became the director of operations for the drugs trade from Italy, while Vito Genovese established warehousing facilities in Havana for reception of the illegal cargoes.

One man who would not witness the start of the Mafia's international expansion was Don Calo himself. He died in his sleep on 13 July 1954, still a resident in his native village of Villalba. Such was Don Calo's fame, or infamy, by then that *The Times* in London was moved to record his death as follows:

> Don Calo, as he was commonly called, had been tacitly recognized for a quarter of a century as head of the Mafia, a secret organization responsible for so many curious and chiefly criminal episodes in Sicily . . . its members were personnel of all classes and types who conspired to promote what they regarded as their just interests independently of the law. Vizzini, a man of benevolent aspect, came from a landowning background which gave a number of sons to the Church. His fortune, estimated at 1,000 million lire and consisting of a sulphur mine, estates and property, goes to his priest brother and three nephews.

The age-old Sicilian paradox re-emerged after his demise: Mafia, yes; bad man, no. The epitaph on the mausoleum of Don Calo is still visible today. It reads: 'Defender of the weak and enemy of injustice.'

In Villalba, the day of his burial was declared a holiday and thousands joined the funeral procession with his coffin held aloft at the front of them. Ordinary men and women lining the streets wept openly. Sorrow at his passing was significantly registered by the Christian Democrats and for eight days, the local government offices and party offices were closed as a mark of respect.

'A good man . . . ,' they said.

And a undoubtedly an extortionist, thief, drug dealer and a killer, but no one would mention such a thing.

CHAPTER FOUR

Mafia Doctor Murders a Child and the Corleonesi Rises

Folklore, says Liliana Ferraro, has a lot to answer for in the international perception of the Mafia and, especially in the intertwining of reality with fiction. None more so than for the Sicilian town of Corleone. Today tourists seek it out, driving from Palermo up into the hills where this community of 12,000 resents the notoriety it has been saddled with through the movie trilogy based upon Mario Puzo's *The Godfather.*

For it is, in real life, the town that also gives its name to the most ruthless of all Cosa Nostra clans, the Corleonesi, whose leaders have been consistently in the frontline of Mafia business.

When I first met Ferraro in 1993, she was basking in the knowledge that the most wanted man in Italy, the head of the Corleonesi, Salvatore 'Toto' Riina, had just been captured by a massive joint task force of the Italian security forces, just a few months after she took over as Director of Italian Penal Affairs. Riina, by then, was the accepted boss of bosses of the Mafia, the head of its military wing and a man whom every other Mafia boss the world over feared.

His name, linked with the man he succeeded as supreme boss of the Cosa Nostra, Luciano Liggio, had become synonymous with Mafia violence in modern Italian history. Between them, Riina and Liggio have been credited with murdering or ordering the assassinations of hundreds of enemies. 'When we finally arrested Riina,' Ferraro told me, 'it was regarded as an historical event, a turning point and a major triumph in the war on organized crime. He is the number one, the big boss, and still is, even though we now have him in prison. Neither he nor his family had been seen for twenty-three years.'

That, in itself, is a remarkable and startling admission, as Ferraro herself acknowledged. Though it was true as far as the the police were concerned that Riina had remained hidden for more than two decades, he could not have existed without *someone* having knowledge of his whereabouts. It is impossible for one so infamous to vanish, who by bomb and bullet has secured control of the Mafia's global heroin business. Riina married a local schoolteacher named Antoinetta in a ceremony conducted by a Mafia priest related to Frank Coppola, and had five children, three of whom were born in a Palermo nursing home. He lived and conducted his business within that city, travelled frequently to other countries on false passports and was in constant touch with senior local dignitaries and VIPs in the political hierarchy. He master-minded some of the worst atrocities in modern criminal history and had a team of financial experts managing his fortune.

And he was never seen for twenty-three years? The only evidence that he even existed was a dog-eared photograph of him taken with his wife during their honeymoon in Venice. As Ferraro said, it is the classic example, the greatest truth about the culture that has existed for so long in Mafia-controlled communities: the code of silence. '*Omertà* was always the greatest hurdle that our police faced,' said Ferraro, 'and it is only in comparatively recent times that it has begun to be broken. In the end, the communities would turn and when Falcone and other colleagues began their greatest attack on the Mafia in the 1980s, that movement of reaction by the people against the criminals finally started to swing in our direction.'

Until then, virtually every major attempt by the law to put the Mafia chieftains behind bars foundered with the collapse of literally dozens of trials through collusion by corrupt judges and politicians, lack of evidence, or the death, disappearance or loss of memory of witnesses.

There is no better example of how the Mafia ruled local communities than the story of the rise of the Corleonesi clan and of its two most infamous bosses, Luciano Liggio and Toto Riina, and with today's knowledge of developments within the Mafia hierarchy it is possible to track the emergence of the modern, ruthless and very rich conglomerate from the feudal, agriculture-based origins in which single, middle-class Mafia families held sway in small territorial regions.

The fictional accounts are confusingly romantic. Ferraro and her colleagues in the Italian judiciary deal with reality, though they accept that historically the Mafia's place in these communities was important. In the flashback sequences of Francis Ford Coppola's *The Godfather* Part Two, Corleone was given an oil-painting image: attractive countryside, pretty young girls and handsome young men with shot-guns strapped to their backs, a place enveloped by traditional Sicilian family values where a girl could only be courted under the watchful eye of a chaperon and whose violence was explained away by the 'vendetta' as if it were an excuse for all that happened. Added to that was haunting music and though you knew the Mafia was bad, the whole scenerio was appealingly attractive even though it was thoroughly stereotyped.

Corleone was and is a shabby little Sicilian town, unremarkable in appearance but sure enough the town has a story to tell. Back in the forties and fifties it was a quiet backwater. Across five decades, very little has changed. The buildings are grimier. Transport is more plentiful and scooters are much in evidence. When the weather is fine, old men will be seen playing *scopa*, the card game, at outside tables in the bar in the main piazza. Around the square are narrow streets lined with small, ugly houses with blank facades. There are few civic facilities, no cinema, no library. And this is where we begin the second stage of our journey of discovery, along that mountainous route to Corleone that leads us to the heart of Sicily and to what also became the mythical beating heart of the modern Cosa Nostra.

In post-war Corleone, the new mayor of the town was Dr Michele Navarra, who was held in high regard in the local community as the local doctor, a career which he pursued in tandem to his other duties as Corleone's *capomafioso* – the head man.

Yet unremarkable though the town was, no single case history from those days more typified the double standards of the so-called men of the 'Honoured Society' of Cosa Nostra than the story of Dr Navarra. He was the man the village people turned to to cure their illnesses and save their lives. He was the man who ran the town, collected the taxes and generally ministered to the needs of the community largely to the benefit of himself, the Cosa Nostra and the landowners.

While saving lives at his hospital, he had no qualms about ending others, indirectly putting various people to death by order. His was the classic biography of a member of the old high mafiosi. He was outwardly a respectable citizen with no criminal record.

During the first two years of his term as mayor, there were fifty-seven murders in the town of Corleone, all of them attributed to Mafia business. They included that of Dr Carmelo Nicolosi who was director of the hospital until one day he was found dead in an alley with two bullet holes in the back of his head. Dr Navarra took over his job.

The most famous incident in Corleone during Navarra's time is still discussed, written about and analyzed by university students, such was its impact upon the community of Sicily. It involved the murder of a poor shepherd boy who had witnessed a Mafia killing of a peasant trade unionist named Placido Rizzotto.

'These murders oblige us,' wrote social commentator Giuseppe Casarrubea in 1994, 'to be precise in our interpretation of the political and social history of Sicily, that after the repression of Mussolini, Sicily was to suffer the repression of the Mafia while the state, for its own convenience, stood looking on and did nothing. The murders of Rizzotto and the shepherd boy are emblematic. They point us towards the exalting battles that small people like Rizzotto, a trade unionist, were prepared to undertake in that period on behalf of his people and yet, when he was killed, no one saw. *Omertà.* Except for the boy who was himself then killed.'

The story began on 10 March 1948 when Rizzotto, a local trade union organizer, had arranged to meet Mayor Navarra to discuss the possibility of forming cooperatives for peasant workers which had been done in several other towns. The co-operatives were a boost to employment and were designed to take up plots of uncultivated land left dormant by absentee landlords. Navarra was against it, and against the activist attitude of Rizzotto whom he considered to be a Communist, though he wasn't: the Mafia hated all Communists. There was no other reason why Rizzotto should be disposed of; he was an honest young man who was engaged to be married and still lived at home with his parents.

That night, around 7 p.m. Rizzotto went out for his prearranged meeting with Navarra. As he reached the main road, three men approached him. One of them carried a revolver: Luciano Liggio, a handsome, flash young mafioso who had recently returned from the US to his native town and strutted the streets with his sleeked back hair and striped American suits. They were Navarra men.

Liggio suggested that they should go for a stroll, an expression which left no doubt in the mind of the victim that execution was imminent. As they walked out of the town, people in the main street drifted back into the shadows. No one saw anything; no one heard anything. Except for an innocent boy, twelve years old and tending his father's animals on the hillside when the three men with Rizzotto arrived. Unaware they were being watched, they shot and stabbed the trade unionist and pushed his body in a gully. It was a popular place for executions.

The boy, Giuseppe Letizia, came running home, babbling. There were suggestions that to silence him Liggio – having heard him scream – had gone over, pulled the boy to the scene of the murder and forced him to stab the victim, thus involving him in the crime. Giuseppe had nightmares and the following day was so distressed his father decided he should be taken to the hospital to see Dr Navarra.

The doctor decreed that he was having hallucinations, administered some drugs by injection, and sent the boy home. His condition worsened and he died on 14 March, killed by Navarra's lethal injection.

Two deaths: Rizzotto in revenge for challenging Navarra's dominion and the boy for witnessing the killing. Nor was the death of Rizzotto an unusual event. He was one of forty-one trade union leaders murdered during the Mafia's campaign against local activists; a war waged against the peasant workers on behalf of political allies. The Mafia, always horribly efficient at eliminating the opposition, political or criminal, would never allow the peasant heroes to get within range of the ballot box.

Liggio was eventually arrested for the murder of Rizzotto and went through three trials, the last being seventeen years after the event. During those years he ran free, committing dozens of other crimes and murders on the way. When he was finally brought to trial he was acquitted for lack of proof.

No one bothered to look for Rizzotto's body in the spot described by the boy at the time of the investigation nor did they until the case was re-examined in an anti-mafia investigation conducted from Palermo in 1970 when an enthusiastic Carabinieri officer, Carlo Alberto Dalla Chiesa – about whom much will be heard later – had the gully searched. By then, several bodies had been dumped in the grotto on the hillside overlooking Corleone, and though reduced over the years to a collection of bones, one of them was identified as Rizzotto by the American shoes he had been wearing.

Liggio was an arrogant killer who murdered his way to the top. He taunted authority and quickly became a major player in the Sicilian Mafia, and found a mentor in Frank Coppola, who reckoned he was destined for great things.

It was soon clear to Navarra that the man who had been his hired gun was now bidding for power himself and so went to war with Liggio and his men. The killings mounted by the day. Between 1954 and 1958, there were 153 Mafia murders in the area around Corleone. They should have included that of Liggio himself. Navarra gave the order for his assassination because he was becoming too powerful. A bloody shoot-out followed in the hills behind Corleone. Liggio was left for dead, but crawled to a neighbouring village where he was nursed back to health.

As soon as he recovered, Liggio planned his revenge. He recruited two young Mafia soldiers who were to be at his side for the next twenty years – the two best shots in Corleone, Salvatore 'Toto' Riina and his friend Bernardo Provenzano. Riina, the son of a shepherd was born in Corleone in 1930 and like so many young men in these communities was drawn to the Mafia to seek his fame and fortune. At fifteen, he made the grade. During an argument with another boy from an opposing family, he pulled out a pistol and shot the boy in the leg.

He died from loss of blood and Riina was given his colours by the Mafia. He was sent to the Mafia finishing school, the Ucciardone prison at Palermo where he spent six years. Inside, he shared a cell with Provenzano and when they they came out, Liggio appointed them his personal aides with a special task in mind – to eliminate Dr Navarra and take over the Corleonesi.

The moment came in 1958, when Liggio put together a gang of fifteen men armed to the teeth. They ambushed Navarra's car as he drove home at night. There was another local doctor with him, apparently innocently accepting a lift. Between them, the two men had 210 bullets pumped into their bodies.

Though a sensational murder – and one of many because Liggio went on to eliminate, one by one, all of Navarra's supporters, a further twenty-eight killings – the existence of a Mafia organization was still being scorned by the most powerful politicians in Sicily. Only the Communists continued to be outspoken, and the local left-wing newspaper *L'Ora* began for the first time to name names, to tie up the Navarra killings with local Cosa Nostra activity.

The paper started a series of articles, detailing the story of Mafia personalities and on the fourth day, published a photograph of Liggio with a caption which read '*pericoloso*' (dangerous). The following day, a bomb blew the printing presses of *L'Ora* to pieces and a special edition, printed on makeshift presses was brought out: 'We will not be silenced . . . this outrage must show to the national government the urgent necessity of a parliamentary inquiry into the Mafia. It is to the forefront of the thoughts of every responsible and upright citizen.' The issue was raised in parliament but though there was talk of an inquiry, it would take another four years – and another major bombing outrage – before it began.

Liggio, under investigation for several murders but still free, was the new Godfather of Corleone, the youngest ever, but in terms of the Sicilian Mafia hierarchy, he was still of fairly low order. He was not even a member of the Mafia *cupola*, although he was ambitious and had plans, and as ever that spelled trouble and the onset of Mafia wars.

* * *

As ever, developments in America had their effect on the Sicilian situation. At the start of the 1950s, US senator Estes Kefauver launched his Special Committee to Investigate Organized Crime in Interstate Commerce – an inquiry which ran for sixteen months, interrogated six hundred witnesses and became the required nightly viewing of television audiences across America.

It was a timely exposure but one which J Edgar Hoover, director of the FBI, attempted to stifle, pouring scorn on Kefauver's claims of organized crime, even to the point of trying to smear him. Hoover, according to his biographer Anthony Summers, was by then already being blackmailed by Meyer Lansky over a photograph allegedly showing Hoover in a compromising state with another man.

Organized crime had run riot in America since the end of the war and Hoover had done nothing to stop it. Kefauver wheeled in mobster after mobster, politician after politician. The life and times of Luciano, Costello, Lansky, Adonis, Genovese and the rest became public property for the first time. The senator concluded that there was indeed an organized criminal network.

Looking back from the nineties it may seem incredibly naive that it took so long to come to such a conclusion, although in Italy such official recognition did not appear until more than twenty years later. But this was, really, the first time it had been recognized publicly in such specific terms.

Kefauver said the Mafia as it existed in the United States was a direct descendant of, and in concert with, a criminal organization originating in the island of Sicily. This was treated as big news even though the American-Italian Mafia had been operating since the end of the nineteenth century and the Italian Mafia in its various forms far, far longer.

One year after the Kefauver hearings had ended, Hoover continued to attempt to discredit its findings. In 1953, his Assistant Director Alan Belmont wrote in a memo for general consumption within the FBI: 'The Maffia [sic] is an alleged organization . . . [its] existence in the United States is doubtful.'

Among the witnesses at the Kefauver hearings was Lucky Luciano's old enemy Harry Anslinger, the head of the narcotics bureau who was far more active in tracking the Mafia than Hoover himself. He had known of the organization all along and continued to insist that the Sicilians were the originators of the increasing supplies of narcotics arriving in the US.

Heroin had been uncovered in mailed parcels from Sicily, on board ships importing everything from oranges to cheese and in the bags of couriers. But Kefauver's hearings only exacerbated the problem. They had a dramatic effect on the US Mafia's finances, which were underpinned by gambling. Incredible figures – for that period in history – were produced estimating that organized illegal gambling turned over approximately $20 billion each year or about 7 per cent of America's gross national product.

When this revenue finally came under attack from the law within the United States, crime families across the US were forced to look for alternatives – and the Sicilian drug franchise would prove to be a favoured substitute which gave the Italian Mafia another timely boost.

Carlo Gambino, ambitious underling of the Anastasia family, who had numerous well-placed relatives in Sicily, had rented warehouse space in Cuba for $1 million a year, into which he received narcotics shipments from his relations, the Gambino family of Palermo. Lucky Luciano and Frank Coppola, who had established supplies of morphine base for processing into heroin in Milan, were also dealing heavily and they were joined by another famous American gangster, Joe Adonis, who had been controlling some of Luciano's rackets in New York.

Adonis was arrested in 1951, went to prison for two years and then faced further charges when he came out following the Kefauver inquiry. The senator described him as 'the most insolent and astute gangster, and in a sense the most sinister of them all'.

Faced with another prison term, Adonis caught the next boat to Italy, docked in Naples and took up residence in Milan to begin setting up his own contacts in the drugs game, allied with various other Mafia activities conducted in alliance with the Neapolitan Camorra and the Sicilian Cosa Nostra. And so, three of America's top gangsters of the thirties and forties, Luciano, Coppola and Adonis – along with half a dozen lesser names who had also fled in the wake of Kefauver – were by the mid-fifties busily setting up their supply routes through Europe to America.

The Sicilians, anxious to meet their demand, began to bolster the narcotics business by buying in from the Middle East, notably at that time through Beirut, North Africa and Asia. By 1957, they had four heroin processing factories in operation, one in Milan and three in Palermo. Their own factories became necessary when the Americans put pressure on the Italian authorities for tighter control of its legitimate pharmaceutical companies which had provided Luciano with almost 1,000 kilos of heroin over a five-year period.

Morphine base, the initial extract in the process of transforming the gum from opium poppies, was refined in laboratories either in Sicily or in the south of France, where Luciano had arrangements with the Corsican dealers in the 'French Connection.'

It was transported on towards the eastern seaboard of America. The methods are now familiar: by boat, plane, courier, false-bottomed suitcases, fake fruit, pottery, works of art; anything which could hide packets of the drug.

As the traffic increased, the US Mafia families began to fight among themselves and through the summer of 1957, a series of killings left control of the Mafia's drug operations in the hands of Vito Genovese and Carlo Gambino. They carved up the narcotics trade in New York. That autumn, the heads of five key Sicilian Cosa Nostra families held a summit meeting at the Hotel del Palmes in Palermo. Suites and a meeting room were booked from 10 to 13 of October.

Also in attendance were Luciano himself, Frank Coppola and a clutch of senior American mafiosi. According to the judicial records from the Commissione Parlamentare, 1976, the meeting was arranged to formally set up an operations group to supervise and expand the narcotics trade. Exactly one month later, the proposals were outlined to the famous Apalachian summit of every leading Mafia boss in the US.

At the beginning of the sixties, the number of registered addicts in America was little more than 50,000. Within a decade, it had exceeded 700,000 and the pattern in percentage terms was repeated throughout the western world. The Sicilian Cosa

Nostra made its quantum leap from its old image peasantry of with sawn-off shotguns to businessmen who dominated the world heroin trade and all its ancillary benefits.

As the sixties proceeded, the whole power structure of the Mafia changed and once again there was blood on the streets, with over 200 killings in America and scores more in Sicily.

In Italy, Lucky Luciano died of a heart attack in 1962, although rumour had it that he had been poisoned by the Sicilians when he arranged to meet a television producer who wanted to tell his life story. Joe Adonis was exiled by the Italian police to a tiny village on the Dalmatian coast. Of the big three Americans operating in Italy, only Frank Coppola, with his strong political connections, remained in business.

Carlo Gambino became the boss of bosses in the US and the pattern was truly set for the Italian-American connection to steer itself into uncharted territories; the era of the narco-billions.

Lucky Luciano's death in 1962 also signalled the onset of the first Sicilian wars among the Mafia that mirrored the jostling for power that had gone on in the United States. In the five years after the drug franchise arrangement was set up in 1957, the price of a kilo of heroin in New York had virtually doubled. Such riches brought greed and greed brought the wars.

Luciano Liggio and the Corleonesi were not in the drugs trade in the early days. He was still reliant on the more traditional Mafia activities. Cattle rustling was Liggio's speciality and he ran his own private slaughterhouse from which stolen animals were prepared for the local trade. He had also taken over care and protection of the local markets which assured him a tidy daily income and he had a side interest on the drugs market, linking up with the Greco family who had bought a fleet of ships to move their heroin around the world, along with other illicit cargoes.

Liggio's control of the ports and harbours gave them free passage, though the Grecos had their own system well rehearsed. Boats that picked up heroin from Marseilles and North Africa would be changed in appearance while at sea. Narcotics agents who were tracking the boats would log them out of the French ports and by the time they reached their destination, they would be renamed and flying the flag of another country.

Towards the end of 1961, the US Narcotics Bureau tried to alert the authorities in Palermo. A special report on the trade between the US and Sicilian families was sent to police headquarters and passed to the new Chief Public Prosecutor of Palermo, Judge Pietro Scaglione who had been deputy in that office for the previous twelve years.

The report ended up on the wrong desk. Judge Scaglione was 'patronized' by the Mafia. Born in Lercara Friddi – the birthplace of Lucky Luciano – he became a magistrate in the late 1920s and apart from two years in Rome, had spent his entire career in Palermo. When the US report arrived for urgent attention, he simply put it in his pending tray – and there it remained for four years.

In the meantime, the Sicilians had begun fighting among themselves as the profits soared. The Greco family – run in two factions by the cousins Ciaschiteddu and L'Ingegnere to whom Luciano Liggio had aligned himself and the Corleonesi – had control over narcotics along with four other families.

The notorious La Barberas, brothers Angelo and Salvatore, led the opposing faction. Both families were represented on the *cupola*, chaired by the head of the Greco family, Ciaschiteddu. The killings began, one a day for fifty days. Many were of lesser mafiosi from either side, but the top members of the families were also hit.

Angelo La Barbera fled, but not far enough. On 24 May 1962, he was in Milan, ensconced in the house of a mistress. He left around 1.20 in the morning and as he started the engine of his Opel, two men appeared at the window and emptied the contents of their heavy revolvers into his chest. He had six bullet wounds, but still managed to pull his own gun and fire at one of the would-be assassins.

He survived and after a seven-hour operation in Milan was arrested, charged with eight murders, sentenced to twenty-two years in 1968, and released under house arrest six years later.

In March 1962, the Sicilian Regional Assembly had, by open vote, called for action, stating that the Mafia was a national problem and not confined to Sicily alone. Even back then, the implications of their plea were evident: 'It is necessary to identify the interests providing complicity and help to the phenomenon of the Mafia . . . we ask that the National Parliament urgently forms a Parliamentary Commission of Inquiry . . .'

The request was granted by an open vote in the Senate in Rome although in the House of Deputies where a secret vote was held, thirty-five MPs voted against. The first all-party commission was formed in April 1963. On 30 June, the Mafia responded to this open threat to its activities when the police headquarters at Palermo received an anonymous telephone call, reporting a suspicious-looking car, an Alfa Romeo, parked in Ciaculli, opposite the house of L'Ingegnere Greco.

A team of army bomb disposal experts went with the police and duly examined the Alfa. They discovered a crude device on the back seat which they quickly defused and thought that was that. Then one of the carabinieri opened the boot of the car. The real bomb was carefully packed inside, and as soon as the lid was lifted it exploded.

Seven policemen were killed.

It became known as the Ciaculli massacre, and the whole of Italy was outraged. The government answered the public outcry by pushing through new laws and the Ministry of Justice in Rome promised that the perpetrators of this terrible crime would be pursued and caught.

It was surely not a coincidence that among the seven victims was police Lieutenant Mario Malausa, the team leader and author of several accusing reports on high Mafia figures, none of which had been acted upon by Judge Pietro Scaglione. The lieutenant had recently completed another report on the collusion between Mafia and politicians in Sicily, a collusion which he said stretched to the highest level.

Few people knew of his intention to submit the report to the new Anti-Mafia Commission but the lieutenant was never interviewed before he was murdered. His report surfaced in Palermo a year after his death when it was delivered anonymously to the newspaper *L'Ora* whose editor courageously published extracts.

Malausa's dossier can now be seen as the first real attempt by any law officer to link the Mafia with those in political office. He had named specifically the Mayor of Palermo, Salvo Lima, later to become a Euro MP and the Mafia's alleged ambassador to Rome and Brussels, who was at the time on the point of being appointed provincial secretary of the Christian Democrats, effectively controlling 28 per cent of the national strength of his party.

His public works assessor, Vito Ciancimino, who would succeed him as mayor, was the man who controlled the building permits. Malausa had put a question mark beside the name of Judge Scaglione and he named several politicians who served in the regional and national governments – all Christian Democrats – who he believed to have links with Cosa Nostra figures.

Huge building contracts were handed out to Mafia-backed companies at the time of the rebuilding explosion that transformed the face of Palermo in the sixties and seventies. The Cosa Nostra, through the individual endeavours of the various families, had formed dozens of front companies, taken over thousands of acres of land by bullying and terrorizing the owners, by burning crops, cutting down lemon trees, and garrotting cattle until they were prepared to sell at rock-bottom prices. They had moved into the whole commercial and business life of Sicily and the south of Italy, and those companies they did not own would face the Mafia's own local taxation – for 'protection'.

Lieutenant Malausa had identified the new breed of businessman of the Cosa Nostra – but it would be another twenty years before anyone began to act on his report.

In Rome, the government began papering over the cracks. On 7 August 1963, the Italian parliament approved nine new measures to give greater power to the authorities to fight the Mafia. They included compulsory banishment to far-away places of known mafiosi, a review of all those registered as possessing firearms, a careful reassessment of civil servants in senior positions in the four provinces of western Sicily, a review of all licences and controls for building contracts in Sicily and southern Italy, and an order that all current trials and court hearings against Mafia suspects should be concluded without delay.

That summer, the clamour for action was such that the law, and the government, had to be seen to be doing something –

a pattern which would be repeated again and again after each outrage in the future. A new strong man was appointed to lead the judiciary into battle, alongside the parliamentary Anti-Mafia Commission.

He was the incorruptible Judge Cesare Terranova, a Sicilian born and bred, who promised he would immediately bring order to the tardy habits of the prosecutory system and demand the arrest and trial of more than 100 members of the Cosa Nostra: the Greco cousins, Luciano Liggio, the injured Angelo La Barbera, Frank Coppola and others, including one young Man of Honour about whom much would be heard later, Tommaso Buscetta.

Within a month of the Ciaculli massacre, Terranova signed the documents authorizing the search and arrest of the *capomafia.*

In effect, he had signed his own death warrant.

According to the testimony of Tommaso Buscetta, who became a major informer against the Mafia twenty years later, the year of 1963 saw the Mafia seriously crippled. The anti-Mafia forces certainly began their onslaught with that prospect and there was a good deal of speculation in the media that this time the Mafia would be broken.

A special force of ten thousand men was amassed in Sicily. The heads of the police, the Carabinieri and army worked out precisely which areas to attack, where known mafiosi were in abundance. Helicopters, armoured vehicles, parachute squads and dog-handlers gave support to mobile and foot patrol units. Secret police and intelligence forces provided telephone taps and surveillance ahead of the raids.

Cities, towns and villages were marked out; whole areas were cordoned off as the troops and police moved in for their dawn raids under the glow of arc lights. Within four months, 1,903 arrests were made, and they included a score of Mafia chieftains. But, of course, the operation was no secret to the Cosa Nostra who had been informed by their spies in the law camps well in advance.

The papers of Judge Cesare Terranova reveal that even before the police operation was mounted, a council of six of the leading mafiosi which included Luciano Liggio and Ciaschiteddu Greco, met in Palermo in the second week of

August. 'By mutual agreement,' wrote Terranova, 'these six decided to suspend all criminal activity that might confirm the existence of organized crime.'

The *cupola* was temporarily disbanded and several of the bigger bosses, and especially those in the narcotics business, did not even wait for its decision. They scattered. Some went into hiding on the island, others heading to the mainland and the north of Italy. A powerful clutch of them, however, left the country on false passports for Britain, Germany, South America, Canada, Mexico and the United States.

Luciano Liggio was found hiding in Corleone. A sickening aside to this discovery was that he was living with the woman who was the fiancée of Corleone's trade unionist, Placido Rizzotto, whom Liggio had murdered on Navarra's instructions sixteen years earlier; the same woman who had once threatened to cut out the heart of her lover's killers. He had chosen her to be his woman, and in the end she had no alternative but to accept.

The arrogance and nonchalance of Liggio came as no surprise to his adversary, Judge Terranova.

'Why are you doing this?' Liggio said, protesting his innocence of any wrongdoing. 'I am a sick man. What could I be capable of?'

Judge Terranova began his preparations for the first Mafia multiple trials for more than three decades. It would be three years before he could begin bringing his most senior mafiosi captives to trial, though many lesser offenders caught in the mass arrests of the police pincer movement were dealt with in Palermo.

Many were acquitted, others were given short sentences and dozens more were subjected to the new banishment orders – known in Italian as *soggiorno obbligato cautelativo* (exile under surveillance).

They were taken to towns and villages in central and northern Italy. Those thought to be especially dangerous were sent to distant islands like Linosa, l'Asinara and Filicudi. The system of banishment on the basis of mere suspicion seemed on the face of it a particularly useful weapon in the police armoury against the Mafia, though in truth it proved to be a farce.

The suspects were free to come and go more or less as they

pleased because it was impossible to hold all of them under twenty-four hour surveillance. As Gaia Servadio recorded on her visit to one of those islands in 1969, she played cards with Ciancomo Coppola, a cousin of the notorious Frank Coppola. She also came across one Calogero Sinatra who asked if she had heard of his relative, Frank Sinatra. Then he complained, 'You would not think they could do this to me. I have no record. I have committed no crime. It is a terrible injustice.'

A new law was brought in which decreed for the first time that arrest would no longer be dependent upon evidence of guilt. It would be sufficient for a suspect to be considered a social danger or being associated with the Mafia and yet, in spite of the efforts of several known anti-Mafia judges and magistrates, the massive attack on the Mafia instigated after the massacre of Malausa and his colleagues eventually foundered, to a large degree, when the trials came to court.

Of the 1,903 originally arrested, around 300 were dealt with on lesser charges ranging from theft to illegal firearms. The hard core of the Mafia elite was whittled down to around 100. The courageous judge, said the media pundits in the north, was fighting the 'impossible fight'.

Undeterred, Cesare Terranova insisted that the myth that the Cosa Nostra was an Honoured Society had to be destroyed. It was exactly the opposite: 'Cosa Nostra, in truth, means oppression, arrogance, coercion, greed, self-enrichment, power and hegemony, against all others. It is nothing less than a total criminal organization regulated by unwritten rules which are maintained by inexorable and iron-rod delinquency that is contaminating all of Italy.'

The charges, running to almost 250 pages, dealt with crimes dating back to the late 1950s, and Luciano Liggio was prominent, as were his henchmen Salvatore 'Toto' Riina and Bernardo Provenzano. The Ciaculli bomb massacre was also the subject of charges against the Greco cousins who, by then, had already fled Italy. The trials dragged on for three years and were held on the Italian mainland, mostly in the Calabrian town of Catanzaro where a school was turned into a courtroom, and surrounded by a permanent guard of 500 carabinieri.

The accused men were brought, day after day, into a huge

cage placed in the centre of a gymnasium and after the impetus of the initial hearings, the interest gradually faded. Where once the Rome adminstration and the media had taken a close interest in developments, now concern about the Mafia had once again subsided. The horrors of Ciaculli had passed into history and the nod went out from Rome that the whole affair should be wrapped up.

All but ten of the the 100 or so Mafia bosses accused were acquitted through lack of evidence. Of the ten who were given prison sentences, half were already elsewhere enjoying a much better life than the Italian prison service could offer – men like the Grecos and Tommaso Buscetta had long ago decamped to distant parts. They were sentenced in absentia. Not one was convicted of any charge relating to the Ciaculli massacre and so the secret of political dealings was once again secure.

Terranova and his anti-Mafia colleagues were naturally furious and not least over the fact that Luciano Liggio was cleared on every charge in the 1968 trials. However, Terranova ordered his immediate re-arrest on nine new charges of murder and a list of lesser charges dating back to 1948.

At the same time, a force of carabinieri was dispatched to Corleone and sixty-nine members of the clan were hauled back to the Ucciardone prison in Palermo to await trial with Liggio. Among them were Toto Riina and Bernardo Provenzano. In February 1969, a series of forty-seven hearings opened once again on the Italian mainlaind. Liggio had continued to run his Corleonesi empire from the confines of a prison cell, or a room in an expensive nursing home in Palermo where he was allowed treatment under guard.

As the trials neared their conclusion, the prosecution gloomily surveyed the wreckage. They had suffered severe setbacks all along. Witnesses who had promised to testify suddenly lost their memories; others refused say anything at all, one crucial figure in the charges against Liggio had been committed to a mental institution and some simply vanished. If that wasn't enough, the Mafia had one more ace to play and Liggio knew it as he sat throughout with his insolent smiles and arrogant guffaws which turned quickly into a murderous gaze into the eyes of any witness who seemed on the verge of saying something incriminating.

As the lawyers began to make their closing speeches, a series of hand-delivered letters suddenly appeared on the desks of the judges and in the hands of members of the jury – protected though they had been by a round-the-clock guard. The words were chilling and to the point:

> You people in Bari have not understood what Corleone means. You are judging honest citizens, gentlemen of Corleone who have been denounced by the carabinieri and the police. We simply want to warn you that if a single gentleman from Corleone is condemned, so too will you be condemned. You will be blown apart; you will be butchered and so will every member of your families. A Sicilian proverb says 'A man warned is a man saved.' It is now up to you.

Two days later, the jury filed back into the courtroom of Bari to deliver its verdict. Every one of the sixty-four members of the Corleonesi clan was acquitted through lack of proof, save for Liggio himself who was found guilty of one charge of stealing grain for which he received a suspended sentence. Liggio, like the rest, walked free again and made a king-like exit into the sunshine surrounded by reporters to whom he gave a press conference decrying attempts to smear his good name: 'I am but a businessman, a poor devil who has been victimized by the police and the media . . .'

Then he climbed into a large limousine and was sped away into hiding, to begin again his activities along with his two aides, Riina and Provenzano. Their incarceration had had little affect on their 'business'.

There was one other unexpected side effect of the attack on the Mafia that the authorities apparently did not even consider. The banished mafiosi in their far-flung locations in the Italian countryside were not long in re-establishing their connections and their business activities which had become so familiar in Sicily.

The Mafia was on the move, and the establishment of new outposts of crime began in the mid-sixties with their enforced movement out of their home towns and villages as the authorities began their purge. Other more senior figures had moved abroad. At least five other escapees from Sicilian justice settled in Venezuela whose 1,700 miles of virtually deserted Caribbean coastline provided havens for smugglers.

Another infamous Sicilian group also moved on, one of them buying a mansion in the south of England from where he set up in the drugs business, while other members of his family went on to Canada, then South America, thus creating a supply route which virtually spanned the globe.

The drugging of America accelerated. By accident, the Italian authorities forced the Mafia to reposition itself, and in strategically important parts of the Americas they took the narcotics business to higher levels. And so what supposedly began as an operation to break the Sicilian Mafia once and for all had completely the opposite effect.

By the end of the decade, when the multiple trials had all but virtually collapsed into a scandalous fiasco, the Mafia was poised for its big bang, aided by startling events already on the horizon in Italian cities.

CHAPTER FIVE

Kidnappers Anonymous, the CIA and the Red Brigades

Liliana Ferraro received the call to Rome to take her place in a world of top-heavy security made necessary by the daily risk of assassination. She was one of the few women in a male-dominated profession where females were mostly secretaries, and if eyebrows were raised at her arrival, it was as much to do with the times, when Italy was under attack from within its own borders. She found herself thrust into what became an all too familiar state of permanent siege for those who work in the ornate, echoing, marble-floored halls of the Ministry of Justice with its exterior ring of steel.

Her arrival in Rome was brought about by pressures on the judiciary which were not the fault of the Mafia – in fact for once the Mafia was pushed into the background. At that time, in the early seventies, Italy was in the grip of a bloody terrorist war, largely conducted by the militants who formed anarchical extremist groups from the left and the right, but dominated by the infamous Red Brigades.

A large handful of high Mafia bosses were also in the thick of it, and there was hefty CIA activity which would reach scandalous proportions. Even today the full extent of their agitation during one of Italy's most troubled periods remains top secret.

The rivalries of the opposing revolutionary factions formed a constant undercurrent to the terrorist campaign which ran from 1969 to the early 1980s. At the end of it, the sporadic urban guerilla warfare had involved more than 10,000 attacks and left 180 people dead and 500 wounded in shootings and bombings aimed at virtually every section of establishment life – judges, lawyers, newspapers, journalists, politicians, businessmen and even the church. The decade also saw the explosion of another Italian phenomenon, kidnappings, which is where the Red Brigades and the Mafia found common ground.

Italian forces of law were stretched to breaking point and that in itself brought a side effect which can be seen in hindsight as bringing great benefit to the Mafia. It also instilled within the Italian nation and the establishment an unprecedented fear of violence which the Mafia leaders themselves would use to great effect. Also, the terrorist war diverted the attention of the judiciary and police so that the Mafia was able to regroup and re-energise itself with far less hindrance from the law than might otherwise have been the case.

At the beginning of the seventies, Ferraro had attracted the attention of the senior civil servants at the Ministry of Justice as a woman of single-minded dedication to her job. Since leaving Naples University in 1966 with her law degree, she had carefully set her course for the future, moving away from a career as a practising lawyer towards the judiciary itself.

As a linguist, she had originally toyed with a move to the diplomatic service, but she proceeded through the lower echelons of court work until, eventually, she became caught up in it and it became her life. She qualified first as a magistrate in Naples in 1969 and was subsequently posted to a small district outside Milan where she dealt with the local casework. In 1973, her propensity for long hours and an obvious ability in the wider aspects of Italian justice came to the attention of her superiors in Rome and she was summoned to the Supreme Court as a young judge.

By then, urban warfare was in full swing. 'I arrived in Rome at a terrible time in our history,' she told me. 'So many good friends in the police and judiciary were being killed, and being new to these surroundings and the close proximity of death, I found it difficult to cope with the grief day after day. At one point, I began to think that we really could not win.'

She was thrust immediately into the judiciary's effort, where eventually she would encounter General Carlo Alberto Dalla Chiesa, who became the hero of the fight against terrorism and later directed his energies against the Mafia. 'At that time,' said Ferraro, 'Dalla Chiesa became exclusively concerned with the terrorists, though admittedly there were times when the paths of terrorism and outright criminality crossed.'

In 1994, when I asked her for her recollections of these dramatic years, she agreed that there were external political forces at work and there were occasions when Mafia and Red Brigades came together as one. It was an important identification of the role of the Mafia in this troubled period and one seldom made. 'The Red Brigades were an ideological organization, and the Mafia strictly criminal. But we now know that when two groups embarked on illegal activities, it was not only possible but probable that their interests should cross.'

For Ferraro, involvement at such a traumatic time brought her into direct contact with, and experience of, some of the most monstrous crimes of violence in Italian history, though it was a precursor to much more that would follow. Indeed, much of what happened in the 1980s with the Mafia, when she would lose even more good friends, had its roots in the 1970s.

The Red Brigades were a uniquely Italian product of that anarchistic age and although they had similarities to other notorious European groups, the links were minimal. The Italian terrorist campaign was born in the wake of the student riots in France in the late sixties, emulated in Italy at a time of social unrest and uncertainty through weak government, rising unemployment and inflation, and later the international oil crisis and a mounting crime wave.

There were many groups on either side of the political divide who were involved in various forms of activism, violent and peaceful. Almost 100 leftist organizations operated in Italy during the seventies under a myriad of revolutionary names and about half as many right-wing groups. The Red Brigades, as a combative organization, considered the Italian Communist Party, democratic labour unions and the Soviet Union to be its enemies.

Even the name 'Red Brigade' was provocatively chosen to

assume the colour of their opponents' banners. The Italian Communist Party had, like its French and Spanish counterparts, ditched its Leninist ideals and had become a model for the new Eurocommunism. This sent the Americans into apoplexy and the CIA operated numerous schemes aimed at destabilizing the trend towards a moderate form of Communism.

There were, much later, strong indications that the Red Brigades were born out of a CIA-inspired plot to discredit the Communists and thus make them unacceptable to the Italian electorate. The Mafia, through its earlier contacts with American intelligence and anti-Communists, became an active participant on the side-lines.

The Red Brigades emerged initially from an organization called Workers' Autonomy which was being funded by the CIA through the American consulate in Rome, a fact established in 1976 by a US Committee of Inquiry under the chairmanship of Senator Otis Pike. Italy was a hotbed of intrigue at the time with all the major powers sticking their oar in: the Soviet KGB, the Bulgarian secret service, the French Sureté, British MI6 and even the military junta in Greece.

The country was swarming with foreign agents – America alone was said to have 5,000 undercover people there at the time – all trying to manipulate events, pumping out propaganda and covertly financing and supporting whichever group best served their interests. The CIA had carried out a drive in American universities to recruit and plant spies and anti-Communist activists within the Italian revolutionary subculture at the universities.

And when the terrorist violence took off, there was a curious overlapping of activity between the Red Brigades and the Mafia, especially in the area of kidnapping. It was no accident and the whole business of the Italian kidnapping phenomenon throughout the seventies was tainted by obscure political involvement and Mafia activity, with background participation by the CIA.

Once again, it was a high-powered Mafia summit meeting that set the kidnappings are in motion in 1972. In May that year Luciano Liggio, head of the Corleonesi, was languishing in Switzerland under the assumed name of Baron Osvaldo Fattori. It was a public scandal that Liggio was still enjoying his freedom. Though wanted on new murder charges, he had been 'accidentally' freed after the trials of the late sixties, following an alleged internal mix-up over his status.

He was allowed to become a patient in an expensive clinic for the treatment of his various ailments, and from there the familiar Mercedes of Frank Coppola arrived to whisk him away to a hide-out from which he travelled freely throughout Europe on false passports. He remained free because of an incredible ruling by Judge Scaglione in Palermo that he could only be arrested in Corleone. This way, Liggio kept one step ahead of the law for quite some time.

His arrival in Switzerland became known to the Italian secret service who were tapping the telephone of another Mafia leader, Gerlando Alberti, one of the Cosa Nostra's new stars of the seventies. He was a small man whose very obvious toupée barely covered his bald head. He had been acquitted of murder in 1956 through lack of evidence and was mentioned during the big Mafia trials of the late sixties, though never charged.

Through Mafia association, however, he was banished from his home in Palermo to the north of Italy in 1967 where in due course he established a new group around him and became one of the biggest dealers in drugs and tobacco smuggling.

The wiretap was on his farmhouse near Milan and though Mafia people were by then notoriously adept at speaking in code on any telephone, the secret police managed to ascertain enough to know that whoever was on the other end of the line – Liggio, in fact though they did not know it – he was Mafia nobility.

Liggio risked the telephone conversations for a very significant reason. At Frank Coppola's behest, he was summoning a meeting of the Mafia *cupola*, long since reformed and active, for important decisions. Ten leading bosses were invited and every one turned up for the conference, which began on 12 May 1972 at the Park Hotel, Zurich.

Liggio was joined by l'Ingegnere Greco, still avoiding arrest and extradition to Italy from his luxurious villa in Beirut, Gerlando Alberti and other names well known in Palermo.

One common factor among all of those who came to the meeting was that they were all wealthy through their involvement in the narcotics business. And yet, Liggio had called them together to discuss what he apparently termed a 'tapping into a vast source of revenue – kidnapping'.

This activity was nothing new in the annals of Mafia history. There was a tradition of kidnapping going back centuries and Liggio assessed that in the wake of the Red Brigades kidnaps, there were rich pickings to be made. It was only part of the explanation for this meeting. The Mafia had a particular role to play in the social calamity which had befallen Italy.

The Mafia would extend and promote the kidnapping phenomenon to a degree that would cause political and public unrest. This new criminal enterprise would go under the name of *Anonima Sequestri* – Kidnappers Anonymous, rather in the style of the old American Mafia organization Murder Incorporated.

Within weeks of that Zurich meeting, the effects began to emerge in what was the beginning of an incredible period of Italian history, when dozens of people from every walk of life were kidnapped and held to ransom. Although there had been a number of kidnappings in the first two years of the decade of the 1970s, there was no pattern. Some had been attributed to terror gangs and subversives, others were clearly the work of criminals, mostly of southern or Sicilian extraction.

The Calabrian 'Ndrangheta, for example, were past, present and future masters at the kidnapping game, and operated from their traditional heartland in the Aspromonte, the mountainous region overlooking the straits of Messina.

The isolated roads that wound up through the forestation surrounding the town of Delianuova provided ample cover and in this little huddle of menace, the 'Ndrangheta would plot some of the most outrageous kidnaps. Many were local, and involved fairly modest sums of between 30 and 50 million lire ($25,000 to $30,000), and as such rarely figured in the news bulletins. A typical rictim was one of the wealthier farmers who had forgotten to pay over to the local Mafia their cut of the EEC olive oil subsidy.

And so, in collaboration with the 'Ndrangheta, Liggio's kidnappers began to flourish and from then on, ever increasing demands were made. Four weeks after Mafia chieftains dispersed from their hotel in Zurich, Aldo Palumbo, a wealthy businessman from Catania, Sicily, was kidnapped and held for a month. The family never disclosed whether or not a ransom was paid, but police estimate that more than 110 million lire was paid over in cash to the kidnappers.

In August Luciano Cassina, son of a Palermo industrialist, was snatched. He was held for 175 days and returned only on the payment of one billion 300 million lire. Pino Vassallo, the son of another Sicilian businessman, Francesco Vassallo, whose own relationship with the Sicilian Mafia in his rise to great wealth in the building boom of Palermo in the fifties and sixties was the subject of an Anti-Mafia Commission investigation, was also kidnapped in 1972.

Pino Vassallo was held for five months, locked in a small room in darkness. Why he was held for so long when Pino himself admitted that his father was ready to pay the ransom almost immediately is not known. The Vassallos gave little away to the police, nor did they reveal how much had been paid to the kidnappers.

Even with such dramatic case histories, the police did not begin to suspect the existence of a systematically organized kidnapping ring until 1973. The extent of the organization only began to come clear when police investigated the kidnapping of a wealthy Milanese engineering boss, Pietro Torielli, after his release for a ransom of $2 million – by then ransom demands had increased to spectacular levels.

Information from a particular source led detectives to a farmhouse near Bergamo, forty miles north-west of Milan. There, in a stable, they discovered a secret trapdoor leading to an underground cell where they found another captive, Count Luigi Rossi di Montelera, who had been kidnapped in Turin twelve weeks earlier, tethered on a four-foot chain.

The ransom demand of $6 million had gone unpaid by his family, owners of the famous drinks company Martini and Rossi. Luigi was one of the very few victims who were released unharmed through this period without a ransom being paid.

From this discovery, police began to assemble clues which all pointed to a Mafia-organized chain. Another clue turned up in their search of the farmhouse. It was a carton bearing the name of a wine company in Milan – operated by two Sicilian brothers. Police began to keep a watch on the place and discovered that a regular visitor was a man named Antonio Ferrugia who was, apparently, more than just a customer and seemed to be giving orders. Later, he was identified as none other than Luciano Liggio – who disappeared from view once again as soon as the count was recovered.

The kidnappings went on, becoming more daring and more expensive for the families who had to foot the ransom bill, and instilling fear in Italian society. The rich, especially, were trembling. Security firms mushroomed. Famous people hired round-the-clock bodyguards for themselves and their families. Self-defence courses were booked solid. The sale of guard dogs rocketed to such an extent they had to be imported from Germany and France.

Even schoolchildren fell victim outside of the country – as demonstrated when five-year-old Graziella Ortiz Patino, daughter of wealthy parents, was seized on her way to school near Lake Geneva. She was freed after a ransom of $2 million was paid. Cristina Mazzotti, aged eighteen, was abducted walking through Italian lakeland, and was murdered by her kidnappers with an overdose of drugs, even after the $2 million ransom had been paid.

The most infamous of all the kidnappings was that of John Paul Getty III, the 22-year-old grandson of the American oil tycoon, kidnapped in 1973 by the 'Ndrangheta and whisked away to the Calabrian mountains where he was imprisoned in a cave. He was held for five months and during protracted negotiations for his release, drawn out by the refusal of John Paul Getty to pay the ransom, the boy's left ear was cut off and delivered to his relatives with the warning that next it would be his hand and so on. Eventually his family paid a ransom in the region of £1,200,000 and he was finally released in December 1973. John Paul Getty III never recovered from his traumatic experience, became addicted to drugs and took a near lethal overdose a few years later which left him both blind and paralysed.

One of those Calabrians suspected of having taken part in the Getty kidnap, Vincenzo Mammoliti, was found dead inside his car from loss of blood through several wounds inflicted with a meathook, and with his testicles cut off and stuffed in his mouth – the classic Mafia way of showing that the man had been guilty of dishonour. That was a mere aside to the continuing kidnap saga.

In 1974 alone, there were forty kidnappings in Italy which netted ransoms in excess of $50 million. The Mafia gangs were being credited with most but confusingly for the Italian public and the judiciary alike, the Red Brigades also admitted responsibility for several major abductions.

In April 1974, Mario Sossi, assistant public prosecutor in Genoa, was kidnapped and released unharmed after thirty-five days of 'brainwashing' by the Red Brigades. Another known Red Brigades victim was Pietro Costa, millionaire shipbuilder, kidnapped in Genoa and released after fifty days on payment of a $2 million ransom.

But by far the majority were snatched by Liggio's loose-knit criminal cooperative, a fact highlighted by an investigating magistrate in Milan, Dr Michele Caizzi, who had identified thirty-two Mafia people involved and issued arrest warrants. More importantly, Caizzi struck another nerve which caused a flurry among the establishment in Rome and Milan.

He pointed out that the organization controlled an enormous flow of 'hot money' running into billions. This was being laundered through legitimate businesses in Italy and through banks at home and abroad, an activity which he insisted was only possible with high level collusion between the criminal elements, bankers and politicians. One name stood out in the investigation, but was kept secret. It was Michele Sindona, one of Italy's best-known international financiers who owned banks and businesses in his own country and had recently take control of a bank in New York.

He was once described by his Prime Minister, Giulio Andreotti, as 'the saviour of the lire' and was an investment adviser to the Vatican, along with his old friend Roberto Calvi, head of the Banco Ambrosiana, with whom he had one other thing in common; membership of the infamous P2 Masonic Lodge.

Sindona was, as events would show, not only a major money launderer for the Mafia kidnappings, but deeply involved in cleaning up billions of dollars of narcotics money, flowing back and forth between the United States, the Bahamas, Switzerland and Sicily. For the time being, his name was kept hidden, but much more would be heard of him later.

Caizzi reiterated what the more courageous among his

profession had said in the past, that in investigating these links it had once again become apparent that politicians at senior level were tied to Mafia activities. Without them, the path could not have been smoothed so easily and in return, as one of Caizzi's colleagues on the bench pointed out, the likes of Luciano Liggio and Frank Coppola delivered votes and money.

Liggio was once again a key focus of the Mafia hunters and it was his old adversary from Palermo, Judge Cesare Terranova, by then a member of parliament and a member of the Anti-Mafia Commission, who continually drew attention to the fact that Liggio and the Mafia had, by the mid-seventies, extended their grip still further, in spite of past efforts to quash them.

The decision taken in the 1960s to banish known Mafia people to far-flung parts of the Italian mainland had now returned to haunt the authorities. In 1974, there were 1,408 living in *soggiorno obbligato*, almost half from Sicily. 'We have inadvertently scattered the bacteria,' said Terranova, 'to every corner of Italy, even into some towns and cities which were once uncontaminated.' A Milanese judge, faced with the sudden upsurge of Mafia crimes in his region, commented that the action was like taking the cheese away from a nest of mice and then letting them loose in a granary.

Luciano Liggio was finally arrested in May 1974 following a new investigation of the Placido Rizzotto murder by carabiniere General Dalla Chiesa, shortly before he was brought back to Rome to head a new onslaught against the Red Brigades.

Liggio was charged with a multitude of crimes from murder to kidnap, along with a whole cluster of other associates. More than 100 were charged, though only 74 were taken into custody and a new set of Mafia trials was put in motion. This time, Liggio would not escape.

Meanwhile, another remarkable series of events began which diverted the attention of media and public from the Mafia and back towards the politics of chaos and mayhem that prevailed in Italy at the time. In June, an investigating judge in Milan pointedly recorded his conclusion: 'Part of the ransom money from the recent spate of kidnappings has, we are sure, finished up in the hands of terrorists. They have ample supplies of explosives, arms and money. It is not a coincidence that many of these acts of terror which our nation is now encountering develop in areas where the Mafia prospers.'

The extent of this connection was seldom publicly pursued at a time when the acts of terror themselves provided headlines enough and with the exception of the obvious Mafia-inspired kidnappings, the terror groups continued to be held largely responsible for the carnage that was all around in Italy.

Later that summer Giulio Andreotti, then Minister of the Interior, also surprised the Italian parliament by producing a secret service report on a number of Fascist and neo-Nazi groups, one of which had planned a right-wing coup d'etat.

In consequence of this report, he said, a number of people had been arrested. He did not mention that among those named was a senior figure in the secret service through whom it was suspected CIA funds were being channelled to right-wing groups. By the mid-seventies, the CIA was employing technicians in several Italian centres, bugging politicians and criminals alike. On one occasion, Italian secret police tried to bug the telephone of an important Mafia figure suspected of links with the terrorists and discovered it had already been tapped, by a man known to have worked for the CIA.

Some agents got themselves into serious difficulties. According to archive documents in the offices of the state prosecutor in Bologna one agent, Ronald Stark, had infiltrated a Mafia narcotics ring which had been based in the Middle East – most likely that of the Greco family – and was subsequently arrested with a group of Italians and charged with drug running in 1975.

While in prison, he had a number of VIP visitors, including Wendy Haines, the US Vice-Consul in Florence. Stark also had visits from the Italian secret service and during interrogation he said he had infiltrated the Mafia narcotics ring in order to make contact with terrorist groups. Later, in May 1976, he warned the Italian agents that a senior law figure in Genoa was to be kidnapped or murdered.

This warning went unheeded and on 6 June 1976, Francesco Coco, chief public prosecutor for Genoa, was killed, along with two of his bodyguards. The Red Brigades admitted responsibility. Stark was transferred to another prison where he remained for two years and was then freed on probation – and promptly disappeared from Italy.

To the CIA, which had infiltrated the terror groups and the Mafia itself, the political scene remained far more important than what the Mafia was doing. Nothing had changed in the CIA's perception of Italy since the days immediately after the war when its precedessor the OSS had installed the Mafia mayors in Sicily and the south. Since then, the country had become a vital strategic springboard for the Americans in the cold war.

The American fear of the Italian Communist Party gaining even a foothold in government had heightened towards an obsession and in 1974, the then Christian Democrat prime minister Aldo Moro had a heated exchange with US Secretary of State Henry Kissinger over Moro's apparent willingness to form a working relationship with the Italian Communist Party in order to stay in power. Not mentioned publicly, but hinted at, were references to the considerable donations Moro's Christian Democrats had received from America since 1948.

Moro, listening to Kissinger loudly and angrily delivering what was tantamount to an instruction that he should drop such plans forthwith, ripped off his translator's headset and walked out of the meeting.

Jimmy Carter, who won the 1976 US presidential election, was so emphatic that Communists should not be allowed to take any role in the government of Italy that on the advice of the then CIA director George Bush, he recalled the US Ambassassor Richard N. Gardner from Rome for talks. Gardner had, for weeks, been sending increasingly urgent cables warning of the deteriorating situation in Italy, and Carter's advisers in Washington were urging him to take action.

The upshot was a stern warning from the State Department which said, 'Recent developments in Italy have increased the level of our concern. Our position is clear. We do not favour Communist participation in government and would like to see Communist influence in any western European country reduced. The US and Italy share profound democratic values and interests and we do not believe the Communists share their values.'

The US warning, decried in Italy as gross interference in its internal affairs, came at a time of renewed violence throughout the country with new factions of Facists and neo-Nazis prominent in the acts of atrocity. Murder after murder, bombing after bombing, were all mixed together in an unfathomable ensemble of political and criminal acts in which it was difficult to distinguish terrorism from the Mafia.

It was the issue of the involvement of Communists in government that led finally to the event which struck at the very heart of the Italian nation – the kidnapping and murder of Aldo Moro himself, which to this day remains an unresolved can of slithering worms with more than enough suspicions to suggest that the Mafia and the CIA were lurking somewhere in the background.

At the time, Aldo Moro, five times prime minister and one of Italy's most distinguished leaders, was on the brink of attempting to achieve political stability by bringing the Communist Party into government. This not only aroused the absolute ire of the Americans but also of opponents within his own party – and, of course, the Mafia, which still held so much sway with its political influence in Sicily.

On 16 March 1978, Moro was on his way to play the final card from his hand and give his casting vote for the formation of a government which would have included Communists for the first time. At around 9.50 on that morning, Moro's government car, a dark blue Fiat 130 travelling in convoy with his bodyguards following in a police Alfetta, was halted in Rome's exclusive Via Sani by a car which drove in front of them. Another skidded to a halt behind and blocked off the retreat.

Within seconds, men dressed in the uniforms of Alitalia air stewards closed in from three directions, raked the Alfetta with machine-gun fire and then shot everyone in Moro's Fiat by pistol – except the president himself. Five bodyguards of the carabinieri were massacred.

Moro was held captive for fifty-five days and the newly confirmed prime minister, Giulio Andreotti, much favoured by the Americans, refused repeatedly to negotiate with the terrorists who were demanding the release of thirteen 'communist prisoners' in exchange for Moro.

Perhaps the most memorable part of this whole business was the despairing letters written by Aldo Moro, dozens of them, passed out by his captors to various members of government. Andreotti remained firm that they had no right to free other terrorists 'to save one of us'. Socialist leader Bettino Craxi agreed, and then changed his mind and thought some dialogue with the Red Brigades was possible. Meanwhile, the police were warily pursuing 'every line of inquiry' but the investigation move forward slowly.

The Red Brigades' directorate crowed contemptuously about its success until finally the threat that had existed since Moro was kidnapped was carried out. On 9 May, his body was found in the back of a Renault 5 with five bullets around his heart. Moro, whose letters had become increasingly harrowing and reflected the cold fury which he so obviously felt over his predicament said in his last note: 'I request that neither state authorities nor party members attend my funeral. I wish to be followed only by those who truly loved me and are therefore worthy of accompanying me with their prayers.'

Andreotti ignored the request and the government attended the funeral Mass. Moro's family, still believing that the Christian Democrat leadership could have done more to save him, did not attend. In the aftermath, General Dalla Chiesa became the hero of the hour, leading a massive crackdown on the terrorists – and is largely credited with smashing the Red Brigades organization itself, though the kidnappings and bombings would continue for several more years. Hundreds of arrests were made but it took four years before the Moro kidnap case ended with a prosecution effort aided largely by a new law which had been worked out at the Ministry of Justice.

It was the law of the *pentiti* – the 'penitents' or turncoats who testified against their terrorist colleagues and received much shorter sentences, and protective measures to ensure their safety, a law which would be revived later under different but equally dramatic circumstances to fight the Mafia.

It was the breakthrough required to secure convictions. In January 1983, fifty-nine terrorists were found guilty of two hundred charges which included seventeen murders, eleven attempted murders and four kidnappings. The convictions were catch-all, unspecific in relation to the Moro killing, and that crime to all intents and purposes remains unsolved. Though thirty-two of those charged were sentenced to life imprisonment, there remained an uneasy 'whodunnit' atmosphere which exists to this day.

The Italian daily, *La Stampa*, summed up the feeling of many – that the trial had failed to answer the most crucial of questions: was the incomprehensible disarray of government agencies displayed during Moro's captivity due simply to incompetence, or was it the result of a political conspiracy?

Conspiracy? Mafia? CIA? The mystery remained, in spite of the long trial of the terrorists. By then, the days of Luciano Liggio's *Anonima Sequestri* were already history. The kidnap phenomenon peaked towards the end of the decade, when the Mafia moved on to greater things. But the money had been fantastic. In 1977, the peak year for kidnaps, £175.5 million had been paid out in ransom money, much of it to the criminal gangs, but no one really knew where the responsibilities truly lay.

The kidnapping era and the terrorist campaign provided the law with so much to do that the Mafia was able to slip virtually unnoticed into what would become its biggest moneyspinner yet: it moved towards total domination of the US heroin market, which poured money into Mafia banks as if from a burst water main.

The nation's new hero, the indefatigable, incorruptible General Dalla Chiesa, who long ago had tried and failed to have Luciano Liggio jailed for the murder of Dr Navarra, for which he was finally convicted in 1974, led the Carabinieri to its final pursuit of the Red Brigades. He saw the Italian terrorist campaign to its bloody end, dying as it did with the decade of 1970s. And it is events to which the general was connected that would provide some devastating evidence that the Mafia was in the background to the Moro kidnap, doing the bidding of political friends.

It emerged in 1994 that the Mafia *cupola* in Palermo had held a special meeting to discuss the 'freedom of Moro'. They argued about it, shouted at one another and, according to the supergrass Tommaso Buscetta, decided to do nothing. This provided confirmation that had eluded investigators, but which was almost certainly known to Dalla Chiesa: the Mafia was in contact with the Red Brigades – and, indirectly, the CIA through Frank Coppola – and had sufficient sway to be able to make decisions which affected the life or death of Aldo Moro.

This was vital evidence and was in line with earlier testimony which curiously had been overlooked. In 1980 the link between the Red Brigades organization and the Mafia was revealed by a convicted revolutionary and former college professor, Carlo Fioroni. He had just been sentenced to twenty-seven years for his part in the terror campaign, and with the new laws for *pentiti*, began telling police everything he knew. In his extensive testimony, Fioroni stated that there had been considerable liaison between the terrorists and the Mafia.

Buscetta, in confirming that the Mafia *cupola* refused to 'approve the liberation of Moro', indicated that they obviously had the power to do so if they so desired. The political ramifications were, in Buscetta's view, the underlying reasons for this and Dalla Chiesa himself was in possession of evidence which also pointed to that fact. One further secret from the period would later float to the surface, like an old wartime mine, trapped in seaweed until it was released years later and exploded.

In 1978 Mino Pecorelli, a journalist who had stumbled across highly sensitive information which was by all accounts dynamite in political circles, had hinted as much in one of his articles. Pecorelli had written a piece for a magazine linked to the Italian secret service in which he suggested that there was much more to the Moro killing than had been revealed, and that the man who knew all the secrets would himself be murdered.

The identity of that man was couched in cryptic terms typical of Pecorelli's writings: 'Unfortunately the carabinieri general's name is known: Amen.' Pecorelli's simple code indicated the name: Amen is said in church. The Italian for church is *chiesa* – thus Pecorelli was predicting the murder of Dalla Chiesa.

Soon after the article appeared, Pecorelli himself was assassinated. As informers revealled later, his murder was carried out not by terrorists but on the orders of two Cosa Nostra *cupola* members, Stefano Bontate and Gaetano Badalamenti at the request of a most senior Italian politician. Dalla Chiesa knew the identity of that politician, and by that information and more that came his way soon afterwards assured his place on the Mafia's assassination list.

BOOK TWO

The Killing Fields

The Cosa Nostra . . . so bold and arrogant as their bosses counted their billions from heroin trafficking, clinically decided that as a matter of policy they would kill in unprecedented numbers all police, judges and public officials who stood in their way . . . it began picking them off one by one, sweeping them from its path.

Umberto Santino, director of the Sicilian Centre of Documentation, to author, April 1994

CHAPTER SIX

A Year in Palermo: Two Judges, Three Police Chiefs, Two Politicians – Dead

In the turmoil of Italy's crisis, exacerbated by the plague of riots, assassinations, bombings, kidnappings and kneecappings, the Mafia had to some degree taken second place. With the threat of continuing terrorist activities after the murder of Lord Louis Mountbatten in Ireland in 1979, the Common Market countries had set up a special anti-terrorist unit to which Liliana Ferraro was seconded as Italy's point of liaison because of her experience gained in the war against the Red Brigades. The years at the Ministry of Justice had been filled with devastating, shattering events which had affected her personally. She came to fear the telephone calls, often late at night, which would announce the death of another of her colleagues or associates in the long fight against terrorism and crime.

She had become an important link in the administration of the judiciary at this most crucial time in Italian history and, more especially, in the security arrangements covering those of her profession who, like herself, were part of the *vita blindata*, the protected life. Though she makes a point of not discussing her personal relationships or her family life for security reasons – every family of every judge and law officer in her position is at risk – the life clearly took its toll. She and her husband, himself a magistrate, separated after six years of marriage and were divorced in the early 1980s.

While the tail end of the terrorist war was being fought and Ferraro's interests were temporarily diverted towards the wider aspects of European events, the Mafia and more precisely the Sicilian Cosa Nostra had risen again and almost unnoticed was on the very brink of its most violent period. It would not be long before Ferraro was drawn into a new, even more frightening arena alongside a man who was at that time unknown to her personally: Giovanni Falcone, then a magistrate dealing with the routine of court work.

The Mafia had demonstrated with ease its phoenix-like abilities and no one in law enforcement in either Italy or the US, where the end product arrived, really appreciated just how rapidly and substantially its business and financial fortunes had expanded in the previous five years or so.

After the 1972 Mafia summit called by Luciano Liggio revenue from the kidnappings provided plenty of cash flow. But it was another Sicilian faction of the Mafia, led by a triumvirate of families which did not include Liggio's Corleonesi, that masterminded the next stage of the Mafia's operations, which was to secure a virtual monopoly on supplies of heroin to the US. Already well experienced in the narcotics business, the Italian Mafia had, up to that point, held only a thirty per cent share of the market. By far the bulk of narcotics passing across the eastern seaboard of America came via the French Connection, run by the Corsicans who were producing heroin by the ton. In 1972, the American Drugs Enforcement Administration identified and broke up the ring.

Next, the French rounded up the remaining Corsicans and shut down their eight heroin-refining factories around Marseilles. By the beginning of 1974, the French Connection was out of business. The Corsicans scattered, tried to move in with the Camorras in Naples but discovered that the Cosa Nostra had already taken over. 'What happened during the seventies,' Umberto Santino at the Sicilian Centre of Documentation told me, 'was that Sicily stopped being merely a point of transit, or the place of birth of the main characters involved in the international drugs traffic, and became the actual refinement centre. After that, everything changed.'

Every consignment of heroin intercepted at John F Kennedy airport between 22 September 1971 and 6 July 1978 originated from Palermo. The Cosa Nostra and the Camorras formed an alliance with the babas of Turkey, bought up control of the poppy field production of the Golden Crescent, the largest opium-producing area on earth taking in Afghanistan, Pakistan and Iran, and by the mid-seventies the Sicilians, with their relatives strategically placed in New York, took virtual control of all heroin being moved into the US through its east coast. Almost overnight, the money was being counted in billions.

The understaffed Italian police and Carabinieri, working at full stretch during the era of kidnappings and terrorism, had no special coordinating units investigating either the drugs trade or the Mafia itself and were sadly lacking in intelligence. The Americans were also slow off the mark. By the time they got to grips with it, the network of heroin distribution was already firmly in place.

The building of the Mafia drugs empire had fallen to principal families of the Cosa Nostra, the Badalamentis, the Bontates, the Inzerillos and the Gambinos, who were in turn linked in the family tree to a mass of relatives in Sicily and in America. Many other families came in below them. At its helm was Gaetano Badalamenti, a small unimposing man but a powerful don from the little town of Cinisi, a few miles west of Palermo. He became head of the Cosa Nostra *cupola* in 1976 after he and his closest confidante, Stefano Bontate, were released from a brief spell in prison.

Badalamenti, until then, was best known as the Flying Gaetano, having been the principal supplier of raw materials to build the new Punta Raisa international airport. He poured literally hundreds of thousands of tons of concrete into the new facility from which he made what would have been an adequate fortune to most men.

But, as for most of his senior henchmen on the *cupola*, the drugs trade beckoned and by 1978, he was operating three heroin refineries in his home town and was among the biggest suppliers to the US.

Badalamenti had been around a long time. He was said to have a 'direct line to' the then Italian Prime Minister

Giulio Andreotti. The turncoat Tommaso Buscetta claimed in 1991, 'Badalamenti reckoned he could always reach Andreotti through Salvo Lima, the political supremo of the Christian Democrats in Palermo, who was in effect the Mafia's ambassador to Rome.'

Badalamenti's closest ally was the young and thrusting new family boss Stefano 'the Prince' Bontate, the forty-year-old head of the Santa Maria de Gesu family and one of Sicily's youngest and richest Mafia people whose connections were said to lead straight to the top, both in Sicily and Rome. He entertained influential businessmen and politicians at his $500,000 villa, encircled by high fences and electronic gates, patrolled by guard dogs and surveyed by constantly monitored close-circuit television cameras.

The third key member of the alliance was Salvatore Inzerillo, another of the seventies stars who had made fortunes out of heroin. The three, Bontate, Inzerillo and Gaetano, along with the Palermo Gambino family, had the strongest connections with the Americans through the Carlo Gambino family in New York. They were suppliers to what seemed an ever-expanding demand in the United States and every other nation in the west. They were all increasingly affected by the scourge of heroin and had rapidly climbing addiction figures.

A friend of the ruling triumvirate was Tommaso Buscetta, a middle-ranking Mafia figure who had fled Italy to South America after the 1960s purges. At the beginning of 1970, he was wanted by the Americans for drug trafficking in the US but the Italian police got in first. Arrested in Brazil, he was extradited to Italy and sentenced to three years for association with the Mafia.

A year later, an American grand jury indicted him on charges of conspiracy to import 170 kilos of heroin into the US and applied to the Italians for his extradition. If he had stood trial there, he would certainly have been incarcerated for many years but the Italians refused to hand him over.

They used the US charges as a base for new court hearings against Buscetta, in which he was sentenced to a further ten years. It was reduced to eight on appeal and rolled up with his earlier sentence, and he was out by the end of 1979.

Those who opposed the Inzerillo faction on the Cosa Nostra *cupola* were allied to the Corleonesi whose head, Luciano Liggio, was jailed for life in 1974, when the influence of the Corleonesi temporarily declined. The clan's involvement in the narcotics business was far less than Liggio thought he deserved. He was still a powerful force and controlled a massive business empire from the comfort of his well-equipped prison cell, to which he had his own meals delivered by a local restaurant. He hired another inmate as a taster to ensure that he wasn't poisoned. Liggio was represented on the *cupola* by his number two, Toto Riina, with Bernardo Provenzano riding shotgun, and he was beginning to get impatient.

Liggio's closest ally was Michele 'The Pope' Greco, linked to the Ciaculli Greco family which was dispersed in the 1963 Mafia wars after their battles with the La Barberas. Police intelligence on the Mafia was so lacking that at the beginning of the 1980s they had no idea that Michele Greco was a high ranking Mafia figure.

To the outside world, he was one of Sicily's most upright businessmen, a tweed-suited model of respectability sitting on the boards of fifteen or twenty companies. He lived in millionaire-style luxury on his twenty-acre estate, La Favarella, six miles outside of Palermo, which was the venue of many *cupola* meetings. His family controlled some of the Mafia's most ruthless killers and he was up to his neck in the narcotics business, with a heroin-refining laboratory hidden in the grounds of his estate.

The American Drug Enforcement Administration had been gathering intelligence on the activities of the Sicilians on both sides of the Atlantic and made several major arrests, but with Jimmy Carter's cost-cutting programme it had been forced to close down its bureaux in Paris and the Far East in the late seventies, just at the very time the expansion of Mafia drug trade moved into top gear.

Furthermore, the concept of the modern Mafia was still not understood or its extent appreciated. Certainly, the DEA at that point was almost as badly lacking in intelligence as the Italians. It was left to individual and honest members of the police and magistracy to begin investigations into particular crimes, and those who took them on were exceedingly vulnerable to personal attack, as was proved in a series of assassinations which began in the late seventies.

An example had already been set. Judge Pietro Scaglione whose career as chief prosecutor of Palermo had been riddled with allegations of corruption and involvement with the Mafia, had been critized by the Anti-Mafia Commission for his tardiness in handling Mafia cases. He was reprimanded for deliberately 'sitting on' a file from the Caribinieri in the sixties implicating Frank Coppola and three members of the Bonanno family from Castellammare in drug dealing and when the case finally came to trial they were all acquitted through lack of evidence.

However, Scaglione's position as both chief prosecutor and friend of the Mafia was inherently dangerous and when he was no longer able to deliver what the Mafia wanted of him, he became expendable. One morning, while visiting his wife's grave at Palermo cemetery, he was shot dead. No one saw his murder and no one was arrested. In his later confessions, Tommaso Buscetta said the killing was ordered by Liggio and carried out by Toto Riina.

Scaglione's murder was a forerunner of many. The systematic killing of policemen, public officials and politicians who threatened the Mafia's activities or connections began almost as the terrorist war subsided. 'What began to happen,' said Umberto Santino, observing all and collating material for his archives, 'was the Mafia clinically decided as a matter of policy to kill, in unprecedented numbers, all those in public office who stood in their way. It is important to draw a distinction – they were not victims of a war against the State itself. Rather, their elimination became necessary when these individuals, often isolated within the very structure of the State and its law enforcement agencies, came to represent a danger to the Mafia organization. In other words, there is no such thing as a Mafia which is external to the State, deciding to wage war against it. What we had, and still have, is a criminal organization which is external to the State in terms of its own structure but is internal to it, thanks to its links with the institutional world. And from that standpoint, it began to pick off and sweep from its path all those who stood before it.'

The beginning of this new era – new in its ruthlessness,

its systematic executions – is marked by the entry of a most respected figure into that terrible memorial known as the gallery of the Illustrious Corpses.

Boris Giuliano was deputy head of Palermo police and had specific duties as head of the elite Flying Squad, the *Squadra Mobile.* He is recognized as the man who first detected the extent of the Mafia's drug trafficking activities, and that discovery would cost him his life. He was in most respects an exceptional law officer. His toughness was tempered by compassion and he was honest. Bribes and deals had been offered in abundance in his years of dealing with the corruption that abounded in his terrority but he had steadfastly refused to be swayed from doing his job – which was to bring criminals to book. The Mafia hated him and respected him in equal measure.

With little in the way of modern technology, the success of police work in Palermo relied upon honest law officers and in the summer of 1979, Giuliano first stumbled across the unequivocal truth that Palermo had become the nerve centre of the world's heroin trade.

From his contacts in the American Drugs Enforcement Administration, Giuliano began to piece together the jigsaw. From 1974, when the last of the French Connection gangsters had been put out of business, supplies had flowed in from South America and Mexico, from the Sicilian drugs ring set up after the Grecos, the Cuntreras and others fled the Mafia purge in the mid-1960s.

For a time, the supplies slowed down and the number of addicts in the US – the only figure from which an assessment of drug trafficking could be made – had declined from its peak of 650,000 in 1975 to less than 500,000 by 1978. It was probably these out-of-date statistics that prompted the Carter administration to cut back the DEA's overseas representation.

But by the end of 1978, the US was being flooded with high grade No. 4 heroin, manufactured in laboratories in Sicily, Naples and Milan. Hiring veterans of the old French Connection production line, the Mafia bosses, predominantly controlled by the Sicilian *cupola,* brought in new methods of production which speeded up the process of refining the morphine base.

Their high-tech laboratories were capable of producing heroin at a faster rate than any previously known technique – one laboratory could produce a ton of heroin a month, worth $525 million in street sales.

By early 1979, the Mafia collectively had eight or nine of these laboratories in production. So much cash was pouring into the Mafia coffers that it became an embarrassment. Sicilian banks began another period of proliferation, and couriers were suddenly travelling the world with body belts full of heroin in one direction and suitcases full of US dollars on the return journey.

In America, the distribution network already in place was being expanded by the Badalamenti, Gambino and Bonanno families in the US who used, among other places, pizza fast food restaurants as their point of sale, with as many as 700 outlets around New York alone.

Even with past experience of Mafia dealing in the drugs trade going back years to when Vito Genovese, Lucky Luciano and Frank Coppola were first active on Italian soil, the American DEA was still unsure of the source of this surge of No. 4 grade heroin which had suddenly hit the streets, though it is hard to believe that the US intelligence network which had been operating in Italy for years had not gathered the information long before. Whatever the reasons the US persisted with its CIA-inspired 'no-go' attitude towards Sicily, there was suddenly no denying the extent of the Sicilians' operation.

On 18 June 1979 a customs officer at Palermo's Punta Raisa airport saw two suitcases on the baggage carousel which had not been collected by the owners long after passengers from a flight from Rome had departed. The bag tags showed that they originated in New York. The bags were opened and were found to contain $497,000 US dollars in small bills wrapped in pizza-parlour aprons. The aprons were later traced to a New Jersey pizzeria run by Salvatore Sollena who in turn was discovered to be a nephew of the Sicilian Gaetano Badalamenti.

Boris Giuliano, head of the Squadra Mobile, soon heard about the discovery and having recently attended a police training course in the US instantly recognized the significance of the find. It was payment money for a drugs shipment.

Though the DEA had targeted Giuliano as a contact in

Palermo for his honesty and integrity, as well as his experience in Mafia affairs, it never had an office or an agent posted permanently on the island of Sicily which it knew harboured the most active bunch of Cosa Nostra families whose relatives were staked out across America. No US agent went there for longer than a flying visit which is what happened in mid-July when the US agency learned of Giuliano's find.

One of the DEA's most experienced undercover agents, Tom Tripodi, flew from Rome for a visit, anxious to discover the source of the heroin and the location of the laboratories. Giuliano drew up his own list of likely suspects. They were names which would become all too familiar: the Bontates, Badalamentis, Inzerillos and Gambinos. He had a number of specific ideas and began carrying out raids on suspect addresses. Tripodi left Giuliano to continue his investigations and returned to Rome.

A couple of days later, on the morning of 21 July, the police chief called into the Bar Lux in the centre of Palermo as he strolled from his home 100 yards away. He ordered an espresso coffee, sipped at it for five minutes and got up to leave.

As he fumbled in his pockets for the change to pay for the coffee, Giuliano – known as the fastest draw in Palermo – was caught unawares and did not even have time to reach for his own gun. A thickset man appeared from nowhere, paused for a second then fired three shots into the policeman's head and another three into his heart as he fell to the floor.

There were more than thirty witnesses to the shooting. All were taken to the police station to make statements and, as one officer later described it, they could not even agree on the colour of the assailant's hair.

The reaction in Palermo was one of horror and fear. Though the streets of Palermo were stained with blood from past killings, this one represented a new turn, completely. A police officer, shot dead in broad daylight. The media voiced its outrage and in Rome officials of the Ministry of the Interior and the Ministry of Justice conferred hastily about what should be done. There was talk of sending a contigent of troops to the island to track down the killers.

In Palermo, the Cosa Nostra sought an accommodation to

have the hue and cry called off but found the new man running the Christian Democrats in Palermo hard to deal with.

Michele Reina, regional secretary of the DC, was a quiet family man, and had the distinction of being what they term in Palermo an 'upolluted' politician. Recently he had joined forces with another vociferous anti-Mafia campaigner, Pio La Torre, in condemning the outrages of the Cosa Nostra, and had promised to help clean up local politics which had traditionally been tied in with local crime families.

Testimony to that could be seen on the western side of Palermo, where a huge carbuncle of development now covered an ancient site – massive concrete apartment buildings and offices put up largely by Mafia-controlled companies seeking to launder their cash. The Sicilian building boom, which had gone on at a time when all other areas were in recession, was one more element of local corruption.

Reina's stance in the past with leading Mafia figures had been one of non-cooperation, a fact which some of his superiors in the party had found disturbingly inconsiderate, not to mention dangerous.

One week after Giuliano's assassination, Reina was drawing away from his apartment on a Sunday morning when three gunmen appeared from behind, opened fire and shot him through the head.

Palermo Communist leader and member of parliament, Pio La Torre, demanded action in his usual impassioned tones and there was sufficient public reaction for the government to take notice and act, modestly perhaps, with one single appointment: the former great Mafia-hunter Judge Cesare Terranova would return to the fray and lead a new attack on the Mafia, through the judiciary.

He would be given extra police to aid the investigation and he spoke boldly to the press about his intention to seek out and imprison the killers of Giuliano and Reina. Terranova, then fifty-eight years old, was already one of the great heroes who had fought long and hard in the battle against the Mafia. In the Mafia trials of the sixties, he had personally sent many key Mafia figures to prison, although most had since been released.

In September 1979, Terranova was as committed as ever to the fight and agreed to undertake the role of chief investigating judge in Palermo, charged with the task of bringing the criminals who had shot Giuliano and Reina to trial and overseeing the continuing investigations into the drugs traffic.

Terranova was a powerful figure, a leading expert on the Mafia and one of the few who truly understood its operations. Years as a judge and as a member of the Anti-Mafia Commission meant that he knew as much as any man on the outside could know about the workings of the Mafia and its personalities.

He also knew that the drugs trade had expanded beyond belief in a matter of months. 'People I saw pushing carts not long ago are now millionaires,' he commented in 1979. He made no secret of the fact that he wanted the Anti-Mafia Commission to press for new laws which would enable investigators to at least question the banks about suspicious flows of money, now so plentiful in Palermo that a new industry had burgeoned: bank security. Terranova believed that by attacking the Mafia's wealth, it could flush them out.

It was a theory that would be left to his successors to pursue. On 25 September, a few days before he was due to start his new appointment, and thus still without the bodyguards that came with the job, he was ambushed in broad daylight, not far from his home. Three gunmen in their twenties opened fire in front of a horrified crowd and sped away.

Terranova's execution was followed by outpourings of great anger, a reaction that was to become all too familiar – and ineffectual – during the coming years.

There were many who insisted that the work that he had pursued for almost two decades would go on, and among those who outspokenly supported a renewed attack on the Mafia on the lines suggested by the judge – i.e. through their pockets – was Pier Santi Mattarella, president of the regional government of Sicily. His father, Bernardo, had also been in politics and was a controversial figure who was said to have accommodated the Mafia on a number of occasions. His son refused to follow this tradition and was dangerously outspoken in his denunciation of Mafia leaders.

Mattarella was the head of the minority Christian Democrat group on the regional parliament and remained in power with the support of the Communist Party of Sicily, whose own leader, Pio La Torre, was a member of parliament, a member of the

Anti-Mafia Commission and a sworn enemy of the Cosa Nostra whose activities he had witnessed since boyhood.

This alliance of two of Sicily's most significant and trusted politicians had similarities to the scenario in Rome not long before: Mattarella himself was a supporter of the Aldo Moro faction of the Christian Democrats, unlike the former Mayor of Palermo, Salvo Lima, an old friend of Mattarella's father, who was firmly in the Andreotti camp and had been a close friend of Andreotti's since 1968.

Pier Mattarella had demonstrated his support of Moro's policy by his own willingness to open dialogue with the Communists and use them to help his own cause, in retaining control over the regional parliament.

In parliament Mattarella and La Torre condemned the Mafia thugs following the execution of Terranova. Mattarella decided to take action through measures which he was convinced would hurt the Mafia. He announced publicly that he intended to call a halt to the Mafia practice of laundering their proceeds of drug dealing through real estate investment and building contracts in the island. He intended to propose legislation to withdraw those public works contracts which ran into billions of lire from all companies which it could be shown had Mafia connections. He would take advice from the Anti-Mafia Commission and from the local judiciary and the public could rest assured that action would be taken as soon as it was possible to so.

Almost immediately, Mattarella received a telephone call from Salvo Lima, the man who with the present Mayor, Vito Ciancimino, had run Palermo for so long they thought they owned it, to inquire if Mattarella had taken leave of his senses. Lima insisted that he had no power to do such a thing and that either way, it was an inadvisable move which would cost the Christian Democrats dear in votes at the next election.

Mattarella refused to back down but before he could move against the Mafia's control of certain public works contracts, the assassins struck again.

On 6 January 1980, a Sunday and the only day of the week he went anywhere without his ring of bodyguards, Mattarella walked to church with his wife and his three children for Mass. 'Not even the Mafia is going to rob me of my day with the family,' he told the police chief who kept insisting that he retain his guard for the full seven days. He refused the offer of round-the-clock protection, and it cost him his life.

As he strolled along hand in hand with his wife, the killers' car screeched to a halt beside them and two men with pistols pumped six bullets into his body. He fell dead instantly.

The cries of outrage were renewed in Palermo and Rome and throughout Italy. A new clamp-down was ordered. Thousands of extra troops and police were flown to the island. Dozens of suspects were rounded up and questioned but not one was arrested for any of the four killings: Giuliano, Reina, Terranova and now Mattarella – all dead within the space of four months.

And yet, even with the island of Sicily thronging with extra carabinieri, searching, patrolling, standing on every street corner with machine guns poised, the Mafia arrogantly continued to send off its packages of drugs. On 16 January a consignment of 24 kilos of Inzerillo heroin was intercepted at John F Kennedy Airport in New York and two months later 40 kilos was discovered in a vegetable truck on its way to Milan, and also bound for New York. The Sicilians were producing so much refined heroin on a round-the-clock basis, the loses were hardly noticed.

In Palermo, another law officer, Captain Emanuele Basile, had taken over the investigation begun by Boris Giuliano into the two suitcases which contained close on half a million dollars and he had decided to direct his inquiries towards possible links between the Mafia and Sicily's bankers and businessmen whose known laundering activities, though at the time entirely legal, were nothing short of a national scandal.

Banks at home and abroad were falling over themselves to take money, in whatever form it was delivered, and that quite often meant people literally turning up with suitcases of it.

As in Switzerland, the Bahamas and the Cayman Islands, those other popular hideaways for Mafia money, the Palermo police had no legal powers to investigate bank accounts of anyone, criminal or otherwise, but Captain Basile remained doggedly persistent in his attempts to improve on Giuliano's list of Who's Who in the Mafia, and who had become very rich in recent times.

There were numerous examples. One of many in Umberto

Santino's Palermo archives involved the Sicilian mafioso Michelangelo Aiello and his front company Industria Derivati Agrumari (Citrus By-Product Industry). Aiello, who served as mayor and a city councillor of the Palermo suburb of Bagheria, founded IDA in 1976 with recorded assets of 200,000 lire. By 1981, the company's worth had soared to 21 billion lire. How? Santino explained:

> Aiello's Mafia collaborators procured morphine from Turkish suppliers, refined it into heroin in Bagheria factories and he shipped it to the USA via the east coast Pizza Connection of Sicilian immigrants Giuseppe Ganci and Salvatore Catalano. In turn, they shipped back the money which was laundered by a Mafia financier through his back accounts in Switzerland, and then on into investment in Sicilian enterprises and London where he maintained an account at Lloyds Bank.

Basile made a breakthrough. He had names and dates and was on the verge of arresting half a dozen senior Mafia figures he believed he could convict on charges of drug trafficking. Inevitably, the Mafia was tipped off in advance and on 8 May 1980 Basile was walking towards the police barracks in Monreale with wife and carrying his four-year-old daughter in his arms. Three Mafia soldiers drove up in an Alfa Romeo and shot him from behind. One was from the Greco family of Ciaculli, the other two were men from the Inzerillo camp. They were arrested the same day on the outskirts of Palermo. One of them was climbing a tall mesh fence at the time and said he was looking for lemons. They were later freed because no incriminating evidence could be found against them.

Soon afterwards, new arrest warrants were issued but by then the three men had been taken off the island by fast motorboat, and on to the US with false passports. One of them even left a goodbye note. Meanwhile, all that the residents of Monreale could do was place a marble plaque on the spot where he was gunned down.

Captain Basile was succeeded immediately by a courageous young officer who was adjudged to have all the qualities of a future leader of the force, Captain Mario D'Alea, who was twenty-nine years old and soon to be married to a local girl. He was just leaving his fiancée's apartment, exactly six weeks after Basile's murder, when he was ambushed in exactly the same way – shot down as he went for his car. So now Captain D'Alea had been swept away.

Basile and others had by then compiled a substantial file on the origination and deployment of Mafia funds in Palermo and one of those files had landed on the desk of Gaetano Costa, Palermo's chief prosecutor, then sixty-four years old and a year or so from retirement. He was a man who worked long hours for years because Sicily's judiciary was permanently understaffed. He had seen much less of his wife of three decades than he wanted and soon he hoped to remedy that failing. He had the respect of the local judiciary and was viewed to be scrupulously honest.

Inevitably, Costa faced an age-old problem in Palermo, one that others less fastidious than himself would have quietly shelved for years until the moment had passed – an incriminating dossier on local businessman and high Mafioso Rosario Spatola who as far as was known had never killed anyone, but made his money by laundering narco-lire in legitimate enterprises.

In 1970, Spatola's volume of business never exceeded 30 million lire in a year. In 1978, he had sufficient funds to be awarded a state building contract worth 10.5 billion lire, and an important role in his obtaining that contract was played by Vito Ciancimino, who at that time was a member of the Commission for the Institute of Popular Housing.

Spatola's business partner was Salvatore Inzerillo, the *cupola* member who was one of Palermo's major heroin manufacturers. Costa was convinced he had enough evidence to proceed and was on the verge of issuing arrest warrants against Spatola, Inzerillo and others.

This information was leaked to Inzerillo by way of spies in the lawyer's camp and Inzerillo was so outraged that he ordered Gaetano Costa's immediately execution, a decision he took without conferring with the *cupola* as was the rule in all such high-level assassinations.

In the heat of the Mediterranean sun, on 6 August 1980, Costa and his wife were preparing to leave the dusty, noisy city for a holiday. A youthful looking man came towards him carrying a newspaper. As he was almost level with the chief prosecutor, he tossed the newspaper aside to reveal a .38 revolver, from which he fired five shots from as many yards, and Gaetano Costa fell dead.

In the the space of a few months, therefore, the Mafia had succeeded in slaughtering the head of the anti-Mafia force, three most senior policeman, Palermo's chief prosecutor, a political party administrator and the president of the regional council.

In the expressions of renewed outrage that followed one voice in particular stood out – that of the Communist leader Pio La Torre who, in the absence of any similar action by his opposite numbers among the Christian Democrats, had begun to campaign with even louder voice for punitive new laws to combat the Mafia. His plan – similar to that which had cost Pier Mattarella his life – was to appeal to the government for powerful new laws to combat the Mafia, though Pio La Torre would not live to see if anyone took up his suggestions. From that moment, he had been placed high on the Mafia's hit list.

CHAPTER SEVEN

The Great War of 1980–2: 1,280 Mafiosi Dead

When they were working together, closeted behind the tight security of whichever bunker-style office they might be in, Liliana Ferraro and Giovanni Falcone would often talk about the beginning of the dramatic sequence of events which led towards the most successful attack on the Mafia ever launched. Often the conversation would drift back to the early days of the fight, at the beginning of the new decade when, as Falcone used to say, he arrived back in his birthplace of Palermo just as things were 'hotting up'.

Falcone was a short, handsome and vain man but tough and a thorough professional. He was the architect of the biggest successes ever recorded in the war against the Mafia, and in 1980 he was just setting out along that road, a winding, dangerous path which he likened to climbing a mountain in fog.

He had been familiar with the Mafia since boyhood. He grew up in Kalsa, one of the most ancient quarters of Palermo, a modest suburb which was noted for its accumulation of mafiosi. He went to school, played football and generally mixed with boys of his own age who would eventually become his adversaries. 'As a child,' he would tell Ferraro, 'I had breathed the air of the Mafia with every breath. The extortions, the assassinations, the great trials that usually ended without a conviction, I saw them all. I was brought up in a progressive family, and was horrified by the murders, the aggression. The Cosa Nostra was like a seven-headed hydra, an inexorable flow of lava, responsible for all the evils in our world.'

While many of the local boys joined the Cosa Nostra, he became a naval officer and then turned to law. In 1974, he became the public prosecutor in the Trapani province of Sicily and thus brushed with some of the most powerful mafiosi. He later became a bankruptcy judge, but returned to Palermo in the autumn of 1979 as the deaths among public officials were beginning.

Ferraro remembers: 'He was a very simple man, although the first impression you had of him was a kind of puzzlement, that you could not quite get through to him. That was because he was initially distrustful. Life had taught him that. Yet at the same time, he had a longing for great loyalty and once those personal barriers had been understood and broken down, he was a very positive man.'

What Falcone discovered on his return to Palermo was a city on the brink of war. He could sense the atmosphere of the place, smell the tension, and at the root of it was money and the struggle for power.

The reason, which he did not fully appreciate at the time, was the emerging spectre of a world flooded by Sicilian-manufactured heroin which began to appear towards the end of 1980 in massive quantities on the American market, and to a lesser degree throughout Europe. By then, many of the leading crime families of Italy were dealing, although the leading suppliers to the US remained the Badalamenti-Bontate-Inzerillo groups.

The Mafia was heading towards incredible new levels of earning capacity, which could only be attained with the cooperation of bankers and corrupt politicians. The new money provided new power and confidence which enabled them to establish a far greater presence in all stratas of commercial life. It won their families major building contracts, major connections to government departments, farming links which enabled them to instigate massive frauds upon the Common Market treasury, and the control of local labour. But above all, it was about drugs. By 1984, global heroin trafficking had reached $1,000 billion a year, of which forty per cent emanated from Italian, and predominantly Sicilian, mafiosi.

Distributors had already fanned out across the world. The Corleonesi's ally, Francesco Di Carlo, moved to London in 1977, to take over the route originally established by the Cuntrera and Caruana families who originated from Siculiana, a province of Agrigento, in Sicily. Those two families were responsible for a large part of the early trafficking to North America from Venezuela where they set up base after the purges of 1963. By 1980 their business extended across Europe and North America.

On the way, the families had also built up a small empire of legitimate companies, based largely in Canada and Venezuela, which were very suitable vehicles for money laundering. Di Carlo took with him to London three senior Mafia figures and was surrounded intermittently over the next few years by a succession of soldiers and couriers, upwards of twenty people at any one time employed by him exclusively to create a major supply route for heroin being distributed in Britain, and a staging post for Europe and the US. Many elaborate systems were employed, including special adapted Lancia cars with electronically controlled compartments in which drugs, weapons and cash could be hidden.

By 1981, Di Carlo had installed himself in a £500,000 mansion in the heart of Britain's stockbroker belt in Surrey where one of the Cuntreras, Liborio, had his house until he died of a liver complaint on 27 May 1982 at the age of fifty-five. Di Carlo's presence in Britain was actually established by Scotland Yard as early as 1980, but they were unable to trap him until June 1985 when he was arrested on charges of master-minding a $75 million heroin racket and was sentenced to twenty-five years by a British court.

Allied to Di Carlo's operation was the industry of financial management made necessary because such huge sums of money were involved. It was run by the Sicilian money-laundering genius named Alfonso Caruana who fled back to Venezuela the day Di Carlo was arrested. He had accounts at Barclays Bank, Knaphill branch, near Woking, Surrey, where he was known to deposit large bundles of used Canadian and US dollars before all British banks clamped down on suspicious money movements. But these case histories were just a few of dozens which were occurring in every major city around the western hemisphere.

Another Mafia associate who has never been arrested on any charge is a British businessman who has offices in the city and a lavish home in the west country. Along with British investigative reporter Andrew Jennings, I published a full account of the activities of this man, whose name appeared at the time on the list of suspected money-launderers at the offices of Italy's Guardia di Finanza, the finance police, who were responsible for tracking movements of Mafia funds around the world.

From the late seventies, according to the Guardia di Finanza, he moved money through accounts at Lloyds Bank in Fenchurch Street, London, vast sums which would later turn up in numbered accounts in Switzerland and Palermo operated by Michelangelo Aiello, the multimillionaire politician and Mafia associate whose business activities were mentioned in a previous chapter.

On occasions, the London businessman was tracked travelling from New York to London and then on to Palermo carrying suitcases filled with US dollars which he then deposited in a Palermo bank. Between 1980 and 1984, he was also overseeing an importing agency through which Britain was supposedly receiving vast quantities of orange juice from Aiello's companies, but the Italian investigators could never trace a drop of it to a British customer.

The files of the finance police, as they are known in Italy, and those of the investigating magistrates in Palermo would become filled with such examples, and demonstrated how Mafia money was moved around the world freely in the international banking system. Suspiciously large movements of money were being tracked by the treasury investigators of seven countries by the early 1980s as various financial scandals began to hit the world headlines. It was already clear that Mafia money was in heavy circulation throughout the system.

The effect locally, in Italy is perhaps best demonstrated by the figures for bank counters open to the public. By 1982, the number of bank counters in Sicily had increased by 124.4 per cent, double the national average of 66 per cent, and Trapani, a supposedly minor province of little influence in Sicily, had more banks than Milan, the commercial heart of Italy. Even in southern Italy the increase in bank counters was 99 per cent – and both these areas remained in the lower regions of Italian economic tables; poverty was still rife.

As Falcone soon assessed, this kind of money had to lead to an explosion among the competing Mafia factions – and it came very quickly as the drugs trade burgeoned to unimaginable heights and numbers. Toto Riina, titular head of the Corleonesi while the true boss Luciano Liggio remained in prison, launched the Corleonesi's bid for total control of the Mafia with all the violence that Kalashnikov armoury can supply, a bloodletting that surpassed anything seen previously in the annals of criminal history. The challenge, as Giovanni Falcone and Liliana Ferraro would chronicle later, was not merely to the Mafia itself but to the State with an arrogance and contempt that sent shudders through certain quarters in Rome.

The meticulous, clinical killing of the police and government officials had already created an atmosphere of fear which in the confines of island living and the village-like communities that exist within political and business life in Palermo, would have a far greater effect than anything the terrorists had been able to engender in their ten-year campaign.

The relentless series of killings listed in the previous chapter was merely the beginning and represented attempts by the Badalamenti-Inzerillo-Bontate faction to stand their ground, and hold their position as controllers of the biggest drugs empire ever created. These statements indicating the scale of what happened may sound clichéd; but there is no other way of saying it. Nothing like this had occurred previously, ever.

The Mafia infighting of the sixties which had littered the streets of western Sicily with bodies and in America had resulted in a totally new regime of Mafia control, was a teaparty in comparison to what would become known as the Great Mafia War of the early 1980s.

And with it was finally buried that romantic image of the Man of Honour, a phrase widely used in various books and articles about the Mafia and its various personalities. If ever there was a time when the word 'Honour' could ever be applied to mafiosi, it was now dead and buried for good.

Toto Riina and his sidekick Bernardo Provenzano finally made their move for total control. By 1980, the Mafia *cupola* had divided into two unequal factions, with the Corleonesi and the Grecos on one side and the supporters of Stefano Bontate and Salvatore Inzerillo on the other. Outside of the *cupola*, but still a very major player, was Gaetano Badalamenti who sided with the Bontate-Inzerillo group. Badalamenti had been head of the *cupola* until 1979, when he was deposed and thrown out in a coup led by the Corleonesi, but for reasons which were never explained.

His cousin and enemy Antonino Badalamenti took his place on the *cupola*. Gaetano Badalamenti realized his days were numbered if he hung around, so he emptied his bank accounts into Switzerland and fled to South America, where he set up shop again.

Tommaso Buscetta, on parole from prison, judged that the power battle was coming to a head between the Corleonesi and the Inzerillo-Bontate faction and tried to intervene by arranging 'peace' talks. He failed and decided to follow Badalamenti and leave the country immediately. His friend Stefano Bontate threw a farewell dinner for him at his villa.

Bontate kissed him on both cheeks and they shook hands. The following day, Buscetta having gathered all the money he could muster, broke parole, drove to Paris and boarded a flight to Rio de Janeiro.

Riina failed to turn up at an important summit called for 6 March 1981 in Palermo. By then, both sides were equipping themselves with an armoury of weapons. For weeks, truckloads of Kalashnikovs, automatic pistols and bombs, shipped in from Turkey along with the usual supplies of morphine base, and from Bulgaria where the Mafia had an arms-dealing link, began arriving at the estates of opposing factions.

Liggio was directing the Corleonesi and their allies in the Greco camp from his prison cell and Toto Riina was ready to move. Bontate decided Riina had to be eliminated otherwise there would be a showdown – but he was too late. The opposition struck first and in April 1981 Italy awoke to a new Mafia war.

The day was chosen deliberately. It was Stefano Bontate's forty-third birthday and having spent the night at his town house, he prepared to leave for his country estate to celebrate with his family. As he left, driving his blue Alfa Romeo in convoy with his bodyguard, two soldiers from the Greco family were watching outside with walkie-talkies.

Two cars fell in behind. As Bontate reached a set of traffic lights, one of the cars pulled out of the traffic and moved alongside Bontate's Alfa. In a second, a gunman opened fire with a Kalashnikov AK47 assault rifle which, on automatic, was capable of firing 100 cartridges a minute. The bullets ripped through the side of Bontate's car. The killers sped away, never to be caught.

Unlike normal Mafia burials, there was a sparse turn-out at Bontate's funeral. The only two important Cosa Nostra figures present were Salvatore Inzerillo and Salvatore Contorno, Bontate's head man. Inzerillo knew he was now in the firing line and he took immediate action. He sent a messenger to Riina carrying two suitcases packed with US dollars, in part payment of drugs money he owed him which had been in dispute. It was a peace-making gesture that had no effect.

On 11 May Inzerillo was leaving his mistress's apartment in a block built by one of his construction companies. He had no time to get inside his brand new bullet-proof Alfa Romeo nor pull the .357 Magnum from his pocket. He was shot to bits in a hail of bullets from five guns which blew eighty-six holes in his body.

Next, Salvatore Inzerillo's fifteen-year-old son was picked up and taken to the Corleonesi torture chamber in Palermo, where his right arm was cut off. He was told it would stop him attempting to avenge the death of his father. And then he was shot to death, anyway, just to make sure.

In New York, a brother of Salvatore Inzerillo was found shot to death in the back of a car with dollar bills stuffed in his mouth and his uncle, Antonio Inzerillo, left his home in New Jersey that same week and was never seen again.

Back in Palermo, Salvatore's closest brother, Santo Inzerillo, was captured by the Corleonesi together with his friend and bodyguard Mimmo Teresi. They were taken to the torture chamber and while they were awaiting death Teresi wept loudly and Santo shouted, 'Stop crying and tell them to hurry up.'

The Corleonesi killers strangled them both, in a drawn-out

death to invoke the most suffering. Giovanni Falcone, in assessing the details of these murders later, attempted to explain the situation, whereby Santo showed courage and thus died as a man worthy of respect and in doing so even his killers 'will have gained prestige as a result of his dignity'.

Falcone went to great lengths to promote an understanding of Mafia atrocities and corruption, and put them in the context of the so-called Honoured Society. Falcone saw this aspect as important – that a sociological and psychological understanding of the way they think and operate would help entrap them. To the outsider, it may often have seemed a fatuous exercise. The Mafia lived by double standards, and led a double life, but Falcone always persisted with those contemplations of Mafia culture.

It was blatant murder, often for the sake of it, usually waged by psychopaths at the butt of a Kalashnikov – as Salvatore Contorno now discovered. He had moved up in the ranks of Bontate's Santa Maria de Gesu family and as such, he was next on the Corleonesi's list. He went into hiding. The Corleonesi tried to lure him out, by shooting some of his relatives, first his wife's uncle and then a nephew. He decided to flee Palermo and was driving to say goodbye to his parents when he was overtaken by a motorcyclist.

He recognised the pillion passenger as the notorious Corleone assassin, Pino Greco. Greco aimed his Kalashnikov AK47 straight at Contorno and let loose with a burst of fire. Contorno was injured, but still alive. The car spun off the road. He saw the motorcyclist coming back. Greco opened fire again, and Contorno fired back with his revolver, five shots in rapid succession and the bike roared off at high speed. Pino Greco was hit but was saved by a bullet-proof vest.

The Corleonesi had set its course – a systematic massacre of all those on the opposing sides. If, as in the case of Contorno and Buscetta, the victim could not be found, they would kill relatives and friends. There were fifty-eight funerals within the Buscetta and Inzerillo families alone, boys and women too, during the period of the war. Often funerals were impossible because the bodies were never found. Buscetta lost his two teenage sons, Antonio and Bennedetto, neither of whom, he claimed, were in the Mafia. They simply disappeared one afternoon and were never seen again.

Then the husband of their sister, Buscetta's son-in-law Giuseppe Genova, was shot along with two of Buscetta's nephews by three gunmen who walked into their pizza restaurant in the centre of Palermo and opened fire.

Gaetano Badalamenti, then in Brazil, called on Buscetta and told him his nephew Nino Gaetano had been killed and suggested they mounted a counter-attack against the Corleonesi. Buscetta said he wanted nothing to do with it, but relatives of Badalamenti went ahead and attempted to ambush the psychopathic Pino Greco who they believed to be one of the main perpetrators of the murders.

The ambush failed and less than a week later Buscetta's brother Vincenzo and his son Bennedetto were murdered at their Sicilian glass factory.

In Florida, police were called to a suspicious-looking car at Fort Lauderdale airport, and found two bodies in the boot – identified as Giuseppe Romano and Giuseppe Tramontana, two of Buscetta's former associates from the 1970s. Both had been shot.

Gradually, Riina and the Corleonesi gained dominance over the old families by methodically promising peace to those who would swear allegiance and assassinating the bosses and their henchmen who demurred. For months, bodies were being discovered daily, sometimes in clusters of four or five at a time, and even the Sicilian law, well used to bloodshed, was appalled at some of the discoveries.

Several headless corpses were found, and then later the heads would turn up, left on the driving seats of cars. Several of those killed had had their genitals cut off and stuffed in their mouths. Many had been tortured and badly mutilated and later the secrets of what became known as the Corleonesi Chamber of Death was discovered when in 1983 an insignificant employee named Vincenzo Sinagra was arrested and began to tell all.

The chamber was in the Piazza Sant'Erasmo, in a scrapyard behind the old Palermo harbour. When police found it, they discovered all the implements of torture that would have done some dictatorial despot proud. There were chains and ropes attached to chairs and tables; acid baths made from metal drums in which it was reckoned a body would dissolve in under an hour. Sometimes, the bodies were dismembered and fed to pigs, or just weighted and dumped out at sea.

Opposition to the Corleonesi was destroyed but the killings seemed endless. Stefano Bontate's family of 115 known members was virtually wiped out. The Inzerillos were also cut to pieces. Several Mafia leaders around the island of Sicily who were earlier associated with the Bontate-Inzerillo-Badalamenti faction were slaughtered. In Agrigento where the 84-year-old boss, Giuseppe Settecase was gunned down, police made another gruesome find – a burned-out car, buried whole and containing the charred remains of three people who had been shot before the car was set ablaze.

Rosario Riccobono, head of one of the Partanna Mondello families and a former member of the *cupola*, survived a tenuous link with Riina until the autumn of 1982 when relations between his family and the Corleonesi finally soured. Riccobono himself was no push-over. He was known as the Terrorist because he was capable of the most hideous atrocities.

Informers later told Falcone that Toto Riina had held a special 'persuasion' party to secure Riccobono's subservience. No expense was spared – there was music, food, dancing, the finest wines, after which Riccobono was finally asked the question by Riina who held out his hand for Riccobono's recognition.

He shook his head. Riina, furious, left the room and gave the signal. Four of his men set upon Riccobono and while three held him, the fourth strangled him with his bare hands. At that moment, other Corleonesi ran through the house and rounded up the rest of Riccobono's soldiers, herded them out onto the lawn and opened fire with automatic Kalashnikov rifles. Their bodies were tossed with that of Riccobono into a bath of acid.

That evening and during the next few days, fifteen other Riccobono men were gunned down, at their homes, in bars, or on the street until virtually the whole clan had been wiped out. 'As far as I know,' wrote Falcone, 'there was only one who escaped with his life from the Riccobono affair – Michele Micalizzi who survived an attack at the Bar Singapore in which three others were killed.'

Among the few survivors of those who were considered to

be in opposition to the Corleonesi were Buscetta, hiding in Brazil but already back in the drugs business, and Salvatore Contorno whose life was saved when he was arrested in Rome and found to be in possession of two kilos of heroin. A week later, the doctor who had tended the bullet wounds Contorno had received as he fled from the Corleonesi killers was shot dead. That brought Contorno's own casualty list to forty-eight: the doctor, seventeen relatives and thirty friends or associates – all shot dead.

The Mafia civil war ran for more than two-and-a-half years and at the end of this most horrific period in Mafia history approximately 1,280 people, including women and children, had been slaughtered. The exact figure is impossible to quantify because many of the bodies were never discovered. It is based upon those known to have been killed, and those who went missing. The Corleonesi had achieved total control of the Cosa Nostra in Sicily and the rest of the Mafia bowed to the new rulers and promised their 'respect'.

A new *cupola* was formed, with Michele 'the Pope' Greco as its head, though everyone knew it was merely a titular appointment. Don Luciano Liggio was the supreme ruler and as ever supremely arrogant, laughing at those who had brought him to trial and demonstrating that they, with all the power of the State behind them, could not stop him. He was saying the Mafia ruled, and for the time being it did.

Liggio himself drew up the new map of operations, dividing up the territories left suddenly vacant by the departing brethren. The Corleonesi became the global controllers of heroin distribution from Sicily, according to a government judicial inquiry in 1984, though it would be imprudent to suggest, as others have, that the Sicilian-American alliances had established a hegemony in the international drug market.

There were still many other groups around the world, even with connections in Italy, that were as active in the market, including the Chinese Triads, Middle Eastern cartels and emerging groups from South America, to mention but a few. There were also some curious anomalies existing within the global drugs market in Asia and the Far East where military generals had emerged as major exporters. An 1984 Australian Royal Commission of Inquiry into drug trafficking, for example, produced clear evidence once again of CIA activity in countries where Communism was thought to be a threat to US interests.

Two senior CIA officers were identified as consultants to a private bank with twenty-two branch offices all over the world, including London, Sydney, Hong Kong and Singapore, which moved drugs money around the world on behalf of a certain criminal syndicate of around seventy people.

The same bank had been involved in laundering black money on behalf of the CIA and of heroin and illegal arms dealers. The bank operated a tax haven policy of absolute secrecy and was, according to the evidence, 'used in the 1970s to deposit illegal incomes of south-east Asian heroin traffic promoted by the CIA to support criminals and reactionary power men in the name of the anti-Communist crusade.'

The CIA, in sponsoring some of the war-lords and generals in the repression of Communism in Asia, was thus aiding men who were also making fortunes controlling the export of opium from their respective countries and whose products would eventually pass through various international cartels, including the Mafia, and end up being shot into the arms of addicts in the western world, predominantly in America. 'It was,' said Umberto Santino in Palermo, whose archive is filled with such examples, 'a ridiculous and tragic merry-go-round.'

Even so, the influence of the Mafia as a single entity was stronger than all others, and could be assessed by the continuing flow of drug money into the international banking system.

One further set of statistics from that era graphically demonstrated the problem that existed within the Italian state: the number of people engaged in criminal activity in Italy during the year 1982 was put at around 600,000 or three percent of the working population, according to Signor Martinoli, chairman of Censis (Centro Studi Investmenti Sociali, 1985).

And since organized crime in Italy was virtually inseparable from the Mafia, particularly in the traffic of drugs and weapons, extortion and blackmail, Martinoli hinted at a high-level conspiracy between Mafia and political and business leaders and provided an intriguing break-down of the personnel involved in criminal activity:

1] A secret top level of very powerful bosses, favoured by political connections, individuals who were above suspicion, well protected by their connections and top lawyers, who truly held the reins of organized crime and numbered approximately one thousand people.
2] Executors of crime, including full-time operatives and sundry criminal collaborators, amounting to tens of thousands of people.
3] People collaborating or 'in connivance' with criminals, i.e. even by carrying out minute tasks or assuming conniving attitudes, such as *omertà*; this sector is very large and, in Mafia strongholds, may include almost the entire population of a small town.
4] Another separate level of people who are not actually involved in criminal activity as such but who take advantage of it through indirect means, i.e. from illegal profits, investments and the like; businessmen whose operations were legal but supported by dirty, recycled money.

As Mafia people tortured, mutilated, decapitated, bombed and shot each other to bits for control of that money, there was outrage, of course, but there was also apathy. Who really cared if the Mafia was killing itself from within? Certainly not Rome, or Milan. But they should have cared, because as Giovanni Falcone identified, the Corleonesi emerged from its war having eliminated all those who would not bow to them or stood in their way and were thus the Cosa Nostra became 'stronger than ever, more compact, monolithic, watertight, rigidly hierarchical and more clandestine than ever'.

CHAPTER EIGHT

Pio La Torre, The Courageous Communist, One Lawyer and Two Bankers – Dead

The atrocities in Palermo which had seen the killing of so many public officials and mafiosi inspired a new anti-Mafia crusade although it came not from the centre of Italian politics in Rome but from the heart of the Sicilian badlands, Palermo itself. As Ferraro recalls, in the great hall of justice beside the Tiber she and her colleagues became aware that senior law officers and magistrates in Sicily were moving towards the formation of a pool of anti-Mafia magistrates and prosecutors to fight the Mafia chieftains in their own backyard, even though this was frowned upon in some areas of the Rome administration.

Certainly, there had been no rush by the politicians to take advantage of the Mafia internal struggles to begin a more determined combative strike. The idea of a pool was planned by a senior judge and prosecutor in Palermo, Antonio Caponetto, a resolute and upstanding figure in the Sicilian judiciary. 'He was a great initiator of the modern war on the Mafia,' Ferraro told me, 'and led his like-minded colleagues in Sicily towards a united effort the like of which had never been seen. Until that time, the magistrature worked individually and there was very little liaison, often through sheer logistical and practical reasons of inadequate communication and undermanning.'

Caponetto put forward a written outline, stating that it was impossible for judges and police to go on investigating the Mafia on an individual basis. They were dealing with organized crime, and there should be an organized response – a pooling of knowledge, a collective force in the judiciary who could lead the investigations and cross-refer to inter-related cases.

The idea had been spoken of before, but had never been proceeded with. For one thing, it was not received with enthusiasm by the political administration in Rome who believed such a pool could wield too much power, and powerful groups had become political hot potatoes. The reason was the sudden arrival of a new national political crisis that rocked the Italian establishment, reverberated around the world and once again knocked the activities of the Mafia from the headlines.

For months, there had been the rumblings of potentially devastating revelations involving people in power, following a financial scandal in which the empire of one of Italy's foremost financiers had collapsed. Coincidentally, and it was exactly that, the crisis for the government began at exactly the moment when the Corleonesi began its bid for power.

In May 1981, one month after the Corleonesi had fired the first shots of its war by killing Stefano Bontate, the attention of the nation had been diverted by a sensational story, and for once the word sensational in newspaper terms was not an exaggeration. The names of 928 members of Licio Gelli's infamous Masonic Lodge, known as Propaganda Two, were officially published as being under investigation as a possible threat to national security and for corrupt business practices.

Uproar followed when it became known that the membership of P2 included two government ministers, three undersecretaries, seventeen army generals, eight admirals, nine senior officers of the Carabinieri, three heads of the secret service, thirty-eight members of parliament, fourteen magistrates and numerous prominent bankers, industrialists and media figures. The government of the day resigned and a general election was called.

The ensuing government inquiry linked P2 to various other financial scandals in Italy at the time and the whole scandal emanated originally from the arrest in 1979 of Michele Sindona, one of Italy's most prominent post-war bankers and a friend of Giulio Andreotti who had publicly applauded his work for the Italian economy.

At the height of his power, Sindona controlled six banks in four countries, an international hotel chain and 500 other corporations. He was special adviser to Pope Paul V1, with a remit covering the Vatican Bank's overseas investment. He was also the very secret special adviser to the Cosa Nostra in Sicily, where he was a close confidant of Stefano Bontate and the Gambino family, a link which extended to the Gambinos in New York.

Throughout the seventies, before his empire collapsed into a morass of financial irregularities leaving thousands of investors ruined, he was laundering close on $1 billion a year of Mafia drugs money. In 1979, Sindona was indicted on ninety-nine counts of fraud and misappropriation relating to the collapse of the Franklin Bank in New York. It was during the page-by-page audit of his accounts by US fraud specialists that the 'black money' was discovered. The laundering operation linked Sindona directly with the drugs manufacturers back in Palermo.

Though this aspect of the Sindona fraud was kept under wraps for the time being, his arrest by the Americans sent tremors through the international banking system, not to mention the vested interests of high Italian society, the Vatican and the Mafia itself. For all three to be mentioned in the same breath showed the extent of the scandal.

Meanwhile, a Milanese lawyer, Giorgio Ambrosoli, was appointed by the government to liquidate the Sindona empire and try to salvage what he could from the wreckage. He too learned of Mafia connections and flew to Palermo to obtain from the police what information he could on the drugs connections and provide estimates of the cash flow which ran into billions of lire.

Ambrosoli flew back to Milan to continue his investigations into Sindona's affairs and three days later, as he parked his car outside his apartment, he was shot five times in the chest by an unidentified assailant. Ambrosoli fell dead. Thus, the Mafia dealt with the threat of Ambrosoli divulging the information he had learned in Palermo.

In New York, Sindona was given bail of $3 million, and

promptly fled to Sicily by way of a fake Mafia kidnap arranged by the New York Gambinos. In Sicily, with the US capo John Gambino at his side, he attempted to blackmail his way out of trouble in the most audacious manner.

Gambino delivered Sindona to the home of his cousin in Palermo, Rosario Spatola, a seemingly upright citizen, a multi-millionaire building contractor who a decade earlier had been one of those Judge Terranova described as 'pushing a cart'. In Spatola's case, it was a milk cart, and he had once been fined for selling watered-down products. Now, his association with the Sindona case alerted the local police for the first time that he was deeply entrenched in the Cosa Nostra affairs, and had been for years.

The establishment was about to be held to ransom by Sindona's public proclamations that he possessed documents which were dynamite and would bring devastation to the ruling class of Italy. He claimed to have a special book which matched the names of secret foreign bank accounts to 530 'very special clients'.

He put forward a rescue plan for his crashed empire – an outrageous scheme that would have left the Italian taxpayer picking up the bill – which he alleged had been approved by the government. He wanted a deal but the government, laid low by public reaction and media exposure about Sindona's affairs, refused and he was re-arrested.

The implications of the Sindona scandal have been analysed over the years and repercussions are not relevant to this work, except in recording the deep association that this once revered 'financial genius' had with the Mafia.

The final chapter to his story which might have revealed the full extent of these connections could never be written, however. Sindona was sentenced to twenty-five years in New York and given a life sentence in Italy, and was then quickly silenced. The day after his trial ended, he was found dead in his cell from strychnine poisoning. The verdict was suicide. But there is little doubt that the Mafia had killed him.

It was during the Sindona inquiry that police searched a villa owned by one of his associates and there discovered the List – a complete run-down of the membership of Licio Gelli's P2

Lodge which was subsequently published amid a huge furore, after which the government resigned.

During the final throes of the Sindona saga came another major financial earthquake which would have similar implications. One of Sindona's former associates, Roberto Calvi, also known as God's banker for his Vatican connections, went missing, leaving his Banco Ambrosiana in turmoil.

Calvi – like Sindona – was a member of P2. Like Sindona, he was also handling Vatican finances – and laundering Mafia money at the same time. Calvi, of course, was subsequently found hanging under Blackfriars Bridge in London in June 1982, a mysterious death which to this day stimulates the juices of crime writers with its undertones of Mafia involvement. Though a suicide verdict was recorded in London, he too was probably murdered.

The ongoing media examination of Calvi's interests and associations filled the newspapers for months, and eventually led back to the equally mysterious demise of Pope John Paul I, after only thirty-three days in office.

The sheer impact of these events, scandal after scandal, corruption in the highest places, the fall of the government, interspersed with other dramatic events in Italy at the time such as the assassination attempt on Pope John Paul II, the Bologna railway bomb planted by neo-Fascists which killed 84 people and an earthquake in the south which killed 3,000, came like a series of continuous shockwaves underneath the Italian seat of power and had a stunning effect.

Media and public alike marvelled at the enormity of it all. In this great succession of dramatic, shocking events, the civil war among the Mafia was virtually overlooked, or at least given rather less attention than might have normally been the case.

The Ministry of Justice in Rome was overwhelmed with the fall-out of national events and the judiciary at large was forced by the horrific violence of the Mafia's war to sit up and take note. Attitudes among the politicians who governed and controlled the police effort drifted under the weight of the scandals elsewhere.

Thus, when the Corleonesi began its bid for total dominion over the heroin traffic, the reaction of politicians and many judges was one of ambivalence and virtually amounted to the view that the Mafia was already beginning to tear itself apart so let them get on with it.

Caponetto and those on the front line in Palermo knew differently. The implementation of his idea – what became known as the Pool – had begun, with the strong support of another senior jurist, Rocco Chinnici, and Giovanni Falcone and his friend and public prosecutor Paolo Borsellino.

Chinnici himself had taken over the files of the assassinated Judge Cesare Terranova. Though with the benefit of hindsight, the pool seemed a fairly elementary idea in the pursuit of the Mafia, it had never operated previously. Each investigation was kept more or less on an individual basis and the Mafia knew it. So it was easy to curtail any investigation simply by killing the law officer handling the case. The establishment of the Pool changed all that and led towards a greater understanding of the complexities of Mafia activity which had so far eluded even the most ardent crime fighters of Sicily.

Giovanni Falcone reckoned that the opening up of the Sindona case showed the true extent of previously unknown avenues of corruption and crime and helped in the formulation of the Pool. 'Through the Sindona investigations and being able to study the evidence,' Falcone admitted, 'the Mafia appeared before me as a boundless world, totally unexplored.'

It was a turning point in the appreciation of the extent of the Transatlantic link that was just one part of the drug explosion. During the coming three years, the investigation reached across Europe into the United States and South America. The Sindona case also allowed investigators on both sides of the Atlantic to finally begin to lift the veil on the movement of the laundered narco-billions.

In Palermo, Vice Commissioner Antonnio Cassara, who had taken over the role as head of the Squadra Mobile in succession to the murdered Boris Giuliano, had begun to put together a team of plain-clothes policemen. It was something of a battle even to do that. His force was underpaid, overworked, ill-trained and badly equipped.

They had a mere half-dozen unmarked cars available, old boneshakers that constantly broke down. His squad's headquarters in the centre of Palermo was cramped even though it was understaffed. For a long time, there was not even a back door, and individual offices had to be kept locked. Security was farcical and infested with Mafia informers.

Cassara ploughed on, establishing his team to begin his own personal crusade. He was already in close consultation with Chinnici and Falcone on what can now be seen as the very beginning of this most concerted attack on the Mafia, moving ahead almost in spite of the establishment.

Though Sicily was engulfed by this world of crime, it was already, and thankfully, endowed with a small consortium of brave and spirited men and women prepared to fight and put their lives in danger, not just in the legal profession. Journalists and editors on *L'Ora* and the *Giornale di Sicilia* had always been at the forefront of the battle and still are.

There were casualties among them, too. Investigative journalist Mauro di Mauro, who worked for *L'Ora*, vanished without trace in September 1970 while working on a Mafia story. The *Giornale*'s crime reporter, Mario Francese, was gunned down in a busy street and his courageous young successor Franco Nicastro, whose views on the current situation will appear in later chapters, was the subject of constant threats to himself and his family.

Churchmen, scholars, university professors and community leaders kept up a consistent attack at considerable risk to themselves. Cardinal Pappalardo, unlike his predecessor Cardinal Ruffini who never denounced the Mafia, became a leading crusader against the criminals and continually implored public officials not to give in to fear. The Jesuit priesthood, gathered at the Centre of Social Studies in Palermo, were similarly outspoken and have included the study and analysis of the Mafia phenomenon on their agenda for many years.

One other man who was a high profile orator on the subject of what he termed the disgusting parasites feeding on Italian society – a term guaranteed to stir the hackles of those so-called Men of Honour – was Pio La Torre, the Communist MP and member of the Anti-Mafia Commission who was continually badgering Rome for something, anything, to be done.

For years, he had argued in vain for new laws which would make any involvement or any association with the Mafia a more easily identifiable and convictable offence. It will be recalled that his friend Pier Santi Mattarella was on the verge of attempting to bring new laws to the regional parliament to attack Mafia finance in 1980 when he was gunned down in front of his family.

Pio La Torre shared this view and it was becoming accepted among magistrates like Caponetto, Falcone and Chinnici that one of the best forms of attack would be through the Mafia's bank accounts. In desperation, as the Mafia wars on his own doorstep escalated, La Torre returned to the subject and drew up a list of demands, to be a minimum course of action by the government, for which he campaigned.

In March 1982, La Torre followed this up with a letter to the new Prime Minister, Giovanni Spandoli, head of the small Republican Party who had come to power through a short-lived coalition of five political factions in the wake of the P2 scandal. La Torre protested that the Mafia's multi-million-dollar drug production business, its international network and penetration into Italian politics 'have transformed it into one of the most deadly serious dangers facing Italy today'.

La Torre went on to demand a series of new laws which he had worked out in detail, the most controversial of which was to abolish bank secrecy and give investigators power to look into bank accounts, make it easier to track the flow of Mafia money and identify those involved. He went further, suggesting that all money and property which was in the possession of convicted criminals should be confiscated – a law which many other European countries picked up on, though not until much later.

These measures, La Torre argued, would go a long way to destroying the accumulated economic power of those who lived by organized crime.

From the public and governmental standpoint, there was one basic flaw in the La Torre presentation: he was a Communist which meant that outside of Palermo, half of the country and most of the opposing politicians were not particularly interested in what he had to say and certainly did not intend to allow him to score political points on such a controversial issue.

On this occasion, however, La Torre was fortunate in that he was not directly up against the Christian Democrats but the more amenable political alliance headed by Spandoli who was anxious to score some points with the public.

La Torre also received a good deal of favourable publicity and appeared to be making some headway. Indeed, what became known as La Torre's Law would eventually pass on to the Italian statute book, but he would not live to see that success materialize.

Though often threatened, La Torre repeatedly chose to tell the Mafia that he would not be cowed by the gun or bomb. He was cautious in his daily routine, though often travelled without a bodyguard even during this crucial time when he knew he had caused anger in the hearts of the Corleonesi and the rest of the Cosa Nostra.

On 30 April 1982, Pio La Torre's car was ambushed as he was driving through Palermo city centre. A hail of bullets from a Kalashnikov were fired in full view of the street crowds, leaving La Torre and his driver Rosario Salvo dead.

A new wave of shock hit Palermo, and incidentally among those now clamouring for action was an unlikely ally for a Communist in the shape of the United States, which had been pressing the Italian government for more positive action to fight the Sicilian drug cartels.

Spandoli and his government finally took heed of the campaign that cost La Torre his life and the Ministry of Justice was instructed to begin formulating new laws which were much in line with what he had suggested.

In the meantime, Spandoli, in conference with the Ministry of Justice and the Minister of the Interior, had already decided to appoint a new supremo to lead the fight against organized crime and he had only one name to approach – the popular hero of the terrorist war, General Carlo Alberto Dalla Chiesa.

CHAPTER NINE

Dalla Chiesa, His Wife, Three Policemen and a Brave Newspaper Editor – Dead

General Carlo Alberto Dalla Chiesa was under no illusions about the job he had been asked to take on. He knew the dangers. Who wouldn't, with those who preceded him having been picked off one by one like sitting ducks. And, anyway, he'd been there before. He'd seen it all, and watched guilty men escape justice to continue their business. He didn't have an answer then and he wasn't sure he had one now. He was under no illusions about the hierarchy, either.

'Dalla Chiesa was regarded as Italy's leading carabinieri general,' Ferraro told me. 'He was a man of great national standing and courage and one of very few people with the experience to attempt to take on this terrible blight affecting our country. He also knew the particular peculiarities of the Sicilian situation which was also vitally important.'

He had seen panic-stricken, vulnerable politicians by the score during the war on the terrorists. He had put up with the banality of a lot of people who were all talk and no mettle. He had dealt warily with a lot of untrustworthy people who would sell him down the river at the drop of a hat. He had witnessed previously in Sicily so-called public servants who were up to their necks in dubious deals who would show him no favours and do all they could to protect the people whose patronage they enjoyed.

Would things be any different this time? He was honest enough with himself to record his exact feelings, or more precisely his misgivings, on hearing that they wanted him to take on the Mafia. Memo to diary: 'It surprises me. It almost frightens me. Once again I think am becoming the instrument of a policy that leaks on every side.'

At the time, he was second in command of the State police, sixty-two years old and only three years away from retirement which he was looking forward to sharing with his new young wife. As one who had experienced a long and action-filled career, he was finding the desk job a bore. In that respect, he welcomed a challenge to round off his days with the Carabinieri though squaring up to the Mafia wasn't quite what he had had in mind.

When Spandoli offered Dalla Chiesa the job he told him he would be made a 'Prefect of the Republic' with powers to coordinate the effort. Dalla Chiesa could draw heavily on his experience in Palermo two decades earlier, when he was in charge of the city's Carabinieri headquarters. He knew the people, he knew the terrain and he knew the vagaries of Sicilian politics better than most – but then, as some pointed out, Judge Terranova, too, had known these things.

In his regular evidence to the Anti-Mafia Commission, Dalla Chiesa had continuously warned of the rise in drug trafficking which had caught the law authorities on both sides of the Atlantic on the hop by the speed with which it had taken off. The money involved had produced a totally new situation and he made this connection with his attacks on the Mafia's political allies.

Indeed, this presented a matter of personal anguish for Dalla Chiesa. His own politics had always been Christian Democrat and he was a personal friend of the party leader, Giulio Andreotti.

It remained a fact, however, that some of Andreotti's strongest supporters in the Sicilian province were tainted by Mafia association, though equally it would be wrong to tar the whole elected force of MPs from the province with the same brush. There were many MPs sent to national parliament under

Christian Democrat colours and local politicians involved in the regional government as DC party members who were staunchly opposed to any contact with the wealthy Mafia families and openly rejected their support.

However, it was an open secret that key positions on the island had at various times been held by Mafia associates who were also closely allied to the Andreotti camp and that he personally relied heavily on their power-base to shore up the often tenuous fortunes of his party.

The same people who had been mentioned in various reports and evidence to the Anti-Mafia Commission were still in power in Sicily in the early eighties, when Dalla Chiesa moved in. Most notable among them was Salvo Lima, the former mayor of Palermo and a member of the national parliament. Lima, who was mentioned on 163 occasions in a damaging Anti-Mafia Commission report of 1976, consistently denied he was a Mafia man.

Dalla Chiesa had a long profile on Lima. He was a serene and calm man of imposing stature who had been in local politics all his life. He became a member of the district council on its formation in 1945 and became mayor before he was forty.

He was one of the three most prominent figures mentioned in the report of the assassinated police lieutenant Malausa in 1963.

In the spring of 1968, Lima decided to turn towards national politics and first met Andreotti when he came to Palermo for the selection of candidates for the forthcoming elections. 'I was impressed by his attitude and general appearance,' Andreotti said of him later.

Lima gave the nod of approval to many of the construction and building deals which ran out of control in post-war Palermo. He moved directly to Andreotti's inner circle, commanding as he did the power to marshal the support and votes from Sicily and the whole of the south of Italy.

It was said that without the votes Lima mustered in Sicily, the Christian Democrats and the Andreotti faction would never have survived. Lima was subsequently appointed under-secretary of state at the Italian treasury, despite loud protests from the left wing of the Christian Democrats, not to mention the left-wing groups in parliament itself. By the mid-seventies he was the leading Sicilian politician in the Rome and locally he was known as the King of Palermo. In 1979, he ran for the European parliament and won handsomely. But always there was an undercurrent of accusation, that as well as being a leading politician, he was also the Mafia's man in Rome and now in Brussels.

And then there was his successor, Vito Ciancimino, still a strong figure in Palermo political circles. So, in a nutshell, Dalla Chiesa knew that once he moved back to Palermo, politics and his new job – if he were to do it without fear or favour – would collide head on.

This troubled him and according to Dalla Chiesa's son, Nando, he had a confrontation with Andreotti before he accepted the job. 'My father told the family of this meeting,' Nando revealed. 'He said he had been to see Andreotti to tell him what he knew about his people in Sicily. According to my father, Andreotti went as white as a sheet.' Dalla Chiesa also made it clear that in accepting the job, he would have no special regard for 'that part of the electorate associated with his [Andreotti's] Grand Electors'.

He laid it out before Andreotti, insisting that this was no ordinary war against criminals. He considered that the Mafia in its present form and with its international connections represented a greater threat to society than the Red Brigades and the 1970s terrorists. 'We are staring down the barrel of a Kalashnikov,' said Dalla Chiesa, 'and it is permanently pointed in our direction. But what we are confronting is far more terrifying than personal danger. It is an insidious, crawling bacteria, a slime, that is creeping through our land and elsewhere that will, if not checked, poison our society with its culture of criminality. You people will grow up aspiring to be Mafia instead of scholars.'

There was one other precaution that Dalla Chiesa took before setting off to Palermo. He wrote a letter to Prime Minister Spandoli setting out his personal misgivings, formally listing his understanding of the job description for which he sought a written acknowledgement. He wrote:

> My possible appointment as Prefect, although indeed a great honour, would not convince me on its own to leave

my present position. The terms of such an appointment as Prefect of Palermo cannot and must not include the fight against the Mafia as an 'implicit' function as this would give the impression that we do not know what the Mafia is, or what is meant by the expression 'Mafia'.

This would also convince public opinion that the declared intention on our part to limit and fight the phenomenon in all its various manifestations is not a serious one . . . It would also prove that the 'messages' sent to some newspapers by the most tainted political 'family' in Sicily have reached their objective.

Far from asking for exceptional laws or powers, it is necessary and honest that the person who is destined to fight a phenomenon of such dimensions should not only receive support from the press – which is not always authoritative or credible and liable to change sides – but that he should also enjoy an openly declared and legally endorsed support from the government. 'Openly declared' because the image of such an appointment must be commensurate with the importance of the task. It must be 'codified' because, as experience teaches, all promises are forgotten, every reassuring statement – 'It shall be done', 'We shall do something about it' – is neutralized and everything is hushed up and limited as soon as certain interests are involved.

I would therefore like to ask you to intervene, in this very important part not only of my career but of my life as a loyal and faithful servant of the state, in a most qualified and confident manner, to ensure that this new appointment will be accepted with serenity, and with the most highly responsible attitude – that of true enthusiasm.

It was a very sincere and deeply edifying letter, which really added up to the general seeking an assurance that he would get the back-up he requested and indeed was promised by Spandoli, to ensure that the hounds were called off, that the politicians, local and national, would not make his job impossible even before he began, that there would be none of the neglect that had wrecked all past attempts at the job he was now undertaking.

He earnestly wanted that 'open declaration' of intent and he did not want the appointment to disintegrate into a mere window-dressing exercise – at which successive Rome administrations have been masters.

As Franco Nicastro pointed out to me in Palermo in March 1994, it was the case then, and was still the case today, that the government and its advisers – the civil service establishment – were most adept at loud exclamations of shock, of promising much but doing little. Giovanni Falcone made much the same point when he recalled that after one assassination, a senior minister in Rome telephoned him and asked, 'Now what can we come up with to calm the country down?'

In other words, they wanted someone or some particular scenario to blame. Dalla Chiesa expressly feared that he might become that scapegoat.

Of course, everyone reassured him it was not the case and that he need not worry that he would upset senior, long standing politicians. 'You are a general of the Carabinieri not the Christian Democrat party,' he was told. But those words would not add up to a bag of beans. He would never know that even as he left for Palermo with his wife Emanuela de Settecarro, a former nurse, then thirty-two years old, that an attempt to veto his appointment was made by the Italian Security Committee.

That august little group consisting of government ministers and the heads of the Carabinieri, the *pubblica sicurezza* and the various branches of the Italian security forces, heavily infiltrated by Licio Gelli's outlawed P2 masonic lodge, voted by an overwhelming majority to oppose the appointment. Only one voted in favour.

And as he and Emanuela packed to leave for Sicily, the Mafia was preparing its welcome and its warning. Pio La Torre's demand for tough new laws, combined with the appointment of Dalla Chiesa, was known to the Mafia families and so Pio La Torre was killed – on the very day Dalla Chiesa flew to Palermo.

It was a signal from the Mafia, not just to Dalla Chiesa but to all those cohorts on the island who might have it in their minds to waver, and support him or even become turncoats. Those who for years had taken Mafia money – even if they were not 'made men' or members of that criminal elite – would be expected to toe the line. It is one of those foregone conclusions in what the Mafia expects of its associates: long-established rituals and warped systems of etiquette in which no words are spoken demand such allegiance.

Put in its simplest terms, if a man goes to the house of a Mafia leader and knows that he is involved in criminal acts, that somewhere in his business he is connected with drug trafficking, the very fact that that person has accepted the don's hospitality is a signal of complicity. The trap is set. Friendship becomes an onerous burden and ultimately a cover, and leads finally to something far more serious from which there is no escape.

Dalla Chiesa was well aware of these little social implications which is why he shunned the social scene like the plague. He guessed that those who had accepted the Mafia's hospitality and their coin would not be long in showing their disapproval of him, and he was right. Salvo Lima, the King of Palermo, publicly put some space between himself and the general's appointment. It was not necessary, he proclaimed. There were sufficient honest men in Palermo who could administer justice.

By then, Lima's motive was unbridled fear. His friend Judge Scaglione had already been murdered. Michele Reina, the former district secretary of the DCs, had been shot because he refused to accommodate the Mafia and halt a certain course of inquiry. Mattarella had been shot because he threatened a political attack. Pio La Torre for the same reason. Lima knew if he stepped out of line, did not do their bidding, he too would get the bullet. It was no excuse for what he did. He had been doing their bidding for so long to service his own ambitions that there was no way back.

There were many like him. A wealthy Palermo lawyer spoke out and claimed that Dalla Chiesa was not wanted in Sicily. If he came, he would ruin Palermo in a matter of weeks. If he halted the drugs traffic, everyone who lived off the trade would be thrown out of work and would turn back to local crime. 'They will sack our homes, hold us up, break into our stores. Our families would not be safe,' he said.

It was an odd kind of logic but one way of attempting to turn the public against the general, for everyone knew that the public was his best source of support. The regional president of the Christian Democrats, Mario D'Acquisto, had already made his position clear, complaining he had not been consulted before Dalla Chiesa was chosen. The mayor of Palermo, Nello Martellucci, likewise grumbled that they did not need an outsider like the general to solve their problems. The shutters came down at almost every level.

The next tactic, well known and well tried among the Mafia and the warring politicians in Sicily, was a whispering campaign. It became rife in the middle-class social set of Palermo where there was at the time a certain hollow prestige in associating with the Mafia. Dalla Chiesa refused point blank to join the cocktail circuit and very soon they were talking behind their hands of rumours, totally false, which centred upon his sexual behaviour and his recent marriage to 'such a young and pretty woman'.

Dalla Chiesa stood alone, completely isolated as far as the political administration was concerned. In spite of the promises, he had been tossed to the wolves. He trusted very few people, and they could virtually be counted on one hand. He dealt mostly with a small group of magistrates including Antonino Caponetto, Rocco Chinnici and Giovanni Falcone, working now to form their Pool of like-minded judges.

Almost from the day he arrived in Palermo, Dalla Chiesa began to ruffle feathers. He announced his attention to look into the construction industry. He knew that the untouchables on the island were the Mafia elite whose fortunes were based on crime and corruption but were legitimized in an array of other businesses. Dalla Chiesa believed that much of this criminality originated from frauds in the construction industry – and any visitor to Palermo will have seen the concrete monstrosities which are a vast monument to this era. A special report on this activity had already been prepared and was in the hands of the Italian finance minister who in turn passed it to Dalla Chiesa.

The report highlighted a convenient local way of laundering drugs money through the building industry. Of $130 million spent on house building in Palermo between 1971 and 1981, less than two per cent of the funding came from conventional bank loans. The rest was financed by cash money, up front, an unheard-of practice in the building business.

Dalla Chiesa made no secret of his intentions. 'The Mafia,' he repeated time and again, 'is now installed in every major Italian city. It has invested in property, commerce and industry and will go on doing so. I am interested in getting to know about this private accumulation of Mafia capital, how they launder the black money, these stolen, extorted lire which famous architects and designers transform into houses, hotels and de luxe restaurants. But I am even more interested in the network which controls the Mafia itself, which may be in hands which are supposedly above suspicion and which having placed itself in key positions, controls political power.'

His investigation into Mafia-linked building companies revealed connections between the financing of a new multi-billion building project and the Cantani Mafia boss, Benedetto 'Don Nitto' Santapaolo. It was an important discovery and one which was confirmed much later, in 1993, by the new breed of supergrass, known as *pentiti.*

The *pentito* Antonino Calderone told investigating magistrates that Don Nitto's rise to power was achieved only with the complicity of the ruling powers and important names in Rome would be mentioned. Had Dalla Chiesa been able to pursue his work on this case, Santapaolo's power would have been cut in its infancy.

In the 1970s, he was a mere chauffeur to the Mafia boss Giuseppe Calderone – who was himself murdered in 1979 – but quickly established his own power-base when he threw his hand in with the Corleonesi. From the early 1980s, he began to acquire large numbers of properties, financed by every traditional Mafia activity of extortion, protection, building contracts and gambling dens, complemented by drugs.

According to Antonino Calderone, Santapaolo took over some of the best restaurants in Catania by the 'usual' method – first taking a protection rake-off and then, by increasing the payments, eventually forcing the owners to sell their businesses to him at ridiculously low prices.

When Dalla Chiesa began his investigations, threatening

to arrest the Catania boss, Santapaolo went into hiding. He was supposedly not seen again for eleven years, until he was arrested in May 1993 during Liliana Ferraro's administration at the office of penal affairs. According to the *pentito*, no one in authority – after Dalla Chiesa – ever bothered to look for him because Santapaolo bought the silence of local VIPs and put out confusing messages that he had been spotted in faraway places.

Yet he and his family lived all the time in a stylish villa in one of Catania's best areas. One man who attempted to expose the connections between Santapaolo and local VIPs was newspaper editor Giuseppe Fava who chose to run an article in his newspaper, *I Siciliani*.

Fava was born and bred in Catania, the city he used to boast was once called the Milan of the south. It exemplified the post-war fifties boom above all other cities on the island. It was an opulent, hedonistic place that attracted industry and business from the mainland.

It was building factories faster than any other city apart from Rome itself and in the early sixties, it held a record for the issue of shop licences: there was one for every forty-five citizens. But just as suddenly, it all turned sour. Billions of lire were poured in in grants and aid, yet the local hospital began to close wards and whole housing projects, funded by 85 per cent government grants, were simply left half finished.

By the late seventies, a new boom was in progress and with it came the birth a corrupt alliance of politicians, businessmen and criminals who between them pocketed the funds. Giuseppe Fava, outraged by these developments, ran his article and described how the leaders of the consortium had taken a stranglehold on development in Catania. He called them the Four Horsemen of the Apocalypse. He hinted at their association with the Mafia leader Nitto Santapaolo who by then controlled the city's underworld.

Santapaolo's men were employed by the Four Horsemen to defend building sites. There was a photograph taken at the wedding of the daughter of one of them at which the local MP, Salvatore La Turco, who was actually a member of the Anti-Mafia Commission, sat with his arm around Santapaolo's shoulder – at a time when Santapaolo was supposed to have disappeared.

Fava's article caused furious anger among those he accused of a cynical alliance between the inter-dependent interests of money, political power and violence. And so one Thursday evening, Giuseppe Fava paid the price. On his way to visit his grand-daughter, he was ambushed by unknown assailants and five bullets were pumped into the back of his head.

No arrests were made though the story would explode later, in the 1990s, when the *pentiti* cast their minds back to the era when Santapaolo ruled supreme in Catania.

Don Nitto was finally arrested in 1993 during a top-secret operation in which thirty special police raided his house, without telling the local force what was planned. But in 1982, Dalla Chiesa first noticed the connection between Santapaolo and a valuable construction contract in Palermo, and asked: 'Why is a company based in Catania on the other side of the island undertaking such a major building contract in Palermo?'

Had he been able to pursue his investigations, Santapaolo might have been stopped then, but he continued 'in hiding' and in business for another decade.

Six weeks after Dalla Chiesa's arrival in Palermo, Santapaolo's sworn enemy, Alfio Ferlito, the boss of a Catania-based family and associate of the murdered Bontates and Inzerillos, was arrested. The Santapaolo clan feared he might give Dalla Chiesa vital information. He was being transferred from a prison cell in Enna to a more secure one in Trapani, with three armed escorts, when they were ambushed.

Three killers from the ranks of the Corleonesi opened fire and killed all four. The attack became known as the *Strage della Circonvallazione* – the Ringroad Massacre.

Dalla Chiesa himself went immediately to the scene to lead the investigation. Ballistics tests identified bullets from the same Kalashnikov that had been used to kill Bontate and Inzerillo. All through the summer months, Dalla Chiesa pressed on but doors slammed shut in his face. There was no enthusiasm among the hierarchy to assist him.

August and the holidays passed without great event and as Giovanni Falcone later recalled, 'The general had not really got into his stride. But I believe the decision to eliminate him had already been taken. Dalla Chiesa was dangerous [to the Cosa Nostra] because he had invested all his commitment and great professionalism in a new job and therefore had to achieve significant results at all costs . . . Sadly he was flung into a situation in which he was to appear as an expression of will and yet did not personify the authority of the State. Thus, the Cosa Nostra believed it could strike with impunity, because he personified only himself.'

There is no doubt the general felt totally isolated, that he had been badly let down. There was even a measure of indifference becoming apparent among the local population and the intepretation hinted at by Falcone was that the Mafia had received the signal: 'Dalla Chiesa is yours.'

In a famous interview with the Italian author and columnist Giorgio Bocca at the end of the summer, Dalla Chiesa said, 'I have been discovering a new fact, which is this: the Mafia kills those [of us] who are powerful and raise our sights to the gentlemen of the Palazzo [the Rome parliament]. I think I now understand the new rules of the game, which is a powerful man is killed when a fatal combination comes about – when he has become too dangerous but can be killed because he is isolated.'

Dalla Chiesa was, that day, being uncannily prophetic. He had been left standing alone in the middle of a wide open space, with guns trained on him from every direction. He virtually said as much to Ralph Jones, the US Consul in Palermo, on the morning of 3 September. According to Jones, Dalla Chiesa was very disappointed that the 'gentlemen of the Palazzo' had not kept their word and he wanted specifically that day to arouse the interest of the Americans.

'He believed that now, only the US government could intervene at the highest level and force some movement,' said Jones, who also recalled the way in which Dalla Chiesa described to him his personal feelings of isolation.

He related a story, going back to the 1970s when he was running the local Carabinieri station. He said he received a call from a Carabinieri captain who had received threats against his life from a local Mafia boss in the village of Palma di Montechiaro. 'I drove up to that village,' Dalla Chiesa told Jones, 'and took the captain's arm and began walking with him slowly up the main street, then back again, and up again. Everyone was looking. Then we stopped outside the house of the Mafia boss, and remained there until the point had been made, that the young captain was not alone.'

The point of that story, the general told Jones, was this: 'All I am asking is for somebody to take my arm and walk with me. At present, there is no one to whom I can turn, and that is why I am here, in your office, now.' Jones promised he would do all he could but of course there was nothing he could do for Dalla Chiesa, even if there had been time.

The US authorities continued to maintain their age-old policy that Sicily was a no-go area for any official presence; no agents of any section of the US investigative community operated there on a regular basis. In any event, it was already too late for any cavalry, foreign or otherwise, to charge in and rescue Dalla Chiesa from his plight.

That evening, the general and his wife Emanuela had decided to dine out at the restaurant in the Hotel la Torre in Palermo. He was always security conscious, though not overtly so. He had his own set of rules, such as changing his route, times, and form of transport so that there was no set routine. That night, they were to travel in his wife's car, a Fiat Auz.

They had only one unmarked escort car with a single policeman, Domenico Russo. As they drove along the Via Isidoro Carini, a powerful motorbike carrying two men began to follow them. Behind, another powerful motorbike and two cars, a BMW and a Fiat, fell into the procession, well behind. Suddenly, the motorbikes roared ahead and drew alongside the little car. The man on the back already had his Kalashnikov at shoulder height as they drew level and fired five or six shots into the face and head of Emanuela.

Dalla Chiesa apparently threw himself across his wife in a vain attempt to save her, and the gunmen gave him enough time to realize what was happening, to see the terrible mutilation of his beautiful wife. Then they opened fire again, killing Dalla Chiesa himself while another assassin pumped bullets into the bodyguard, who died a week later in hospital. The BMW drew up and another assailant climbed out, and fired again at the bodies of the general and his wife to make sure they were dead.

Later, a police investigation team discovered the assassinations had been meticulously planned, using an eight-man team with two-way radios tracking the Dalla Chiesas from the moment they got into their car. The two cars and one of the motorbikes were later found abandoned. All had been set on fire. The ballistics report on the bullets in Dalla Chiesa's body confirmed that it was the same Kalashnikov that had killed Stefano Bontate, Salvatore Inzerillo and Alfio Ferlito.

On a wall near scene of the killing, where flowers were placed, someone had chalked up a phrase which expressed the feelings of the island: 'Here dies all the hopes of the people of Sicily.' Sadly, it was not a sentiment with which the bourgeosie wholeheartedly concurred, the preservation of the Palermitan status quo having been, for the time being, assured.

The shock waves from Dalla Chiesa's death had travelled far beyond the island of Sicily, to Rome, Milan, the EC countries and on into America. That 'local' problem could no longer be passed off as such and Italy was deeply moved by the death of the general of whom much had been expected. In the mass of tributes, it was clear that Italy had believed that he had been armed with special powers and a suitable troop of Carabinieri to protect him when he had not; the special powers simply never materialized.

There was considerable reaction to the curious fact that Dalla Chiesa had been travelling without an effective bodyguard when he was shot and there was a note of some apprehension about that from within his own ranks. Giovanni Falcone pointed out that when the general arrived in Palermo, the newspapers emphasized his professional abilities, his self-confidence and his courage. 'So people were amazed that when he was assassinated he had been virtually unprotected,' said Falcone. 'The criticism of lack of prudence is classic when "illustrious" homicide has been committed. There is a lesson to be learned from all this, however. Those who represent the State in enemy territory are duty-bound to be invulnerable. At least within the limits of what is feasible.'

It was a curious statement which seemed in a way to be putting some of the blame on Dalla Chiesa himself, though as time wore on Falcone amended his view as so many others began to be cut down, even though they had taken all the precautions that were feasibly possible.

The fact remained, and it was emphasized by later developments and revelations, that Dalla Chiesa had been left exposed like a general going into battle without troops. The new anti-Mafia laws proposed by Pio La Torre did not go before parliament until after the general's death, rushed through in the aftermath as the 'gentlemen in the Palazzo' began their public relations exercise to quell the alarm and despondency being displayed in the media. There were already rumblings of a conspiracy.

Even though Dalla Chiesa had not gone far down that path of discovery, those who feared him knew that he would get there in the end. As the tributes said, 'He was a remarkable man.' So there were many people who were interested in seeing him disappear from the scene either by discrediting him and forcing him to withdraw or by killing him. Since the first option was an unlikely one, given his stature as a public figure, the second was the only alternative.

The evidence pointed to the usual Mafia killing machine that had disposed of so many of its enemies in the previous eighteen months or so, but a number of eminent commentators were strongly of the belief that the assassination of such an important person as Dalla Chiesa could not have been carried out without a nod of approval from a higher level. A good deal of public speculation began for the first time to suggest that word had come from above the Mafia *cupola* which pulled the strings on matters of importance such as the disposal of a troublesome public official.

Facts filtered out during the next decade, piece by piece, that suggested Dalla Chiesa's death was certainly more than a fight with the Mafia. Skeletons of the Aldo Moro kidnap and murder were in several cupboards, and in Dalla Chiesa's safe hidden in his bedroom. The safe, whatever it contained, was cleaned out by persons unknown. Four years later, in July 1986, it emerged from new interrogations of Dalla Chiesa's staff that the safe contained incriminating papers, providing damning evidence of the Mafia's links with politicians and with a key figure in the Italian secret service.

The revival of this speculation provided the starting point

for a whole new inquiry, which took in the original hints by the journalist Mino Pecorelli – murdered in 1978 – that the assassination of Dalla Chiesa had been ordered because of what he knew about the Moro killing. But politics and the Mafia remained, for the time being, a no-go area of inquiry for the Palermo judges and so the lid was kept firmly on that particular can of worms.

Nando Dalla Chiesa, the general's son and a sociologist at Milan's Bocconi University, in the wake of his father's death pointed an accusing finger at where he believed the blame lay. 'The police should be looking among the ranks of the Christian Democrats in Sicily for those who ordered the killing,' he said. Later, he added that he believed there may have been a connection between his father's death and that of Aldo Moro. Certain politicians in Rome, he claimed, lived with a constant fear that his father would reveal damaging information about the kidnap and assassination of the former prime minister which would have deep implications for the political power structure of Italy.

They believed that Dalla Chiesa, having decided to attack the political and business affiliations of the Mafia, would eventually expose the secrets that only he knew, as the former commander and supremo of the anti-terrorist forces of the seventies. In November 1992, when more Mafia supergrasses came crawling out of the woodwork in profusion, further allegations were made that the deaths of Dalla Chiesa and Aldo Moro were linked. A leading informant, Tommaso Buscetta, said that the Mafia would have had no interest in eliminating Dalla Chiesa in 1979 'unless he was inconvenient, very inconvenient for the State and for a particular politician'.

Nando Dalla Chiesa, commenting on these later disclosures, said, 'I always thought the Moro case might have something to do with my father's death. I had never suspected they planned to kill him as early as 1979. It is no coincidence that we now find that past political leaders were not just people who took votes from the Mafia, but exchanged favours with outright criminals.'

The scenario was blurred and misty. Past events mixed with the present to form a threat which was considered by Dalla Chiesa's enemies too great to leave unattended. In making his declaration of intent to expose the Third Level, to cut a deep swathe through the secret machinations of the politicians and businessmen who were in league with Mafia chieftains, Dalla Chiesa was the author of his own death warrant. Once under way such an inquiry would have undoubtedly revealed facts which people in power, not just in Italy but America, too, wanted to remain hidden.

Dalla Chiesa had to be eliminated.

His personal knowledge, that which he kept stored in his brain, was buried with him and what evidence existed in his bedroom safe was quietly stolen away. His killers had at least halted a possible imminent exposure of a political conspiracy surrounding the murder of Aldo Moro but the great boulder he upturned to reveal Mafia secrets was already rolling. Little new light would be shed on the Moro case but the biggest-ever attack on the Mafia and its high-level protectors and associates had begun and was unstoppable.

CHAPTER TEN

Two Judges Leading the Attack on the Mafia Hierarchy – Dead

Liliana Ferraro today identifies the killing of Dalla Chiesa as a turning point in the fight against the Mafia. In the wake of his death, the anti-Mafia crusade moved on several fronts, and the first major contact between Italian and American law enforcement agencies began. 'It was at this precise moment, in the autumn following Dalla Chiesa's murder, that significant developments occurred,' Ferraro explained. 'It marked the launching of bi-lateral cooperation between Italy and America and the passing of the first batch of new laws that would strengthen the arm of the prosecutors.'

Above all, the new initiatives stemmed mostly from the single-mindedness of a small group of Sicilian magistrates determined to break the mould, aided by the worried government agreeing to push through the Pio La Torre laws, and by the Americans' own mounting concern at the incredible rise in the narcotics business.

Another brave Sicilian policeman, Commissario Antonino Cassara, had provided some timely ammunition. One of the few policemen Dalla Chiesa took into his confidence, Cassara had with the help of Giovanni Falcone and Rocco Chinnici prepared an explosive report which was the culmination of months of investigations by only the most trusted men in his Squadra Mobile and which picked up from where his predecessor Boris Giuliano had left off when he was murdered.

On 16, July 1982 Cassara presented his dossier to Chinnici and Dalla Chiesa. Headed *Greco + 161,* it was as close as anyone in Palermo had ever come to dissecting the current state of play within the Mafia. It identified for the first time that Michele Greco, the respected businessman and public benefactor, was the head of the Cosa Nostra *cupola* and principal ally and subordinate to the Corleonesi chieftains Luciano Liggio and Toto Riina, a fact which had been discovered by Giuliano but as yet had not been made public. Cassara recommended the arrest of Greco and 161 leading Mafia figures whom he named, on charges ranging from associating with the Mafia to heroin manufacture and smuggling.

Though far short of what Giovanni Falcone himself eventually learned about the Mafia from his series of interviews with the *pentiti,* Cassara's report would send shock waves through Palermo society if and when it became known. It was the most effective and damning indictment ever produced and became the working document for the attack that would be launched on the Mafia from this small group of dedicated lawmen over the next two years, each one knowing that they may well end up paying with their lives.

The Cassara report was the key element of what now became a much wider investigation as Judge Antonio Caponetto's scheme for a coordinated effort by the magistrates began to take shape with the formation of a pool of judges, initially ten in number. Rocco Chinnici, head of the training office at the Court of Palermo, overworked and obsessively secretive, was a family man who saw Mafia gunmen around every corner and he was right to expect that they might be.

With the death of Dalla Chiesa, he had assumed a heavy case-load and was in regular contact with Giovanni Falcone and the recently appointed chief prosecutor for Palermo, Paolo Borsellino. Under Caponetto, they created the nucleus of the anti-Mafia Pool which would go on to score stunning victories.

Chinnici, a strong, thickset man, demanded and eventually received armoured cars and a constant ring of bodyguards with machine guns for himself, Falcone and the most senior members of his pool scattered around the island of Sicily who from then on would begin to work towards some kind of coordination of their intelligence, such as it was.

Liliana Ferraro recalled for me: 'I first met Falcone at a conference we called on organized crime after the death of Dalla Chiesa. The courage and dedication of these men was incredible. We were all agreed about the necessity of a much greater liaison and support between the Ministry of Justice in Rome and the central law enforcement agencies with those working in Palermo, who clearly believed they were out on a limb. Later, I was given special charge to form that link and so I spent my time going between Rome and Palermo, going down to support the judges and magistrates in the fight against the Mafia. The Pool was already in operation and it was seriously needed. Until that time there had been no organization, no central unit within our judicial system that was strong enough to launch a war against organized crime.

'When I went to Palermo, I saw that they were in desperate need of back-up, not merely from the people within our profession, and the weight of the Ministry of Justice, but help with matters right down to minuscule requirements, such as paper-clips. Unbelievable, perhaps, but true. They had nothing. They were working in tiny little offices, some rooms in a building in the centre of Palermo, with a few desks and broken furniture. They had absolutely no electronic aides at all. It was pathetic that these men who were leading our action against the most ruthless killers should be so exposed. My first task was to organize a round-the-clock guard because there was no doubt they had already become listed targets of the Cosa Nostra. We found a suitable building for them to work in and installed proper furnishings, chairs, desks and finally a fairly modest computer system – until then they had none of these things.'

They became familiar with bunkers and armoured-plated motorcades, and were surrounded by men carrying cocked machine guns, ready to fire.

Using Commissioner Cassara's report as a model, the judges began to cast their net. The American DEA and the FBI were, coincidentally, by then very anxious to form a cooperative link, having finally been given the powers to combat organized crime. They were positively pushing for action now as the heroin trade reached epidemic proportions and was being made worse by the burgeoning traffic of cocaine from the

Columbians finding its way onto the east coast by way of the Bahamas and to the west through Mexico.

The Americans' keenness to form a liaison link with the Italians stemmed from President Reagan's 1980 declaration of war on organized crime and new laws known as RICO (the Racketeer-Influenced and Corrupt Organizations Act), which enabled US agents to make much wider use of wiretapping. Naturally, a lot of the conversations they were listening in to were in Italian. After Reagan's declaration, Rudolph Giuliana, chief district attorney of New York (and later mayor of the city), was charged with setting up a new group which brought agents of the DEA and the FBI together for the first time as the Organized Crime Drug Enforcement Task Force. It represented the first major nation-wide attack ever mounted against organized crime, and the Mafia in particular, by the US law agencies which had until then still laboured under the inheritance of denial of the Mafia by J Edgar Hoover – even though he had died eight years earlier – to the great benefit of major criminals everywhere.

Even before the assassination of Dalla Chiesa, one of the top operatives of the US Justice Department, Carmine Russo, of Italian ancestry, was assigned to forge contact with the Italians and flew to Rome in June 1982 to open discussions at the Italian Ministry of Justice. It was the first time that the two authorities had ventured a serious exchange of information.

He carried with him a three-inch thick packet of paperwork giving a precis of the rapidly growing files on heroin distribution in the United States, with names, dates, places and sources, most of which related back to Italy. Russo, however, returned to America disappointed, complaining that the material the Italians gave him was out of date and patchy.

At that stage, the Americans did not understand the Italian system in which judges like Chinnici and Falcone combined the functions of the judiciary and the investigative forces, akin to the US Grand Jury procedures. Thus, once a police file had passed into the hands of a magistrate, it was governed by the laws of secrecy as it would be when it was passed to a US Grand Jury investigation.

Similarly, the Italians did not understand the US procedures, and considered it something of an insult that they had to prove the need for the evidence from America which they required to support their own prosecutions in Italy. The Americans desperately wanted to gain access to the files of the Sicilian magistrates but the legalities of the two opposing systems prevented it.

In an attempt to circumvent these problems, Chinnici and Falcone were invited to the FBI headquarters at Quantico in Virginia, USA, in October 1982 for what was the very first official meeting between the enforcement agencies of the two nations. There were speeches of welcome and then representatives from both sides gave their talks about their respective investigative activities.

Rocco Chinnici, who was one of the chief promoters of the idea of setting up a joint liaison group, gave an emotional summary of recent events and tears welled up into his eyes as he recounted the deaths of so many of his friends and colleagues. Falcone gave a broad picture of the present lines of investigation while Carmine Russo and other American officials outlined their own investigations.

Both sides were able to identify Sicilian connections with a cluster of drug traffickers exporting from Venezuela and Brazil and the direct association between the Mafia families of Sicily and the main distributing franchisees in the US. They could track the routes of Sicilian heroin through Europe and on to Canada in the north and from South America and up through the Bahamas in the south, or directly into American airports and harbours. They were beginning to pursue the millions of dollars that washed to and fro until they were clean, and were then deposited in safe havens.

To this had been added a new problem. When South America became the hiding place of several important Mafia figures who fled the 1963 crackdown after the Ciaculli massacre, it also became an early staging post for heroin traffic into the United States. Now the Columbian cartels were pushing up their production of cocaine.

A mere 20 million tons of the coca plant were in production in South America in 1980, 60 million in 1985 and 160 million by 1989. By the end of the decade, the line showing its quantity and value would run off the graph at the DEA investigations centre.

A lot of these discussions covered completely virgin territory and law officers were basically starting with a clean sheet. It seemed an incredible situation, given the knowledge and well publicized activities of the Mafia on both sides of the Atlantic for almost 100 years that it was only then, in 1982, that they were beginning to get to grips with their joint problem. At that meeting, it was agreed to seek approval from both their respective administrations to set up the first Joint Italo-American Working Group, targeting four specific areas: the sharing of information on drugs trafficking and organized crime; joint police operations, the coordination of transatlantic investigations and money laundering. Even then, it took almost another two years before the first meeting of that new group took place in Washington on 2 October 1984.

In the meantime, the individual departmental heads agreed to liaise on an informal basis. A few weeks after the joint conference, Russo went to Rome and then on to Palermo. This time, he was more insistent than on his previous visit to Rome. The Americans wanted current information on deals and shipments that were going on then and there, gleaned from phone tapping and informers. Chinnici and Falcone obliged, and through the auspices of the Italian secret service supplied wiretaps on a number of leading bosses, and provided as best they could a run-down on the Mafia families.

The US investigators had discovered that very substantial supplies were originating from the Trapani province of Sicily, the home district of a number of influential businessmen and the centre of the highest proliferation of banks anywhere in Italy. The Sicilian judges knew that, of course, and were able to cross-relate some important names and families.

Trapani had historically been an important centre of Mafia activity, especially in the narcotics trade, dating back to the early days of Lucky Luciano and Frank Coppola. Like the Palermo Cosa Nostra, its families had traditional links with relations in America.

Dalla Chiesa himself had pin-pointed the province for his own investigations and had been warned off by the local prefecture. Trapani had all the sophistication of a wild west boom town: it was completely lacking in an effective police force, had no investigative unit to speak of and a dilapidated courthouse that was designed only for use by small-time lawbreakers and traffic offenders. Yet beneath the facade of what its leaders described as a 'hard-working law-abiding area' – which for 90 per cent of the population, it was – lay a veritable hotbed of mafiosi.

For years, the region was controlled by a ruthless mob headed by Salvatore Zizzo, of whom a Carabinieri report once said: 'He has spread so much blood and terror in the region – always associated with the worst criminals.'

Zizzo was banished from Sicily to Campania in 1970 between various trials for murder and extortion from which he usually emerged unscathed, and he was particularly noted for his exploitation of victims of an earthquake. Government aid for the victims and rebuilding contracts found their way into construction companies controlled by the Zizzos and for years afterwards the homeless victims lived in an old army barracks and makeshift homes until the state intervened with more money.

By the eighties, Trapani was operating some of the biggest refineries for heroin, which went directly to the Gambinos in New York. One of the laboratories discovered by the police was equipped with the most modern refining technology, imported from Bulgaria, capable of producing almost five tons of heroin a year worth $250 million wholesale.

Couriers of every description were used to get it across the Atlantic. Sailors, aircrews and even little old ladies 'visiting relatives' in New York. Once, police picked up two middle-aged women with their girdles stuffed with packets of heroin and their passports stamped by US immigration on so many occasions that their relatives must have been sick and tired of seeing them. When they were caught, police in Sicily searched their peasant cottage in the tiny hamlet of Torretta, between Palermo and Trapani, and found it luxuriously and garishly fitted out with marble floors and gold taps on the bath, even though they had no running hot water. It was an amusing example, but also tragically serious, demonstrating the way in which Sicilians of all walks of life were benefiting from the narcotics business.

But, as Dalla Chiesa always said, and as the Sicilian pool of magistrates well knew, there were much bigger fish to fry in

Trapani. One of Dalla Chiesa's first priorities in a task which he was never able to complete was to call for a report of evidence to the Anti-Mafia Commission that stated the Christian Democrat party in the Trapani Province of Sicily was 'in the hands of a power grouping dominated by the Salvo family. The same Salvo family has provided the financial backing for those engaged in major international drug trafficking.'

And yet public funds were also the source of much of this financial wherewithal, by courtesy of another remarkable political backhander which three decades earlier had placed the operation of Sicily's 344 revenue offices in the hands of three families who held the State concession to collect an average of 10 per cent of the earnings of every Sicilian working man, for which they received a commission, and use of the capital as it passed through their bank accounts.

A report by the Anti-Mafia Commission in 1976 concluded that 'it is an anomaly that has become a vehicle for political corruption and for Mafia activities'. Even so, eight years had passed and the Salvo cousins had never been investigated.

The two cousins, Ingazio and Nino, were from Salemi in the Trapani province. They were two suave-looking men with a life-style of mansions, yachts and chauffeur-driven Mercedes. They were renowned for their expensive parties which might end with everyone going aboard a chartered aircraft to Paris or Monte Carlo. They made their fortunes running the tax-collecting companies until the franchise was eventually given over to a syndicate of banks. Nino used to boast, 'We are the most important financial group in Italy. Our funds are unlimited.' Indeed, they were. They were veritable captains of industry and multi-millionaires.

Their interests extended to major construction and shipping companies based in Palermo and throughout Italy. Political sweeteners helped move their businesses into top gear. They donated heavily to the Christian Democrats and bought Salvatore Lima, the MP and former mayor of Palermo and close ally of Giulio Andreotti, a bullet-proof car and gave his son Marcello a job.

The Salvos, courtesy of the government franchise, acquired huge agricultural holdings, a 320-acre vineyard and took over a wine production cooperative producing 60 million gallons of new wine every year, aided by favourable state loans and Common Market benefits, including one for opening up export markets in the Soviet bloc.

But the Salvos were in the Bontate camp. The Corleonesi, to show their displeasure, kidnapped Nino's father-in-law, Luigi Corleo, and set the ransom at $6 million. Nino pleaded with Stefano Bontate to intervene, which he did and got the ransom cut by half. According to Nino, the money was paid over but Luigi was never seen again. His body, it is believed, was tossed into the acid bath that the Corleonesi kept in their torture dungeon in the heart of Palermo. Investigating magistrates also tracked down other financial dealings Nino had with the Mafia and the cousins were identified by Anti-Mafia investigators as members of a clandestine, all-powerful, politically-linked group of Mafia associates.

According to the thesis of Giovanni Falcone, these people were never members of the Mafia as such, but were linked by association, through business and socially, exchanging favours and receiving protection. The Mafia would ensure that businessmen were allowed to operate without hindrance, offer security arrangements for the company directors, ward off potential kidnappers, protect them from vandals and thieves, ensure the security of building sites and that the labour force did not cause undue strife.

This is what the Mafia traded upon, and few dared to resist. Those who did seldom lived long enough to enjoy their life. Once the practice was accepted, and the Mafia continued to accept payments that the industrialist or businessman considered reasonable fees for their security, friendships would develop between the businessman and the Mafia bosses. Gradually, the insidious arrangement entraps all who fall into it and these intertwining relationships have more importance than the rule of law.

On 19 December 1980, Nino Salvo made a 'loan' of 300 million lire to a member of the Greco family using a bank draft drawn on the Banca Commerciale in Palermo. Two further amounts were paid the following month, using fictitious names. Later, when Falcone began his own investigations into the Salvo cousins, he suspected that the loans were a front, and that Nino Salvo was laundering money to clean up Mafia narco-lire. The truth was that he had switched sides – from the losers in the Bontate-Inzerillo camp – and was buying insurance against future trouble with the Corleonesi.

Dalla Chiesa had set this investigation into motion. On his desk at the time of his murder was a report from the finance police in Rome which showed that £387 million in public funds had recently been awarded to 'a restricted number' of companies, several of which were fronts for the Mafia. In some cases, a company which presented the winning tender for a major contract would exist only on paper, and then would be absorbed into another company, usually owned by a Mafia figure.

Until then, no one in any area of criminal investigation had begun to attempt to unravel the political connections and vested interests that existed between the Mafia, supposed legitimate businessmen and politicians. It was the most complex and dangerous area of all, and one which eventually Falcone took up, aware that it would lead to the biggest unheaval in Italian politics since the war.

By the end of 1982, after the visit of Carmine Russo to Sicily for consultations with Rocco Chinnici and his team, the investigating magistrate for Trapani, Judge GianGiacomo Ciaccio Montalto was in the final stages of concluding a devastating indictment against more than three dozen leading figures in the Trapani Mafia.

Like so many of the Italian outposts of justice, Mantalto worked pretty much on his own during his thirteen years as the representative of justice in Trapani. His facilities were poor, much as Liliana Ferraro had described on her arrival in Palermo – cramped accommodation and not even a personal computer, let alone any kind of networking system. He had provoked the indignation of local VIPs and politicians who decried his efforts to investigate the Mafia and warned him he would be forced out if he persisted. He was threatened often and, like Dalla Chiesa, felt very much alone. No one had seriously tackled the Mafia in Trapani since the days of Mussolini's clear-out of the surrounding hills.

By Christmas 1982, Montalto was ready to take them on. He had only just begun to acclimatize himself to Rocco Chinnici's plans for a pooled effort, although he had made use of the new La Torre laws to take a look at some interesting financial transactions. He had linked up with another colleague, Judge Carlo Palermo, who was investigating an arms and drugs smuggling operation in the north of Italy and on 14 December, Montalto received confirmation that a $3-million payment for one of these shipments had turned up in a Trapani bank.

More substantially, and through his personal efforts, he had tracked down stocks of refined heroin ready for shipment from the Trapani laboratories worth a staggering $750 million and established its route from Sicily, to the south of France and on to Canada for dispersal in North America. By the turn of the new year, he was in a position to issue arrest warrants against forty suspects, including some big names in the Mafia hierarchy.

On 18 January 1983, the brave judge returned home at one in the morning after a heavy day at work. Unlike his counterparts in Palermo, he did not have a ring of steel, just a small group of men of the local Carabinieri who looked after him singly in shifts. He was alone as he reached his home and the Mafia lay in wait. Inside, his mother heard the crack of gunfire. Two Mafia assassins opened fire with machine guns and Judge Montalto fell dead under a hail of bullets. One more name was added to the gallery of Illustrious Corpses, and others were soon to follow.

Back in Palermo, Chinnici and Falcone were deeply involved in their own judicial inquiry, a long and detailed study of events and people, using the report of Commissioner Cassara as their outline. As always, it was a brain-numbing task of attempting to assemble watertight cases against groups of people, rather than single individuals, that would stand up to the vagaries of the Italian judicial system of trials and appeals.

They also had to find a way to overcome those special peculiarities that had traditionally dogged all major Mafia trials – such as loss of memory, disappearing witnesses, sudden illness, *omertà*, lack of proof and death threats to jurists which had in the past usually meant the accused Mafiosi walked free.

For many months, Chinnici and his colleagues burned the midnight oil. 'They believed they were on the verge of a major breakthrough,' Liliana Ferraro told me. 'There was subdued excitement which was tempered, naturally I think, with some apprehension as to where it would lead them.'

By the end of June, indictments had been prepared, witnesses assembled under protection, and Chinnici was ready to sign arrest warrants for close on 200 Mafia, the biggest round-up in years. The rumour mill was in overdrive, and it was being suggested that he planned to arrest the Salvo cousins, linking them officially with Mafia activity. He was also ordering the arrest of Michele Greco, the Corleonesi chiefs Toto Riina and Bernardo Provenzano and a host of other big-name operators.

That, at least, was Chinnici's plan, but he was never able to finish the job. On the morning of 28 July 1983, he was leaving his apartment for work. As he reached the street below, a cordon of guards were waiting, guns poised, glancing all around for potential attackers. The engine on the armoured car was running and Rocco Chinnici glanced up to the window of his apartment where his wife stood, looking down and watching him climb into the back seat.

At that moment, there was a massive explosion. A car parked nearby and packed with 100 lbs of gelignite was set off by remote control, and blew everything around it to pieces. Chinnici, three of his bodyguards and the caretaker of the apartment house were killed; little remained of their bodies.

In spite of all the new security measures, Rocco Chinnici, the Consigliere Istruttore of Sicily, had been eliminated by a terrifying change of tactics by the Mafia. Unable to get a clear shot with a Kalashnikov, they blew up the street.

CHAPTER ELEVEN

The Very First Informer, Leonardo Vitale – Dead

'The year of 1983 was the start of the fight back by the anti-Mafia forces. It was an incredible period,' Ferraro said, 'filled with high drama, great detective work and intense personal feelings among those involved.' At that point, the bloodthirsty leadership of the Mafia, principally under the control of Luciano Liggio, in prison, and Michele Greco and Toto Riina in Sicily, feared no one, no power, no state intervention, nor even the forces of the US crime agencies. They carried on as if they were truly untouchable and the systematic killings spread far into mainland Italy, and on throughout the world. Bodies were turning up everywhere.

The official death toll for 1982 alone listed 373 murders in the Camorra territory of Campania in central Italy, of which 255 were in the province of Naples itself. To the north, in Lombardy, there were 112 murders and in the south, in 'Ndrangheta strongholds, 147 killings. On the island of Sicily there were 330 murders, of which 151 were in the province of Palermo and 77 in Catania.

Confidential research by Italian security agencies for the Ministry of the Interior showed that a majority of the Mafia-linked murders were indeed the result of the ongoing feud between the 'new' families supporting the Corleonesi alliance, and the families who did not conform.

On the mainland, there had been limited success as the

government once again poured troops into the worst-hit areas. A major heroin-refining laboratory had been discovered at a shoe factory, and 80 kilograms of pure heroin, which would make 160 kilograms of the 'cut' version of the drug when it was sold on the streets, was found. It was destined for New York, and was listed as the biggest single seizure of heroin ever made in Europe.

The last remaining pockets of terrorist activity still hampered the progress of the judiciary. In the first ten months of 1982, 807 people were arrested for terrorist offences in Italy – almost three times as many as Mafia-related arrests. And to the last, there remained strong rumours, if not clear evidence, that the Mafia and terrorism were linked. General James Dozier, the American NATO forces commander in Italy, was finally released after being held in a Red Brigades kidnap cell for forty-two days after police and the army raided a flat in Padua.

Strong rumours at the time indicated that the police had been sent to the hide-out as a result of a tip-off which came directly from the Mafia itself, and that Toto Riina, boss of the Corleonesi, wanted to rid himself of involvement with international politics.

Back in Palermo, the investigating magistrates had at last been able to see some tangible results from their liaison with the Americans. In November 1982, two months after Dalla Chiesa's murder, the trial began of the forty-two Mafia prisoners rounded up months earlier but whose trial, ironically, was only made possible by the new La Torre laws rushed through parliament after the general's death.

Until then, the police had no power to investigate bank accounts, which provided them with vital evidence. In every respect, the Mafia had brought this trial upon themselves, by murdering first Pio La Torre who had campaigned for the new laws and then Dalla Chiesa whose death secured their place in Italian judicial history.

All the forty-two accused – and another thirty-four who were being tried in absentia – were the sworn enemies of the Corleonesi and in many respects they were being regarded as 'the losers' in the Mafia war. For them, the humiliation of a trial came on top of the loss of so many of their allies.

The trial was the result of the discovery of an abandoned

packing case, found at John F Kennedy Airport in August 1979. It contained 45 kilos of heroin. A month later, with the DEA now keeping watch, an airport freight worker named Frank Rolli was arrested carrying a suitcase containing 115 kilos of the drug. Rolli agreed to collaborate with the US prosecution in return for immunity and a new identity. He was one of the first to do so, and it set the law agencies on both sides of the Atlantic on the trail of the Sicilian-American drugs connection. In the coming months, acting on the information Rolli provided, several more shipments were intercepted, containing a total of 220 lbs of heroin.

The trail led back to the Palermo families whose relatives in New York were the major distributors. The courtroom at Palermo's vast Tribunale building was the scene of intense security and great public interest when the men were first brought to trial in November 1982. As the trial wore on, however, the courtroom became almost deserted. Even prisoners themselves could not be bothered to turn up, and preferred to remains in their cells in the Palermo prison.

One who did turn up, day after day, was Rosario Spatola, one of Palermo's business elite, a multi-millionaire who little more than a decade ago was 'pushing a hand cart'. A man in his mid-forties, he was always smartly dressed in blue blazer, grey slacks and a chestnut hairpiece. Beside him were two brothers from the Adamita family, equally immaculate in newly pressed clothes.

These men were the so-called new Mafia – the nouveau-riche of the drugs business. They were arrogant and unbowed. Day by day, the story that would become all too familiar in the coming years began to unfold, and it revealed in detail for the first time the set-up – the networking of 1980s' Mafia families.

The world's press arrived at the beginning to listen, but gradually as the Italian judicial system ground painfully and slowly through all its processes, they too became bored and went home. The evidence, however, gave confirmation of how the morphine base was brought into Italy by sea, air or long-distance lorry. It told how Sicily had achieved the near monopoly of the refining process, having taken over from the Corsicans after the clean-up at Marseilles, how in that year 60 per cent of all heroin imported into the US had a Sicilian connection.

Rosario Spatola, the chief confederate in Sicily of the international financier Michele Sindona and at one time accused of Sindona's kidnap was, according to the prosecution, the chief accountant of a drugs manufacturing combine which included the Inzerillos and the Bontates before their decimation by the Corleonesi. He was the final link in the complex web of financial transactions for this particular group of families that turned millions of narco-dollars into hotels, factories and high-rises in Sicily and throughout Italy, through a system that was originally planned and masterminded by Sindona himself.

The prosecuting lawyer Giusto Sciacchitano spelled out in no uncertain terms the importance of this case: 'Four families living part in Sicily and part in New York form a single clan so large that it is unique in both Italy and the United States – perhaps the most potent family in the Cosa Nostra. John Gambino is the converging point in the United States for all the group's activities in Italy and the final destination for its drugs shipments.'

The assessment that this grouping was the most 'potent' in Sicily was premature. It was certainly important, vitally important, and strong. It had been right to the fore in the expansion of Mafia drugs activities since the early seventies. But even with their knowledge of the Mafia at that time, neither Sicilian law enforcers nor their American counterparts truly appreciated the extent of the tribal conflicts that were being played out before them, with all the killings.

Falcone and the Pool was on the very brink of a far greater discovery that would broaden their horizons and provide a completely new perspective. Before leaving this aspect of Falcone's inquiries, it is worth mentioning, too, his disappointment at the case. Though Spatola himself was found guilty of various offences at the end of the trial, he appealed and was freed in 1986. He vanished from Palermo and surfaced later in New York, where he was re-arrested. Later, however, he would return – and turn state's evidence against his former associates.

Meanwhile, attention switched to South America. The Corleonesi had put out assassination contracts on two of the last remaining important escapees from the Great War, Tommaso Buscetta, still resident in Brazil under an assumed name, and Gaetano Badalamenti who was operating from Rio until the summer of 1983, continuing to organize and receive drug supplies from his Sicilian relatives and shipping them on to New York.

The continuing murder of the relatives of the two men remained their constant worry. The most recent killings were of two of Badalamenti's great nephews, Matteo and Salvatore Sollena, who were found shot in New Jersey.

DEA agents had still not linked Badalamenti to a particular supply route, but were fairly sure he had set up a completely new distribution network through a pizzeria chain in the US. At the end of 1983, they gleaned another clue as to his whereabouts from a local newspaper report about the death of another of his relatives: 'The lifeless body of Antonio Badalamenti was found in his car with a bullet in the back of his head in a street in the suburbs of Buenos Aires . . . According to Giovanni Badalamenti, brother of the Italian businessman who was forty years old, Antonio was the victim of an aborted kidnap attempt. The Badalamenti family own an ice cream parlour in the centre of the capital and a similar place in Palermo . . .' There was no mention of the real scenario behind the murder.

Gaetano fled, first to Paris and then to Spain. But he was still in business. The DEA was sure of that and the effort was concentrated on breaking the network. The Americans had made several arrests, had wiretaps all over New York and other centres.

Tom Tripodi, the DEA agent who met the Palermo police chief Boris Giuliano shortly before he was murdered in 1979, had reported the heavy links to Mafia exiles in Venezuela, notably the Cuntreras who were still running drugs on a supply route from the east, on through England where four *capomafiosi* were in position, then to Canada and down into the US, and from the south they were already stoking up the cocaine industry.

What happened next would provide Giovanni Falcone and the Americans with their biggest ever window on the Mafia's global network. Tommaso Buscetta and Gaetano Badalamenti had been named in a US investigation, along with others, as being prime suspects involved in the flow of heroin from

South America since 1981. The DEA told the Brazilians that Badalamenti had also been spotted in one of the main regions of cocaine production in Bolivia. The report was sent on to a special Mafia unit which had been set up within the Brazilian Federal Police Force to investigate the smuggling of cocaine and heroin within Brazil.

In the early hours of 22 October 1983, they arrested Buscetta in Sao Paulo where he had arranged to meet his wife, then living in Rio. At that moment, Tommaso Buscetta became the most celebrated mafiosi in history. He was never a hugely important figure in the Mafia hierarchy in Sicily and in any event would have been shot on sight had the Corleonesi assassins ever caught up with him.

Months of internal wrangling followed between the police departments of Brazil who wanted to accuse him of varying crimes, the Italian Ministry of Justice in Rome and the FBI in Washington who had both filed for his extradition. But at least, now, there was a considerable measure of cooperation between the Americans and the Italians. In January 1984, a working group of law officers from Italy, the United States and Canada held a conference in Ottawa to discuss the unfolding evidence in the case that would become known as the Pizza Connection.

As one described it, the Italians and the Americans discovered that the situation was comparable to a dollar bill torn in two; they were each holding half.

In the meantime, the Americans were on the verge of another major breakthrough. A combined task force of the DEA and FBI had been tracking the heroin and cocaine distribution network across America through pizzerias for many months and with hours of telephone taps and the evidence of informers to go on, were approaching a crucial stage of their investigations.

The routes, the suppliers, the laundering set-up had all been monitored and the US law agencies' biggest ever onslaught against the drug traffickers rested upon the apprehension of a particular figure, known from the wiretaps as the Uncle. They had been listening to him on the telephone for weeks on end, taped dozens of hours of coded conversation, and were convinced that they were actually listening to none other than Buscetta's good friend Gaetano Badalamenti. But they could not be sure.

Then, astonishingly, the US task force agents heard him personally arranging a drugs deal which would send one of the largest ever shipments of heroin into America, through Fort Lauderdale. They heard him say 'I have two factories ready.'

Badalamenti himself planned to officiate largely because there had been some last-minute disagreements over money. So he wanted his nephew and chief negotiator in the US, Pietro Alfano, to perform certain tasks and collect money from distributors and bring it directly to him in Spain, prior to the drugs deal being effected.

The FBI team heard Badalamenti instruct Alfano to take some of the money to a currency broker at the world trade centre in New York. Then Alfano was to fly to Madrid, where Badalamenti was living, to bring him a suitcase full of US dollars bills. The FBI task force was placed in a dilemma. It could wait to see if the drugs deal in Florida developed, and take a chance on Badalamenti arriving on US soil where he could be arrested. But there was always the possibility that something might go wrong.

They decided they had to act quickly rather than allow the situation to drift on and perhaps lose the opportunity of taking Badalamenti. It had taken four years, literally tens of thousands of man-hours of surveillance, 1,500 rolls of surveillance photographs and more than 11,000 intercepted telephone calls across the country and the globe to reach this final act – the one which would go down as the biggest drugs bust in American history.

Alfano travelled from his home in Oregon to Chicago airport where he boarded a KLM jet to Amsterdam for an onward connection to Madrid. He paid no attention to two men who boarded behind him – one was a DEA agent, the other an FBI man. At the other end, Spanish police were waiting to monitor the movements of Alfano. He was picked up at the airport by Vito Badalamenti, Gaetano's son, and was taken to an apartment in a smart area of Madrid.

The following morning, the DEA and FBI finally had Gaetano Badalamenti, the former boss of all bosses of the Sicilian Mafia and one of the most hunted criminals in the world within their their sights. A smallish man with greying hair, wearing a smart grey suit and white socks came out of his apartment with Alfano. As they walked along, the police decided to take them. They were surrounded and arrested and taken to Madrid police station.

Meanwhile, another squad raided Gaetano's apartment. There they found Signora Theresa Badalamenti setting the breakfast table. Her son Vito, who had met Alfano at the airport, came out of the bathroom in his robe. They were all arrested.

Within minutes, the news was flashed to Thomas L. Sheer, coordinator of the task force investigation in the US, and he subsequently telephoned Giovanni Falcone. The second stage of the operation swung into action and FBI agents and US marshals began a pre-arranged attack. Wearing flak jackets and armed with automatic weapons and sledge hammers, they crashed down doors and forced their way into homes and apartments across the country.

In all, seventy people would be arrested in the US, although only twenty-two would eventually face trial.

The Italians also filed for the extradition of Gaetano Badalamenti on charges of murder and extortion. The US wanted to do a deal. Falcone and his American counterparts conferred and decided to split the spoils. The Italians could have Buscetta first if they could keep Badalamenti. And so it was done. The Americans withdrew their extradition request for Buscetta and in effect handed him to Falcone.

The Sicilian judge had already made contact. As Liliana Ferraro explained to me:

> Giovanni flew to Brazil at the end of 1983, and again at the beginning of 1984 while awaiting the completion of extradition procedures, and took statements from Buscetta. He was very cautious at the beginning, but it was the start of a huge breakthrough in our fight against the Mafia – an explosion of material, you might say. The information eventually given to us by Buscetta would be important on two levels. It provided the police with a vast amount of previously unknown information about the activities of

> the Cosa Nostra and also gave us a complete overview, a totally new insight into our actual understanding of the criminology of these people. Buscetta would be the key to unlocking many of the mysteries of the past, the ritual of membership, the so-called code of honour that bound members of the Cosa Nostra, the feudal system of the hierarchy and, of course, eventually he gave us names. It is impossible to exaggerate the importance of this man's evidence at that particular time in our history. Falcone more than anyone, I think, appreciated that it was the biggest breakthrough that had ever been available to the law enforcement agencies of this country, and he principally took charge to ensure that nothing was lost.

Reaching the point of Buscetta's maximum cooperation was, however, like walking on glass for Falcone and the other key negotiator, Gianni De Gennaro, a brilliant police executive who led Italy's Anti-Organized Crime unit in Rome. For one thing, Buscetta was seeking heavy assurances about his own safety. His wife had already made visits to the US embassy to negotiate for asylum for him there in exchange for assistance.

He considered the prospect of being returned to Palermo was nothing short of a death sentence. If he had been transferred to the Ucciardone prison in Palermo, he would have been murdered by the Corleonesi within hours of his arrival; no amount of security could have saved him. Indeed, no prison in Italy was safe and even after giving Falcone the word that he was prepared to cooperate, he decided there was only one other solution to his dilemma.

On 7 July 1984 he was travelling under guard to the prison medical centre in the Brazilian capital for a check-up before being finally released into the custody of the Italians when he suddenly turned blue and collapsed, writhing on the floor. It was discovered that he had obtained a small phial of strychnine, which he had managed to get into his mouth.

The Brazilian lawmen, aghast at the possibility of losing their most prized captive, took him straight to the casualty ward where a doctor pumped his stomach, and saved his life. He remained unconscious for twenty-four hours and was kept in hospital for a week. He was still feeling the effects when

Falcone arrived to escort him back to Rome. Buscetta was ready to talk and the doors to the Mafia's secrets would be unlocked at last.

On 15 July Buscetta arrived back on Italian soil, landing at Fiumicino Airport which had been given a blanket security mode for the occasion. Police and Carabinieri surrounded the perimeter and patrolled all public areas. The Alitalia 747 in which he travelled was guided to a special area surrounded by the proverbial ring of steel and after clearing immigration swiftly, he was taken in convoy in armoured cars to Rebibia prison on the outskirts of Rome.

Ferraro recalls that the immense security which surrounded Buscetta signified the importance the Falcone team gave to the task at hand. Though there were strong rumours at the time – and since – that the support from the gentlemen of the Palazzo was not entirely wholehearted, even a touch reluctant, Ferraro maintains that they received all possible support. It was only later that things began to go wrong, when certain politicians and certainly some judges and their courts began to turn against Falcone.

At the time, Falcone and the Pool were jubilant. He had arranged for his most important informer to be buttoned up in a bunker at the prison specially built to house a group of Red Brigades terrorists, and where Dalla Chiesa himself had spent many hours interrogating his suspects.

In what were by then dingy prison rooms, a contingent of two dozens guards, all vetted and chosen by the judges themselves, worked in shifts around the clock, armed with machine guns. Buscetta, Falcone and De Gennaro were watched day and night, with guards present even while they slept or carried out their daily ablutions and the calls of nature. Every caller, whether judge or policeman, passed through a security check. All food was double tasted for poison. All drinks were tested before Buscetta consumed them.

For the next sixty days, Falcone carried out his own interrogations which began formally and developed gradually into a progressive conversation in which they talked for hours on end. Each night, Falcone worked until late, writing his reports and cross-checking and cross-referencing to his own material, especially the reports of Inspector Cassara in Palermo which represented the Sicilian judiciary's own most important findings, especially about key figures in the laundering of drugs money.

Falcone, Ferraro recalls, was working sixteen-hour days, compiling his evidence and debriefing Buscetta. They travelled back and forth in time, corroborating the names of Cosa Nostra members, discussing the Mafia wars in which Buscetta and the rest had lost so many family members and putting names to the men who had ordered the killings of all of the Sicilians, police and politicians murdered in recent times.

As time went on, and Falcone gained Buscetta's confidence, the *pentito* began to confirm the international drugs set-up, put names to the key operations, describe the territorial and family demarcations and the workings and machinations of the Mafia *cupola*.

It represented a historic coup in the war against the Mafia, lifting the lid on a terrifying labyrinth of crime stretching across the globe. No one single informer, before or since, has given so much away, and even then, Buscetta held back some of the political intrigue on the grounds that 'no one will believe me and dismiss it as the ramblings of a madman'. Only later, in 1993–4 would he begin to unravel some of the Mafia's long-held political connections – and by then he had plenty of corroborators, with many more *pentiti* singing their confessions.

His testimony in 1984 was merely the beginning, the precursor to all that followed. He ended with the words:

> I have made these statements of my own free will and I am in full possession of my mental facilities. In doing so, I have been guided solely by my own conscience and not by the desire for revenge or vendetta . . . the truth is that I have realized for some time that the times in which we live are incompatible with the traditional principles of the Cosa Nostra and that the latter, correspondingly, has been transformed into a band of ferocious assassins inspired solely by the thought of personal gain. I do not fear death, nor do I live in terror of being murdered by my enemies; when my turn comes I will face death serenely

> and without fear. I have chosen to follow this road and there is no turning back. I will fight with all my strength to see the Cosa Nostra destroyed. I will not retreat one inch and will seek to convince all those who are still undecided to follow my example in order to put an end once and for all to a criminal organization that had brought nothing but struggle and desperation to so many families and has contributed nothing to the development of society.

The words smacked somewhat of official guidance, words that Falcone needed to have on his testimony in order to convince dubious members of the Italian establishment above him that Buscetta was indeed a credible witness. All too often in the past, such evidence had been discredited and discarded and those charged with terrible crimes acquitted.

Falcone had to make it watertight. At the end of the sixty days, he had compiled a report running to almost 800 pages, packed with names and accusations. Midway through, the US Attorney's office sent one of their key men, Charles Rose, to discuss the prospect of Buscetta joining the American Witness Protection programme to ensure his safety. There was little doubt that the longer he stayed in Italy, the greater the chance of him being eliminated.

Once the Italians had completed their interrogation, Buscetta would be flown out and put in deep security in the US, to give evidence at the series of drugs trials planned in America. Under conditions of strict secrecy, a US Air Force C-130 aircraft was brought to Rome airport, and Buscetta was taken aboard for the flight to New York, but despite the American's efforts to keep Buscetta under wraps, word leaked out and a media circus developed in America.

The C-130 was diverted to a smaller military airport, and from there Buscetta was transferred to a light aircraft and flown directly into a US marine compound at LaGuardia airport, New York, where a mass of US marshals, police and agents from the DEA and FBI stood guard as he was whisked away to a secret bunker to begin his next round of talks with the law.

Simultaneously the Italian judiciary, largely through the efforts of Falcone and his pool of anti-Mafia judges and police, opened up unprecedented lines of communication with the

Americans. A working party, formed the previous year, met in Rome to try to cut through the baffling red tape that had stifled attempts at Italian-American cooperation in the past.

Falcone made it clear that on the basis of Buscetta's statements, the Sicilian judiciary was moving towards a massive arrest programme and the resultant trials would run pretty well concurrently with the Pizza trial being planned in New York.

At last, the traffic of communication between the two groups began to take on an immediacy that had never previously existed. Real information was being passed between the two countries and it was followed with an exchange of officers. FBI agent Carmine Russo whose previous trip to Rome, it will be recalled, was an immense disappointment, found himself in the heart of the Italian investigative procedure while the most important policeman in Falcone's own investigation team, Ninni Cassara, made many trips to New York where he was sworn in as a temporary US marshal so that he could join the local field work.

He would go out in the unmarked vans fitted out with a galaxy of electronic gear that was new to his experience in the impecunious Sicilian police force and would listen for hours to intercepted telephone conversations between pizzeria owners and their Mafia contacts until the US task force had built its case and made its arrests.

Back in Palermo, Giovanni Falcone's team prepared for their own spectacular round-up. Their list of names, provided in part by Buscetta's testimony to Falcone and in part from the earlier work by Falcone and Cassara's Squadra Mobile, read like the *Who's Who* of the Mafia. Unlike their American counterparts, the Italians could move on the charge of membership of the Mafia which was in itself sufficient for arrest, and towards the end of September 1984, the Carabinieri had held top secret meetings with the judiciary to plan their strategy.

It would come in two waves, each precision planned with the back-up of Army, carabinieri and police units. The first, code-named Operation San Michele – or the St Michael's Day Blitz as it was dubbed – was launched just before dawn on 29 September 1984 with the target of arresting 366 suspected mafiosi. Under cover of darkness, the 3,000 carabinieri and police officers sealed off huge areas of the city of Palermo.

At the appointed time, a squad of helicopters flew in and armoured cars and a fleet of vans and buses began to move in. As dawn broke the task force began its massive round up, the largest in the history of law enforcement in Sicily and certainly nothing like it had been seen since Mussolini's purges of the late twenties and early thirties. They burst into houses, apartments and office buildings, arresting dozens of suspects as they went, and detaining relatives and associates as well.

More than 200 people were taken in chains that day to the Ucciardone prison. Others were taken direct to the Punta Raisa airport where an Alitalia DC-9 was waiting to fly high-level prisoners to Pisa, and on by armoured vans to jails in Florence, Livorno and the island of Pianosa.

They ranged from ordinary Mafia soldiers to high-ranking personalities, although for the time being many of the key figures on the target list, like Michele Greco, Toto Riina and Bernardo Provenzano, eluded the police. Within the next four or five weeks, a further 140 arrest warrants would be issued and on the Italian mainland, a further 66 arrests were made in various cities across the country.

The spectacle of leading mafiosi being hauled away to jail in chains brought the world's press to Palermo and Giovanni Falcone and his colleagues ensured that there was full co-operation with the media. On the face of it, the Sicilian judges had launched the most significant attack on the Mafia in history and together with the Pizza Connection investigations and arrests in America, this would be heralded as the beginning of the end for the world's most feared criminal organization. Soon, such headlines as 'The Decline and Fall of the Mafia', 'The Last Days of the Sicilians', 'The End of the Line for the Cosa Nostra', began to appear.

Sure enough, the Falcone Pool in conjunction with the combined forces of the DEA and the FBI, along with help from the Brazilians, had delivered a massive blow, and more would follow in sensational manner as the Italians began to talk of the 'maxi-trials', running concurrently as they did with the Pizza trials in the US.

There seemed, at that time, absolute justification for euphoria and indeed there was; but as events would quickly show, to talk in terms of the Mafia – and especially the Sicilian Cosa Nostra – being wiped out was wholly premature. As I write this chapter a decade later, it still is not true, nor anywhere near it.

Palermo took on the appearance of a city under siege, with police sirens and wailing wagons dashing through its streets, carrying convoys of prisoners and, with even louder sirens, streams of armoured vehicles carrying the judges and senior policemen around the city. The lives of those at the forefront of the attack on the Mafia had been transformed overnight.

Though most had long ago become used to the tiresome routines of their personal security and that of their families, the advent of the Buscetta era and all that followed made it necessary for even stricter rules. They lived and worked in conditions of absolute protection. The judges and the policemen preparing for the maxi-trials were in stressful conditions on a round-the-clock basis. Families were moved to secret addresses and for Falcone and his team of investigating judges, another problem loomed large on their horizon.

'It was important,' explained Liliana Ferraro, 'that the judges searched for confirmation of what Buscetta had been telling Falcone. We needed corroboration. Standing alone, Buscetta's evidence could be attacked and put in doubt at the trial as coming from a man perhaps seeking revenge or to save his own neck.'

The first of what would, in due course, become a veritable stream of new *pentiti* was a man already in custody – Salvatore Contorno, who it will be recalled had been arrested in Rome after fleeing assassination attempts by the Corleonesi in 1981.

Contorno, who had been the right-hand man of the murdered Stefano Bontate, was a thickset ex-butcher. He was at the heart of Bontate's activities from the early seventies and was linked to drug deals and most of the other usual Cosa Nostra action before the Greco/Corleonesi faction killed his boss and sent him running.

Falcone had him brought to see Buscetta who had been on the same side, although under a different family. On entering the room, Contorno kissed Buscetta. They talked for a few minutes and Buscetta explained that he had decided to cooperate with the law. Before he left, Contorno had agreed to do the same and since much of his knowledge was also related to the Pizza Connection in the US, he too would be offered the ultimate security of the US Witness Protection Programme.

One more vital piece of evidence came out of the blue, on 2 December 1984. It was a Sunday morning and a young man named Leonardo Vitale was walking home from church in Palermo when he was shot and killed. The murder had mysterious connotations and was one which initially baffled the police because Vitale had only recently been released from a mental hospital. It was only when a check into his past was made that an incredible background was discovered.

The story went back to 1972 when a group of mafiosi were arrested in connection with the kidnap of Luciano Cassina, a member of one of Palermo's most powerful families. Those arrested were held for a month or so, and then released through lack of evidence. It was an episode described to me as 'one of pure routine' at the time.

Six months later, however, in March 1973, one of the mafiosi arrested suddenly appeared at the police station and declared he belonged to the Cosa Nostra. His name: Leonardo Vitale.

He was interviewed and began describing all kinds of local Mafia activity in which he had been involved. He told of the code of the Mafia, the structure of the organization and the so-called Men of Honour. He began talking of their methods and their terrible crimes which he had witnessed or knew of; he named names, began accusing many people, and some very important ones at that, of serious matters. He spoke of the rise to power of Luciano Liggio and of the financial operations handled by Giuseppe Pippo Calo, the Mafia financial genius stationed in Rome at the centre of a political and high-profile business connection.

Leonardo Vitale was the first man in history to tell of such things, to break *omertà.* When asked why he had decided to make such allegations, he said he was troubled by his conscience and had converted to religious beliefs.

The investigating judge asked for a psychiatric report. Vitale was examined and was thought not to be suffering from delirium or hallucinations, though he was obviously a troubled young man. Even so, the judge declared him insane, acquitted his codefendants through lack of evidence and locked Vitale away in a mental hospital for eleven years.

When his file was recovered after his death in 1984 and delivered to Falcone, he was amazed to discovered that a good deal of what Buscetta had told him about activities and personalities running the Mafia in the early seventies was mentioned by Vitale.

Falcone wrote:

> Vitale's statement offered confirmation on important points: the precision of the information given years later by Buscetta [and others] and the profound inertia of the State [at that time] towards those with the Cosa Nostra who decided to speak. In 1973, Vitale gave the police clues which should have set the police and magistrates in the right direction. He talked about Toto Riina as one of the bosses of the Cosa Nostra. And he recounted an emblematic episode about a heated discussion as to who should receive a certain bribe. Vitale was almost certainly psychotic but he was the source of many genuine pieces of evidence that deserved greater consideration. The State, after taking these statements, locked him away in a lunatic asylum and forgot about him.

Clearly, the Cosa Nostra had not forgotten him and, at a time when the Falcone team was pressing its attack, he was considered, even then, to be too dangerous to be on the loose. Soon after his release from the asylum, they shot him. The killing also pin-pointed another aspect – that the Cosa Nostra must have been aware, through its spies and allies, of the contents of Vitale's original statement, especially that regarding Toto Riina.

CHAPTER TWELVE

Police Chief Cassara, a Mother and Her Twin Children – Dead

The confessions of Tommaso Buscetta and Salvatore Contorno opened up a huge window on the terrible world of the Mafia. Their stories would make headlines around the world and Sicily became the focus of international attention as the media criminologists, feature writers and analysts poured in to report on this remarkable achievement in the fight against organized crime.

The Sicilians were preparing for the biggest trial in history and apart from amassing the evidence to support the hundreds of charges, the sheer logistics of bringing four or five hundred people to court, daily, housing them locally and then taking them back to prison was in itself exceptionally difficult.

Falcone, Borsellino and three other judges were to spend the next six months completing their interrogations of witnesses and suspects, and writing up the depositions and charges. The logistical and security problems of the great trial were handed over to Liliana Ferraro and her role in this historical event is today set in stone, a monument that is the courthouse at the side of the Ucciardone prison in the heart of Palermo. Ferraro explained:

> Quite apart from the dire lack of equipment in Palermo, the accommodation for such an undertaking was virtually non-existent. The Pool of judges, the lawyers for the

prosecution and the defence, the clerks and the secretaries would require basic commodities and, of course, protection. The paperwork involved was several mountains high. It was so difficult. They had to deal with the dossiers on a mass of crimes involving possibly 700 suspects, dozens of murders and literally hundreds of other crimes. Even at the beginning, we had 476 people who had been arrested and charged. There was simply no courtroom or prison in Palermo which could accommodate such numbers – so we had to set about building a new courthouse, attached to the Ucciardone prison with its own cells and iron-strung cages capable of holding the large number of accused who would be brought to court on a daily basis. Nothing like it existed. Nothing.

By then, we knew that there were going to be hundreds of arrests and that ultimately the court would have to be in session for many months, possibly years, and so there had to be the facilities put in place to allow this to happen, even down to secure accommodation for judges and lawyers for the prosecution who would face the threat of assassination once they stepped outside of the court.

What we needed was a totally new security compound which required government approval. We selected a site next to the prison so that the prisoners could be transferred daily without causing further disruption to the already chaotic traffic conditions of Palermo city centre with road blocks and the like. I must say, once we had laid out our proposals and shown the need for these trials, we received excellent support from Rome. Later, there would be a subtle change. But in the meantime, the building work went rapidly ahead and we set a provisional date for the start of the maxi-trials at the beginning of 1986.

Ferraro recalls these events in a dry, matter-of-fact way. At the time, there were those who were ready to taunt, especially because it was a mere woman who had been presented with this mammoth task. There were plenty around who would say, 'You will never do it. You will never stay alive to complete it. You will never get so many Mafia to court.' The months ahead were filled with great tension, long, long hours of discussions and planning. The law enforcers' lives became even more enclosed by the need for top-level security; they were in constant danger of assassination. They all knew that.

Another glaring problem at the outset was the inadequacy of the Sicilian system of handling the mountains of paperwork. Though she does not comment on these subsidiary aspects which would give away too much about systems and security, it is known that Ferraro was also heavily involved in the massive task of computerization which again was virtually non-existent. She brought a particular skill to this vital installation without which the sheer volume of data would have been impossible to handle during the trial itself.

Meanwhile, Giovanni Falcone was always ready to talk to the press and ensure that the public was well aware of their work, and of the dangers they all faced daily in their fight. And rightly so. For too long, the Italian Anti-Mafia Commission had been a toothless organization which had a tendency towards understatement.

The case of Leonardo Vitale represented something of an indictment against past administrations in Palermo. Falcone saw that. If only someone had taken note earlier, he said, many innocent lives might have been saved. But he knew it could never be as simple as that. Were the people of Palermo, and Sicily as a whole, or even the Italian mainland, dogged as it had been for years by the continuing expansion of the Mafia across the length and breadth of the boot, really so unaware of events that nothing could have been done earlier? No, that could not be so.

True, it was a proven fact that Vitale had provided a good deal of the same information that Buscetta was giving ten years later. It could be asked – and was asked – why the carabinieri could not have arrested all of these known villains long ago. There were enough of them.

Evidence gathered by the Anti-Mafia Pool in 1983–4 was being presented as a 'brand new' devastating and fresh understanding of the Mafia which had previously eluded everyone. The Anti-Mafia Pool was also able to deduce the motives behind several of the recent killings which have been explained as they appear chronologically only with the benefit of hindsight and access to modern documentation. At the time, the motives were less clear to the investigators.

Boris Giulano, it was now finally understood, died because he had discovered the links between Palermo and the Trans-atlantic heroin traffic and the money-laundering connection between the Mafia and Michele Sindona. 'He proceeded blindly,' Falcone noted, 'unaware of the dangers he was stepping into.'

Judge Cesare Terranova was killed because he was convinced of the importance of Luciano Liggio and the Corleonesi in the emerging geography of criminal power and had sworn not to rest until Liggio was put away for life.

Dalla Chiesa was murdered because of his planned attack on the so-called Third Level of Mafia association and because he was the first to discover the importance of the Catania and Trapani Mafias whose existence had in the past been denied by those in authority.

Rocco Chinnici was blown up because he was about to arrest the tax-collecting Salvo cousins, which had been Dalla Chiesa's ambition. All of these aspects were identified by the Falcone Pool in the wake of the confessions of the *pentiti.* And yet, as Falcone himself virtually admitted in his assessment of the Leonardo Vitale case, much of this evidence had been in the hands of the law for years and had never been acted upon, or 'when it was, those arrested were usually acquitted'.

In his first tour of duty in Sicily in the late sixties, Dalla Chiesa had pursued Liggio for the murder of Dr Navarra only to see him acquitted, and later escape from prison altogether.

The Salvo cousins had been hand in glove with politicians and known *capomafiosi* for years. The former mayor, Vito Ciancimino, had been criticized as long ago as 1976 by the Anti-Mafia Commission for having family connections with a building company (his wife held 10 per cent of the shares) in which the co-directors were 'quite undesirable characters'.

So these facts were not so new. The underlying information about Mafia codes was new to a degree, although as we have seen from the early chapters of this book, even that was fairly well established by writers as long ago as the late nineteenth century.

The real difference lay in the fact that at last the judiciary

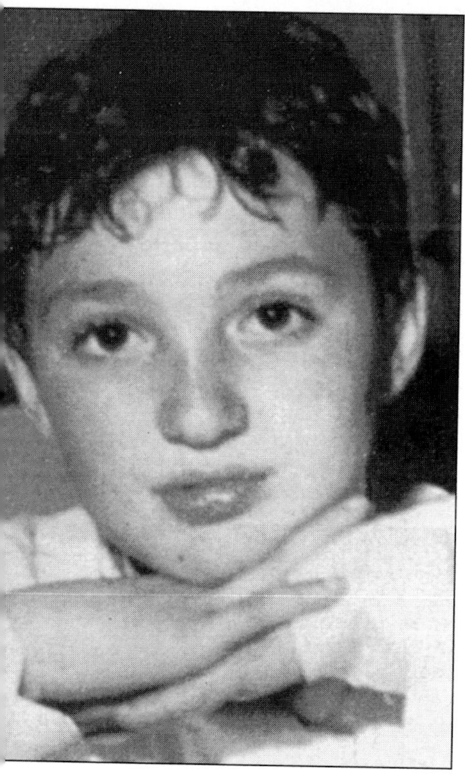

Nothing Changes: (top) Liliana Ferraro's huge courtroom bunker with cages for its prisoners built for the maxi-trials in the 1980s and (below) the first ever Mafia trial in 1896.

The building of the court brought horror for the family of Claudio Domino (left). His father, who ran a cleaning company, refused to give cover to Mafia hitmen and Claudio, then just 11 years old was shot dead outside his home the next day

Arrogant to the last and claiming he was just a poor farmer, Salvatore 'Toto' Riina (above), head of the military wing of the Cosa Nostra, succeeded his old friend Luciano Liggio, the boss of bosses and head of the Corleonesi. He had not been seen for 23 years when he was arrested in 1993, trapped when the FBI produced a computerised 'ageing' photograph from this old snapshot (left). Now he is accused of ordering the murders of Falcone and Borsellino, along with several dozen others

Changing places and faces: Liliana Ferraro in her various guises (top right) with Giovanni Falcone (1991); and in three pictures posed for the author; (above) at the UN Conference in Naples in November 1994; (middle right) with then Prime Minister Silvio Berlusconi; and (bottom right) in her Rome office in March 1994

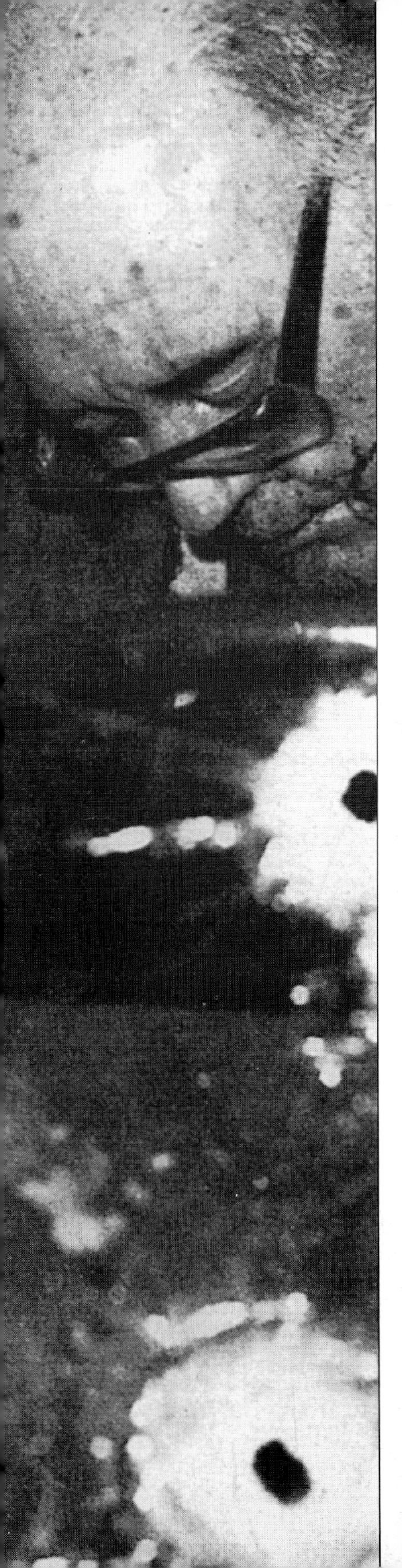

The Illustrious Corpses: (top right) New York policeman, Joe Petrosino; (middle) General Carlo Alberta Dalla Chiesa and (above) his wife; (left) Judge Cesare Terranova; and (bottom) the Palermo politician Michele Reina

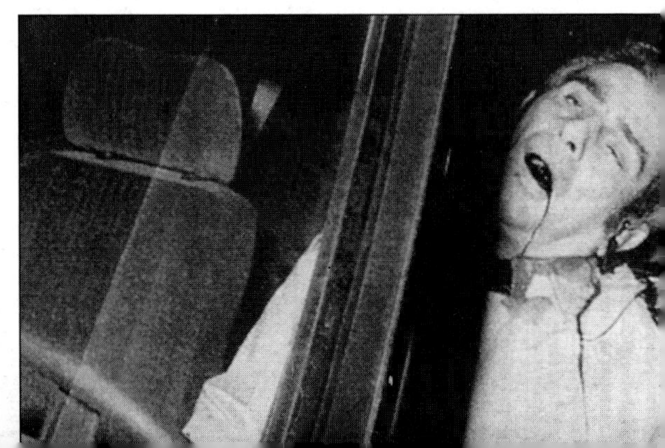

Mafia hunter extraordinaire, Giovanni Falcone (top left) was surrounded by a machine-gun guard from the outset (above). Unable to get close, the Mafia blew up the motorway as he approached (Top right)

Falcone's closest friend, (below) Paolo Borsellino suffered the same fate, blown up as he visited his mother's house in Palermo on a Sunday afternoon (left)

Making friends and influencing people: three top American gangsters who led the Italian Mafia into the drugs trade: (top left) Charlie "Lucky" Luciano, on the day he was deported from the US in 1945; (top right) Luciano settled into Naples high society; (bottom right) politician's friend, Frank "Three Fingers" Coppola; and (bottom left) the ruthless Vito Genovese

Supergrass Tommaso Buscetta is brought to Italy to begin naming names (right). He paid dearly. Virtually the whole of his family was wiped out, including his brother Vincenzo (below), his two teenage sons and Vincenzo's 15-year-old son

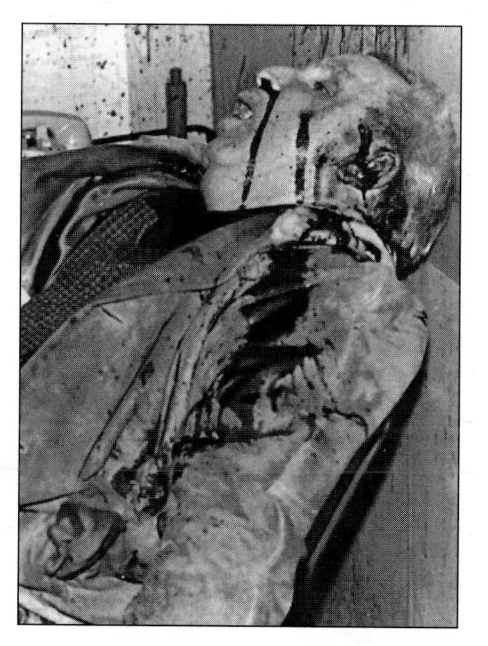

The Mafia Wars: The Corleonesi take control by murdering Stefano 'The Prince' Bontate (right). Over 1200 mafiosi were killed in the two-year war (below left) including a member of the Riccobono family (below) who was decapitated. Many others were tossed into acid baths in the Corleonesi torture chamber

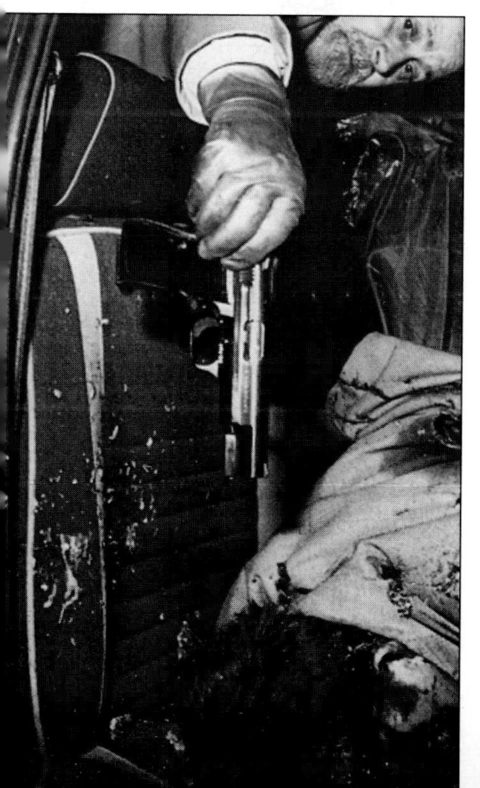

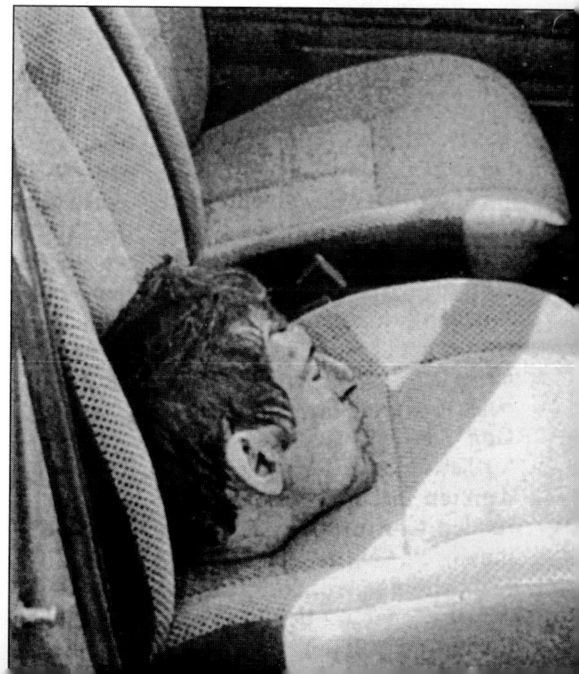

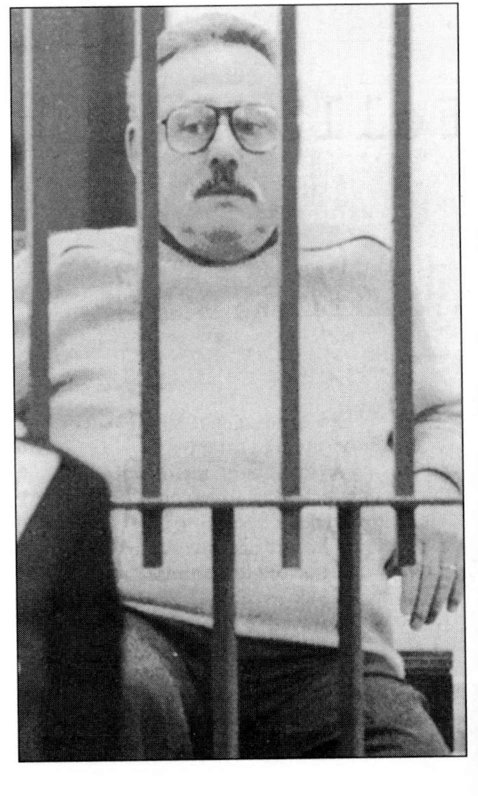

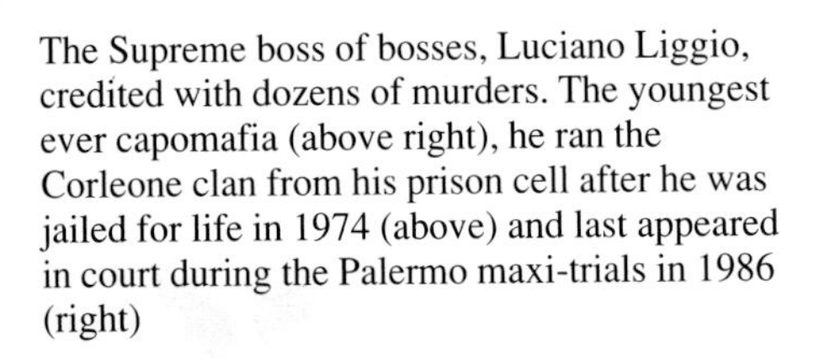

The Supreme boss of bosses, Luciano Liggio, credited with dozens of murders. The youngest ever capomafia (above right), he ran the Corleone clan from his prison cell after he was jailed for life in 1974 (above) and last appeared in court during the Palermo maxi-trials in 1986 (right)

had the weapon of the *pentiti* – just as Dalla Chiesa had when he tackled the Red Brigades in the late seventies. They now had authentic, authoritative witnesses prepared to go before the courts and tell all – name the killers, name the extortionists and reject *omertà*.

In the whole bloody history of the Mafia, there had been only two such similar occurrences: when Joe Valachi told all to a congressional committee in 1963 and, though of far lesser importance, when Vincent 'the Fat Man' Teresa became a turncoat in 1973.

Unlike Joe Valachi who was an illiterate thug, Tommaso Buscetta had the appearance and even gentility of an Italian statesman. He spoke three languages fluently, he had lived all around the globe, owning large properties. His police files dated way back into the distant past and at one time or another he had had dealings with every major Cosa Nostra figure of the last forty years.

Falcone and his colleagues, perhaps understandably, were prepared to overlook the fact that he gave a glowing account of his own life which he initially claimed was without sin, and that the only people he ever admitted killing were a few Nazis.

There were many gaps in his first testimony, though over the years he has more or less filled them with an almost continuous round of interviews with Italian and American law officers and later a succession of biographers and ghost writers. The fact that he would become an international celebrity was not even considered as a possibility back in 1984, as Falcone put the finishing touches to the 2,400 pages of evidence he presented as an initial indictment against those whose had been arrested.

Among the latest arrests were, sensationally, men considered to be among the Third Level; Vito Ciancimino himself, followed soon afterwards by the Salvo cousins. These three figures, out of the 563 people arrested by January 1985, caused most comment.

On 31 March, another leading figure, Giuseppe 'Pippo' Calo, the Mafia's chief cashier, was arrested at dawn with two bodyguards as he stepped out of his car, heading for his luxury apartment in Rome.

This was a major blow to the Mafia and an absolute triumph for the Sicilian judges. In recent years, Calo had become the central figure in the handling of Mafia drugs and kidnap money. He associated heavily with the bankers Michele Sindona and Roberto Calvi. He was a financial genius who was entrusted with huge sums of black money which he transferred with ease into legitimate investments – many still hidden in place today – and succeeded in moving the Mafia into a new area of activity, in elite real estate investments in the expanding tourist industry, notably on the Sardinian Emerald Coast. The following day, nine of his associates were picked up in Rome and Milan.

Two factors made all of this possible. First the testimony of the *pentiti* backed up the evidence in the hands of Inspector Ninni Cassara which he had prepared for Rocco Chinnici shortly before he was blown up. Second, with a clear case to put forward to the judiciary, Giovanni Falcone and his Pool could now bring in the finance police to examine the bank and company records of people like the Salvos and Ciancimino.

Ciancimino was the first of the Sicilian elite to be brought in. When detectives arrived at his apartment, he fainted and had to be carried downstairs to the waiting police wagon where press and television cameras were waiting to report on his fall from power.

When he recovered, he protested loudly. He was the man, he said, who had spoken out courageously against the Mafia on many occasions in the past. He had also been a senior figure in politics, and a leading light in the Christian Democrat Party for thirty years. He counted Giulio Andreotti, whose faction within the party he supported, a personal friend.

The political connections, though speculated upon from time to time, had never been thoroughly analysed. The Mafia was an important vote-gatherer for the Christian Democrats and sent a crucial contingent of representatives to central government in Rome. As such, the power of Ciancimino, the Salvo cousins and others in that particular lobby controlling the political system of western Sicily had never been challenged by Rome, the gentlemen of the Palazzo or even the local forces of justice.

In all the years of suspicion about Ciancimino, he had never been investigated, in spite of some very damning evidence contained in a report of the Anti-Mafia Commission ten years earlier which had never been acted upon. It lay dormant and ignored. Yet he had a record of great activity in Palermo, and had been one of its most prominent citizens since he left his home village of Corleone to start up in the construction business when he obtained contracts with the state railway company.

More than three decades later, Falcone had put his feelers out and discovered an unknown and secret world attached to Ciancimino. From that moment, when the Palazzo in Rome saw there was no point in attempting to defend him publicly, Ciancimino, the Salvos and others who had built an extensive political power-base in Sicily found themselves in a void of non-support.

Falcone's right-hand man in Palermo, Paolo Borsellino, went on record at the time to say, 'When hard evidence gave us the opportunity of reaching Ciancimino, he was already in a state of political isolation such as he had never experienced before. Practically until the moment of his arrest, he had enjoyed the protection of political allies. Once this stopped, it became much easier for us to delve into his background and discover the evidence we needed to secure a prosecution.'

The same applied to the Salvo cousins who were powerful members of the political clique of western Sicily. From this initial financial base, they had enjoyed a fabulous life-style and built up their empire spanning real estate, agriculture, shipping, vineyards and finance. Rumours of their joint affiliations with both leading Mafiosi and senior political figures on the Italian mainland had been circulating for years and they had been a prime target of both Dalla Chiesa and Rocco Chinnici.

Now, Falcone was able to move against them, too, and as with Ciancimino, they quickly discovered that their protection at both levels evaporated overnight. No political might could intervene, and the *capomafiosi* had too many troubles of their own.

They were confronted by Falcone soon after Ciancimino was arrested. A heavily-armed squad of carabinieri raided the offices of one of the Salvos' many companies and arrested Ignazio Salvo, suave and immaculate. Later that morning, they arrested his cousin Nino as he prepared to drive to work in his BMW. They were both taken under armed guard to carabinieri headquarters and later were transferred to Punta Raisi airport where a plane was standing by to take them to Rome.

Two of Sicily's wealthiest and most socially revered businessmen suffered the indignity of confinement at the shabby top security prison, in which Tommaso Buscetta himself had given his testimony during the long hours of conversation with Falcone which had provided the basis for the arrest of the Salvo cousins.

Falcone himself interrogated them, as he did with Ciancimino. They all told the same story, that doing business anywhere in Sicily made it impossible to avoid contact with the Mafia at some time or other. They denied knowing Buscetta, even though he had said in his testimony that he had once stayed at one of their seaside villas during his flight from the law.

Nino Salvo acknowledged contact with the assassinated Stefano Bontate but maintained that it was an obligation resulting from the kidnap of his father-in-law, Luigi Corleo, in 1975.

Bontate, he said, acted as the go-between to achieve his release though he admitted that even after a ransom had been paid, his father-in-law was never seen again. 'You have to keep good face in times of bad fortune,' Nino Salvo told Falcone. The cousins rejected all charges against them and protested that they were the victims of a plot engineered by the Sicilian Communists.

Even so, within a matter of months their $30-million business empire was placed in the hands of a receiver and the finance police began the enormous task of sifting through thousands of documents and scrutinizing bank accounts. Nino himself did not survive to face further questioning or trial. He died of cancer in 1985.

For Falcone and his Pool, the workload of physically investigating and preparing cases against the 563 defendants against whom arrest warrants had been issued during the previous few months was enormous, and it thrust them into a new world of high finance, previously unexplored by any of the Italian judiciary.

It meant seeking the cooperation of banks in Switzerland, Great Britain and North America which in some cases was never achieved. Gradually, however, after encountering initial reluctance to divulge secret information, he began to obtain what he termed a brief glimpse at the enormity of the money laundering network around the globe.

In those early days of the investigations for the maxi-trials, however, Falcone had great difficulty unravelling the mysteries of global money transactions. While investigating Vito Ciancimino for example, he gained permission from the Swiss Ministry of Justice to examine documentation relating to three bank accounts in Switzerland, held in the name of an important Italian figure, apparently unconnected with the Mafia. Because of the sudden and significant movement of capital, he assumed it was related to drug trafficking. Almost as soon as he was granted the necessary permission, the accounts in Switzerland were stripped bare. Obviously, the suspect had been tipped off.

However, Falcone was able to follow the money over a period of three years. Five million dollars was sent to a Panamanian company bank account, where it was divided in two. Half went to a bank in New York, the other half was moved to a bank in Montreal. Later, the five million came together again, having been moved around the world, and ended up in a Guernsey Bank, in an account of a Guernsey registered company.

The bank had no idea of the illegal nature of the funds. But by then, the money had already left Guernsey. It had been divided into five parts, and deposited into five separate accounts in Switzerland, in a bank next door to the one from which the journey started.

Very soon, the balances in those five accounts began to build up, until there was more than $15 million on deposit. Finally, with Falcone putting on pressure in the background, a Swiss magistrate ordered seizure of the money in 1991.

This was one small example of the money-go-round that the Italians were chasing. Similar successes on an even larger scale were being racked up by their American counterparts during investigations for the Pizza Connection trial and they were constantly amazed by the numbers involved and the ease with which the money had flowed through the international banking system, either by way of transfers, bonds, securities or plain old-fashioned cash being dumped on bank counters in holdalls and suitcases.

From respectable finance houses on Wall Street, to the dignified city banks of London; from offshore tax havens in the Caribbean to the secrecy of the banking halls of Switzerland and Liechtenstein, the money was turned around and around like linen tumbling over and over in an automatic washing machine, until it came out the other end, cleaned up and untraceable. It was all made possible because of the willingness of banks around the globe to accept these deposits with no questions asked, in spite of the suspicious nature of many of the couriers who might turn up with sports bags crammed with dollar bills of low denomination.

The Americans tracked down the movement of no less than $1.6 billion during a four-year period of the Pizza Connection operations, from 1980 to 1984. That was by no means the whole amount, and represented a fraction of the total drugs money floating around the system.

The DEA/FBI chart showing the money-flow for the Pizza Connection revealed the way in which the Sicilians relied upon old and long established connections for the transfer of narco-dollars from the US. By far the largest sums were flown by private plane to the Bahamas and deposited in banks in Nassau in tranches of no less than $1 million at a time. The money was allowed to languish there for a short time and would then be telexed on through the international system, on a route which invariably ended in Switzerland. From there, millions at a time were transferred directly to suppliers of morphine – a supply line which at the time was largely controlled by a Turkish cartel which had long ago filled the void as Lebanese and North African supply lines closed down.

The remainder was moved back and forth, much as Falcone himself had discovered, but invariably concluded its journey in business investments throughout Italy or private accounts in Sicily – sometimes aided by the blind eyes of bribed bankers in shady operations. As the Sicilian judges and police began to move towards establishing their own version of the US money charts, Falcone warned everyone in the Pool to be on their guard. There were still powerful men they had not reached and those who were under arrest still had the ability to order assassinations virtually at will.

The gathering of evidence against the hundreds now facing

trial would continue for many months and one of those at the forefront of the financial investigations was Judge Carlo Palermo who in 1980 was the first member of the investigating judiciary in Italy to discover the Turkish partnership with the Sicilians which he identified as trading exclusively in morphine base and arms.

At the time, he was assigned to the province at Trento in the far north of Italy. Over the next four years he pursued his mission with a tenacity that angered many politicians, including the then Prime Minister, Socialist party head Bettino Craxi. In 1983, Craxi had personally admonished Judge Palermo after he issued a search warrant for the Milan offices of a well-known financier who handled the investments of the Italian Socialist party, as well as Mr Craxi's own.

Craxi complained to his superiors that the judge's motives were 'clearly persecutional'. Palermo then produced a 5,898 page document backing up his investigation which showed that Trento had become the transit centre for one of the largest drugs and arms smuggling rings in the world. Arms bought clandestinely from France, Italy and Bulgaria by the Mafia were being exchanged for morphine base through the Turkish and Middle East connection. The arms were then turning up in the hands of rebel regimes in Africa and other trouble spots around the world.

The list of armoury that the gang had been selling was incredible and was valued in multi-million-dollar shipments. It ranged from Leopard tanks to Exocet missiles, ships to plutonium. In 1983, Judge Palermo issued indictments against twenty-five Italians, nine Turks, two Syrians and one Egyptian on charges of drug trafficking and illegal arms dealing.

Among the nine Turks named was Bekr Celenk who was later charged with complicity with Mehmet Ali Agca in the attempted assassination of Pope John Paul II in 1981, just one more ironic twist in the mix and match events of Italian crime and international politics.

Craxi still persisted that Judge Palermo was overstepping the bounds of his judicial duties and so the judge sent his massive dossier to the Chairman of the Chamber of Deputies and the Senate. Thereupon, accusations that he had displayed too much zeal in his Trento investigations were dismissed by his colleagues and superiors who attested to his professional integrity and dedication.

Clearly, he was being blackballed by the establishment in the north and still anxious to pursue what he believed to be a vital link between the arms trade and heroin traffic involving the Turkish connections and the Bulgarians, Judge Palermo, then thirty-nine years old, requested a transfer to Trapani, Sicily, the financial capital of the island and which, as we have already noted, had more banks than Milan.

He was released from his duties in the north to join the Sicilian effort in early February 1985 and moved to Trapani – the provincial home of the Salvos and some very strong *capomafiosi* – and resumed his investigations into the Turkish supply line of morphine base.

For security reasons, he lived in the military-style compound of the heavily guarded police headquarters. He quickly established that the Turkish route now supplied the largest quantities of raw materials to the Sicilian heroin producers and there were rumours that one of the biggest refining factories was operating within Trapani.

Since 1982, the Corleonesi faction of the Cosa Nostra had controlled most of the imports from Turkey. Luciano Liggio, through his associates on the outside, had bought up the franchise for $11.5 million after their previous largest customer, Nunzio La Mattina, supplier to the Bontate-Inzerillo consortium, had failed to pay all his dues and was shot.

Toto Riina arranged to have the money paid over instantly to the Turkish supplier, Yasar Musullulu. Almost half, $5.5 million, was wired direct from New York to a bank in Bulgaria. The rest, $6 million in dollar bills, was packed into six Samsonite suitcases and delivered by couriers to Zurich.

Judge Palermo was getting closer to these facts and was already preparing indictments for the arrest of five local businessmen on charges of money laundering when on 2 April 1985, less than two months after arriving in Trapani, he was driving to work in the now familiar police convoy that accompanied all the Sicilian judges wherever they went.

The wailing patrol car ahead of his own car slowed down in traffic. At that precise moment an enormous bomb estimated to contain around 1,000 kilos of explosive packed into a parked car, was detonated by remote control. It was not his car or the one carrying his bodyguards that took the full force of the blast – but tragically a private car which was being driven by a young mother taking her twin daughters to school.

The force of the explosion was so violent that the car and its occupants were blown to pieces. Though the mother's body remained identifiable as a human form, little remained of her children. Police given the gruesome task of collecting remains found shreds of bone up to 200 yards away, and the largest piece was a foot, discovered in the garden of a nearby villa.

The real target for the attack, Judge Palermo, was injured by metal shrapnel and sustained severe leg wounds when his own car overturned. Two of his bodyguards were also seriously injured. The horrific details of the atrocity once again brought outrage and shock to the Sicilian public. The Cosa Nostra had sent its message. Judge Carlo Palermo was the one who should have been blown to shreds for seeking to close the Corleonesi's Turkish supply route.

Judge Palermo had a special unit of the carabinieri brought in. By the end of the month, they had located and closed down the largest heroin-refining plant in Trapani province, capable of producing $1 billion worth of the drug a year. More arrests were made, and by then the prisons and the cells of Sicily and southern Italy were filled with Mafiosi.

Ferraro acknowledges that the Sicilian judiciary and senior law men were in the gravest danger in the months prior to the opening of the trial. Though hundreds were in jail, many hundreds more were not, including the two most dangerous of all – Toto Riina and Bernardo Provenzano – and various Grecos, including the Godfather of the family, Michele. There was little doubt that the Cosa Nostra, having failed to kill Judge Palermo on 2 April would strike again, especially now that one of its key heroin-refining factories had been knocked out.

In the summer of 1985, Falcone and colleagues were still working round the clock in the bunker conditions from which they emerged only briefly at weekends for reunions with their wives and children, always under close protection.

Another key figure in the forthcoming trials would be Ninni Cassara for whom the round-up of so many Mafia people represented a significant achievement. It was his initial report to Dalla Chiesa that first Rocco Chinnici and then Falcone used as a blue-print, though Cassara knew that without the testimony of Buscetta and Contorno he would have had trouble making his charges stick.

The road had been a long one. Five years' work had gone into his own contribution to the present euphoric successes against the Mafia and he was proud of it. It had been carried out, incidentally, in between all the other non-Mafia crimes which he and his Squadra Mobile had to handle.

Ninni Cassara remained doing the best he could in his pokey little headquarters with its broken back door. He was also alone. Policemen in Sicily did not have bodyguards.

On the hot night of 6 August 1985, with temperatures still in the eighties, he decided to pay an unplanned visit to his family after days of working with the judges in their confined surroundings. He called in at his office and then left for home. It would take him about fifteen minutes. In that time, someone from within the building, or watching it from the outside, had tipped off the Mafia.

By the time he arrived home, there were ten snipers with Kalashnikovs posted nearby. As he got out of his car, they opened fire. Cassara was murdered with terrible ferocity – in a hail of more than 200 bullets.

Reaction on the Italian mainland, far removed from the centre of the Sicilian violence, was strong in tone but had a certain resigned predictability. Prime Minister Craxi immediately pledged 'extraordinary measures against the bloody offensive by the Mafia' and convened an emergency meeting of his cabinet. The upshot was to send another 1,000 carabinieri to the island without delay to give the judges and the police additional protection and support.

The government and its anti-Mafia stance spearheaded by the Interior Minister Oscar Luigi Scalfaro, sounded serious in tackling the Mafia problem once and for all, and pointed to the new bilateral anti-crime treaties between Rome and Washington as a dramatic improvement in combined transatlantic efforts.

The problem remained, however, that the many-headed monster had permeated throughout Italian life and beyond as a massively wealthy, multinational corporation that could call on an unlimited army of 'soldiers' and protectors to do its bidding. The loud noises of protest and promises of action from the gentlemen of the Palazzo still appeared remarkably sterile in their effect and the front line of the war was still tought by that small band of untainted and courageous judges and politicians in Palermo.

Shocked but undaunted, the judges carried on. Outside, in that hot, oppressive summer air, the people of Palermo expressed once again their horror of what was going on in their midst, and yet Cassara's memorial mass was hardly one which befitted a hero of the city where he had devoted his life, and finally given it, in the battle against the criminals.

Fewer than one hundred people attended, largely colleagues and family. It was in every respect a sad reflection upon Palermo itself but more so upon the state his office represented.

CHAPTER THIRTEEN

The Mayor of Palermo, and a Small Boy Named Claudio – Dead

Ferraro worked day and night on the logistics while Falcone and his team were engaged on the investigative effort. Her courtoom bunker appeared with miraculous speed at the side of the Ucciardone prison and the Sicilian judges prepared for the stage of the maxi-trials which would consume their energies and all their waking hours for the next four years. In the midst of the preparations, a new hero came to the Palermo stage to assist in the local denunciation of the Mafia.

Professor Leoluca Orlando, then thirty-seven years old and a practising lawyer, was elected mayor of Palermo in the 1985 election, and more surprisingly in view of the recent history of the political alliances in Sicily, he was a member of the Christian Democrats.

Surprising, that is, because he would be written into history as the first mayor of that city who was openly and vociferously campaigning on an anti-Mafia ticket. Not since Pier Mattarella, the president of the regional government who was assassinated by the Mafia on 6 January 1980, had any local official been so outspoken.

It took courage and an ability to actually avoid dealing with the Mafia, which was so clandestinely wrapped up in local business and community life. The previous incumbent in the mayoral office, Giuseppe Insalaco, also a Christian Democrat, had lasted only a few months. He was elected in April 1984 but was forced to resign towards the end of the year when it was discovered he had sold land to builders linked to Mafia companies.

He was immediately arrested on charges of taking bribes and interrogated by Falcone and his team. He was suspended from the Christian Democrat party (although he was later readmitted) and was edged out of political life. Insalaco decided he would repent his sins and cooperate. He denounced several former holders of the mayoral office, including Vito Ciancimino, and told the judges the time had come to clean up the connections between Mafia and politics. He was a man who knew too much and of course was destined to pay the ultimate price. Having been released back into community life, he was driving home one night to his house in an exclusive area of Palermo when two helmeted men on a motor cycle pulled alongside him in typical Mafia assassination style. The pillion rider raised his Kalashnikov to his shoulder and emptied a complete magazine of bullets into his body.

Giuseppe Insalaco had been silenced for good.

Now, Leoluca Orlando, a married man with two young daughters, had taken over the hottest seat in Sicilian politics at the most tense time in Palermo's history. 'Yes, you can say that it was with a good deal of trepidation,' he admitted when interviewed for this work in 1994. 'It has been a regular feature in Mafia history that it buys politicians with the promise of votes and those who are not for sale get killed. It took me a long while to get used to all the security measures. Our life, as a family unit, changed completely. But however unnatural and difficult it is, and I am speaking now from a distance of nine years since it began for us, you can get accustomed to anything.'

Orlando was born in Palermo in 1947 and thus spent his childhood and youth in a city which had witnessed the progression of Mafia violence. He studied law in Palermo and followed with post-graduate studies in Cambridge and Heidelberg, and eventually returned to his home city to become a professor at the University of Palermo and a practising lawyer. There was considerable anguish in his household when he chose to pursue an alternative career in politics, and especially when he moved towards the hot seat itself, speaking in strong oratorical fashion of his determination to rid local politics of its Mafia influence.

He declared his intention to sever the city and public works building contracts that used to go to Mafia-run companies. He also had to avoid bringing further national and international resentment and scorn of the island of Sicily, and Palermo in particular. In recent times, it has been common in newspaper articles reporting on events surrounding the assassinations and the arrests by Falcone's team for Palermo to be referred to as a sewer and a rat-infested swamp. To the outside world, of course, it was.

But inside this city of 700,000 inhabitants, and elsewhere on the island, ordinary folk still had to go about their daily lives, Mafia or no Mafia. The image of the city and of Sicilians in general had taken a severe beating over the years, and there was nothing on the horizon – except the work of the few untainted men like Orlando and Falcone – that could change it. 'We are one of Europe's great cities,' Orlando would say, 'and we are steeped in great history. But we are being isolated by the image of violence and corruption and the Mafia thrives on such isolation.'

With this in mind, Orlando flew to Rome for a meeting with Prime Minister Craxi. He called for a 'direct line' of aid and cooperation between Rome and the city of Palermo which had never existed before. 'Either there is national action on a concerted scale,' Orlando told Craxi, 'or Palermo and Sicily will be lost entirely to the Mafia – in spite of the recent arrests. As has been seen with the assassination of Cassara, they have arrogantly sent their message of contempt for the work of Falcone. We will lose any hope of being saved.'

Craxi's reaction was a predictable show of temporary force and a promise of government consideration for greater co-operation and financial help. But, as ever, in the volatility of the Italian political scene itself, the problems of Palermo and Sicily would soon be back on the back burner.

Orlando returned to Palermo with dissatisfaction and distrust in his heart. His feelings were unchanged when interviewed in 1994: 'The engagement and the fight against the Mafia cannot only be against the armed hand of it. The Mafia is not just a military operation; it is also a connotation of power. We cannot defeat the Mafia simply by sending its bosses to prison, although that must be the start of it. We must also arrest the financial and political brains, to wipe out the alliance of Mafia and political power. Toto Riina, the military head of the Mafia, would not have had the power he had without that protection. So we must ask ourselves what we have done to root out the links and alliances.'

The first major steps in that sequence Orlando spoke of were taken towards the end of 1985. In December, Orlando's most notorious predecessor, Vito Ciancimino, was formally arrainged on charges of association with the Mafia and of illegal currency dealings. He was placed under house arrest and had $6 million in property and cash confiscated under the new fiscal laws.

Across the Atlantic, the Pizza Connection trial opened in New York, with Gaetano Badalamenti and his twenty-one associates facing a mass of drug trafficking charges and murder. It was set to become the longest trial in American criminal history. And even as that trial opened, a spokesman for the US Drugs Enforcement Administration cast a reflective eye towards the events in Palermo and stated categorically and without hesitation: 'Mafia labs in Sicily produce 90 per cent of the heroin sold on the east coast of the US and 50 per cent of the country's total consumption. They are now also heavily involved with the cocaine cartels and if these mafiosi are not convicted, we are going to see the same people, directly or indirectly, out on the streets again.' A prophetic assessment.

Tommaso Buscetta and Salvatore Contorno who had been under guard in the FBI witness protection programme since they were flown out of Rome in October 1984 were among the earliest witnesses at the Pizza trial so that they could be returned to Sicily to give evidence in the first of the maxi-trials which were due to begin in Palermo in February 1986. Their evidence had now been supported and added to by twenty-eight other Mafia turncoats who had given themselves up to Falcone.

At the start of the new year, Prime Minister Craxi flew to Palermo to give Orlando and Falcone a last-minute show of support and a judge in Venice organized a one-day visitation by judges from all over Italy to mark their support on the first day of the maxi-trial on 10 February.

There was, unfortunately, a good deal of theatre about the commencement of the biggest, most spectacular, most internationally followed trial in global criminal history. The fact that it was a situation to which all those adjectives and more could be applied made it a natural event for media overkill. In its cost (estimated at $100 million), its scope and complexity, it was without precedent.

Yet its importance to Italy, and more precisely to the likes of Giovanni Falcone and the people of Sicily, would be overshadowed by the fact that it became a media event – a show trial to compare with great political courtroom dramas; Moscow and Nuremberg spring to mind, though it was by no means as important to the outside world in terms of what it represented, though its significance to Sicily was great.

For the Italian establishment, it represented something quite different. Immediately after the unification of Italy it suited the incoming political masters to describe the insurgents as a criminal, rather than a political, conspiracy. That is what the gentlemen of the palazzo wanted in 1986 – to promote the maxi-trial as involving criminals only and leave the politics out of it.

For the thronging journalists and cameramen who arrived in abundance it was in every way a story about gangsters, about the Mafia. Political undercurrents were ignored. The trial was a stunning spectacle, a good story, a riveting focus for a few nights of television news coverage, until the interest faded.

How many times can you tell the world the Mafia is an evil bunch of murderous thugs who have made themselves into multi-millionaires drugging a sizeable percentage of the population of the western hemisphere and that a small unit of judges and policemen are risking their lives to fight them? In soundbite terms, it is never possible to convey the drama of the history or of the heroism or the killings.

Liliana Ferraro's brand new $18-million bunker-like compound, attached to the nineteenth-century Ucciardone prison by a 150-foot-long underground tunnel, looked to all the world like a military command post. On the opening day, as every other day for many months, it was surrounded by blue armoured personnel carriers, each with an attachment of carabinieri in full battledress, helmeted and carrying sub-machine guns. This scene in itself aroused all the purple descriptive powers of reporters and media analysts from around the world and Falcone played to them with the language of his team's 8,636 page indictment: 'This is the trial of the Mafia organization called the Cosa Nostra, a very dangerous criminal association, which with violence and intimidation has sown death and terror.'

But though it may have had the appearance of theatre, and Falcone seemed at times to be the star of an epic drama of Hollywood proportions, there was a supreme seriousness to the whole business that was perhaps lost on the rest of the world, where the news media were obsessed with the Godfather syndrome. In telling the story of the round-up of so many Mafia people, the real story tended to be overlooked.

The stage, if that is what we must call it, was set for a heroic battle and few would really appreciate the implications of what Falcone and his team had taken on, nor indeed did they themselves when they first started. It began as an attack on the Mafia but had long ago sailed into murky political waters, not merely of Italian origin. The truth was that it affected virtually every major country across the globe, from the Far East, Africa, Europe, Australasia and the Americas – that was the extent of the Italian Mafia's spread of activity in the drugs business and the enormity of it was only matched by the scandal of international inertia in the face of the problem.

For two decades and more, since the drug business began to expand to the proportions reached by the mid-1980s, no country anywhere had ever managed to sever the distributive system of the Sicilian Cosa Nostra, or the Triads and the other international gangs for that matter. Only France, in the early seventies, had managed to halt the Corsicans and the French Connection – yet even that action was eventually turned to the benefit of the Mafia; they simply moved in to fill the void and used it almost as a launch pad for expansion.

The rest of Europe had notched up numerous drugs busts, but at the courier and retail level where there were always ample replacements to fill the arrested men's shoes. Britain had managed only one major arrest which connected back to the Sicilians, in 1985, yet the Cosa Nostra had had at least three *capomafiosi* operating in the country since 1979.

The United States, with all its international resources and agencies, had been able to root out one major ring – that of Gaetano Badalamenti whose trial was currently running in New York. There were other successes of course, but the fact that the Pizza Connection trial was being billed as the 'biggest ever' was evidence enough that the Sicilians had for years outmanoeuvred every major law enforcement agency in the countries through which their products passed and in which they were finally sold on the streets and in the ghettos.

The trial in Palermo was not just another big court case, arranged for the displeasure of a bunch of hoodlums, gangsters and fiscal crooks who could be herded together under the collective heading of 'Mafia'. It had, as Ferraro pointed out to me, a double emphasis: to pursue a serious judicial attack on its most dangerous and complex criminal organization, and, second, to send a message to the international community at every level that the time had come for global cooperation in attempting to stamp out, or at least curtail, the channels through which the interrelated flow of drugs, arms and cash had continued to flow.

These were the real undercurrents when the first of the maxi-trials opened in Palermo on 10 February 1986 and it was only there, with the very visible evidence of maximum security for all concerned, that one other aspect of the whole situation tended to be overlooked: the sheer bravery of the judges, the lawyers, the jurors, and the policemen. Each was under threat of losing their life.

In spite of the show of support from judges who had travelled from all parts of Italy prior to the opening, and in spite of the words of Prime Minister Craxi, there remained an air of detachment. It was Sicilian business.

There was one other problem. After the many months of build-up and publicity which had preceded it, the opening of the trial was always in danger of becoming something of an anticlimax, and to a degree it was. At 8 a.m. on the first day, just over 100 of the original 467 defendants named in the indictments were marched through the tunnel from Ucciardone prison to take their places in the 30 separate steel-barred cages fitted with benches along the rear wall of the fan-shaped courtroom.

Of the remaining accused, 115 were still at large, including heavy names like Toto Riina, Bernardo Provenzano and Michele Greco and his brother Salvatore, known as the Senator because of his political connections. Both the Greco brothers had been hunted by police since 1982. In 1984, they had been sentenced to life imprisonment in absentia for planning the car-bomb killing of Judge Rocco Chinnici. Another 40 suspects arrested in the big-round up in 1984 had been released under house arrest and 113 were freed on bail, all to appear later in the hearings.

In front of the cages were long tables at which the 307 lawyers engaged in the case, either for the prosecution or the defence, would come and go with distracting frequency. To the right of them was seating for yet another group, the plaintiffs in a number of civil actions.

Soon after 9.30 a.m., the presiding judge Alfonso Giordano took his seat beneath the tall crucifix on the wall behind him. In front of him was a panel of television monitors which were capable, with the press of a button, of zooming in on the faces of the accused to gauge their reactions. There was also a computer screen on which the judge could have instant access to the 200,000 pages of trial documents.

With the judge sat sixteen jurors wearing identifying sashes in the Italian colours of red, white and green. Elsewhere were the press benches and the public areas, filled for the first day and for many days to come, though eventually attendances would become spasmodic.

The parade to the cages was led by Luciano Liggio, undisputed boss of bosses, head of the Corleonesi who had been flown in from his maximum-security prison in Sardinia. He had grown fat in prison, where he had languished for twelve years, though according to the indictments, this had not stopped him running his empire from his cell. He was smart and well manicured.

He paid little attention to the early business of the court, which was to listen to the monotonous reading of the indictments. His insolence, long ago noted by his arch enemy Judge Cesare Terranova, whose murder was among the 97 killings listed in the charges against the 467, was as apparent as ever. He sat casually reading a newspaper, and smoking a black Tuscan cigar, occasionally raising his head to glance around the courtroom.

He caused an initial flurry when he got up and spoke, demanding that he wished to dismiss his lawyers and take no part in the trial. He complained that the newspapers had published some unpleasant things about him which were totally untrue. The judge ruled that it was the law that every man should be defended, and Liggio was no different.

Next to Liggio was Giuseppe 'Pippo' Calo, fifty-eight, the Mafia's treasurer and underground ambassador to Rome. Much would be made of his influence in the financial world, controlling as he did the investment of the dirty billions in respectable establishments with the aid of people like Robert Calvi before Calvi 'committed suicide'. Alongside him was another of the Mafia's financial wizards, Tommaso Spadaro, forty-eight, whose bank account in Lugano, Switzerland, according to the trial indictments, received $600 million from drug trafficking in the United States in a two-year period, between 1981 and 1983.

Eleven days after the trial opened, they were joined by Michele Greco, 'the Pope', who Buscetta had named as the head of the Mafia *cupola,* who was arrested in a farmhouse twenty-four miles outside of Palermo on the night of 20 February 1986. He entered the cages looking completely out of place – distinguished, well groomed, silver-haired and wearing expensively tailored clothes, usually blazer and slacks, and hand-made leather shoes. He carried a copy of the Bible and would sit reading it in court as the witnesses paraded forth to make their terrible accusations of murder and mayhem against him and the rest.

In addition to charges of planning the killing of Rocco Chinnici for which he had been sentenced to life in his absence, he now faced additional charges, including that of ordering the murder of Dalla Chiesa. 'The Mafia? I don't even know what it is,' he would protest daily. 'I am a god-fearing, respectable businessman of this city. How can they accuse me of such things?'

Michele Greco's brother Salvatore sat nearby and together they joined the other personalities, including a distant relative,

Leonardo Greco, boss of the Bagheria Cosa Nostra clan. Next to him was Gerland. Alberti, protesting, 'I am just a hard-working fabrics salesman,' but who according to the indictments controlled most of the heroin refineries in the Palermo suburbs, had strong historic connections with the Corleonesi and whose telephone had been tapped years earlier during the kidnap era by the CIA and the Italian secret service at the same time.

For Falcone's team, it was a major disappointment that several other key figures named in his charge sheet were still at large and it must be said that many of the others who were herded daily into the cages were relative small fry, the Mafia soldiers who had played their own part in terrorizing Sicily for years but against whom charges would, at best, secure fairly modest prison sentences or heavy fines.

These men, from the lower echelons of the Mafia power structure, were placed apart in adjoining cages, from which there oozed reverential respect for and subservience to the *capomafiosi*, though none for the authority and dignity of the court. They dressed casually, and wore sunglasses as if it was expected of them. They laughed and joked with each other, they would shout, jeer, and wave hellos and goodbyes to relatives and associates who filed daily into the visitors' gallery like passengers disembarking from a train. Their arrogance and air of invincibility remained. They would stare, icy, murderous stares as the prosecution began to call the *pentiti*, brave men in their own way because apart from Buscetta and Salvatore Contorno, they had no protection.

The Italian law of the *pentiti* at that time did not permit special treatment. Their confessions would be used as their own damnation and the best they could hope for was a less severe penalty than they might otherwise have received, and yet they were vital to the Falcone team's penetration of the Mafia secret society. So, unlike the US, the *pentiti* remained unrewarded for their efforts and perhaps in some respects, given the circumstances, this was just as well, as it more or less assured that evidence given was free of either promise or intimidation.

Gradually, these men – whose ranks would be swelled later – began to talk and tell, and all the romantic myth and legend, the stuff of fiction writers, began to fall away like dried leaves on a dying tree. The Mafia they described was, in the words of one of Falcone's pool of judges, Giusto Sciacchitano, 'global, unitary, rigidly regimented, vertically structured, governed from the top down by a *cupola* with absolute powers over policy, money, life, and death. It is only now that we can see this global nature, but it was always there.'

Then came the moment of high drama when the prosecution produced its first witness and star of the show, Tommaso Buscetta, brought to Palermo under the most stringent security conditions especially for these hearings before being whisked back to the US again to be blanketed by the FBI's protective cocoon. As he was called for his eight days of testimony, hundreds of Sicilians queued from dawn each day down the narrow streets to the Ucciardone gates for one of the seats in the public gallery.

The intensity of the hatred of the men in the cages towards this super-informer was overwhelmingly evident. The atmosphere was electric as the armed escort delivered Buscetta to the bullet-proof glass booth in which he was placed to give evidence, with his back to the men for whose arrest he was largely responsible – the same men who as a collective had destroyed his family, murdered his sons, and wiped out his friends.

Buscetta, however, showed no sense of strain or of being ill at ease in spite of the insults and taunts hurled at him from the cages. Liggio called him a slimy lizard. Pippo Calo chose to insult his wife, calling her a prostitute and a tart. Buscetta showed not a flicker of reaction as he began to give evidence in his husky baritone voice, clinically and dispassionately.

He wanted to say at the beginning that he did not consider himself a *pentito* because he had done nothing for which he had to repent. He was clearly intent on trying to convince the jury, if not the world, that he was an original Man of Honour, that really there were the good guys and the bad guys in the Mafia, and he of course fell into the first category. He spoke almost with nostalgia for the old days, when Mafia leaders – like those installed by the Americans after World War II – wielded local justice and ruled like an alternative government.

He said he had upheld the honour of his family and had

pursued the rules and code of the Cosa Nostra which had been his life since his youth. He had not changed in his outlook or views; he had not broken faith. It was, he claimed, the Cosa Nostra that had done that by its switch of emphasis. The change began after 1970, as kidnappings became rife and the drugs trade was on the brink of take-off. It was at that point everything changed, he said, and the movement emanated entirely from the Sicilian Cosa Nostra once the French Connection had been put out of business.

His evidence was colourful and at times, it must be said, untrustworthy and with many evident gaps and flaws which can be identified with greater clarity with the passing of the years. He denied his friends and relatives murdered in the Great Mafia War of 1981–3 were drug dealers. And, of course, he himself had always been a good businessman who conformed to old Mafia traditions.

Falcone himself had said in his original assessment of Buscetta's testimony that he came from an era of the Mafia which was founded on the age-old principles of virtue and vice, respect or vendetta. Falcone had placed great emphasis on this 'understanding' of the Mafia which he believed was necessary to successfully prosecute it.

Buscetta spoke at length of the 'virtues' that made up the unwritten laws of Mafia membership, such as family values, the oneness of the organization, the territorial traditions, bravery in the face of opposition, courage in the face of death and so on – all those dubious credentials of Mafia membership which we have examined in earlier chapters but which were only then, as Buscetta and the *pentiti* gave evidence, being confirmed.

The vices, those which Buscetta knew, were all the traditional forms of employment of Mafia members which included illegal gambling, kidnap, extortion, theft, smuggling, blackmail, arson, bombing and murder. The premise that 'it wasn't as bad as drugs' would be offered up as some kind of placatory excuse. For some reason, there was a degree of acceptance of this view, when in truth it was simply a matter of varying degrees of evil and awfulness.

He maintained the modern leaders of Cosa Nostra – notably the Corleonesi – had subverted the 'ideals' that, although frowned upon by those who live within the law, 'are beautiful for us, who live inside this association'. Thus he tried to pass off his membership of the 'old' Cosa Nostra and disassociate himself from the 'new'. That is why he did not regard himself as a *pentito.* His life had been governed by a set of rules which he was bound to honour.

The criminality did not have to be explained. The Cosa Nostra existed for the furtherance of its members' interests. Killings and vendettas were integral to the system, and always had been. The difference was that the Cosa Nostra, and the wider Mafia, before the seventies, had operated by its own internal self-imposed laws. He reckoned it would not kill women and children, usually avoided killing policemen and judges and everyone was beholden to maintain the standards of the Men of Honour.

Buscetta thus reinforced the romantic Robin Hood image which was an utterly false one and always had been, although the notion lingered still among the dozens of towns and villages in Sicily and the south of Italy where Mafia chieftains had 'looked after' the local populace since the organisation's inception. Women and children had never been excluded from the Mafia's sights if their liquidation was deemed necessary – Dr Navarra, the old head of the Corleonesi, himself killed the boy shepherd who witnessed the murder of a trade unionist.

Buscetta, however, stuck to his theme and maintained throughout that he was outraged by what the Cosa Nostra had become in its battle for domination of the heroin market, and so wanted to destroy it. By and large, Buscetta also kept out of politics and the so-called Third Level of Mafia connections in this first stage of his evidence. He opened up on that score much later when biographers and Italian sociologists began interviewing him for their books in the early 1990s. For the time being, he identified only Vito Ciancimino as a Mafia associate 'run by the Corleonesi' and confirmed that the Salvo cousins had powerful connections on both sides of the law.

Buscetta was followed into the witness stand by Salvatore Contorno, a gruff, unsophisticated soldier. He possessed none of Buscetta's intelligent eloquence. Contorno's words were rattled out fast in B-movie jargon that lawyers could not understand, and one even protested to the judge that he should be instructed 'to speak Italian'. It was, however, a gripping narrative, perhaps because it was told by a man who looked and sounded like everyone's idea of a Mafia hood.

He was rather more open than Buscetta about his own grounding in the seedy world of the criminal brotherhood and admitted that he had been on his way to murder Pippo Calo – who was now sitting in the cage immediately behind him – in Rome when he was arrested. He wanted Calo to die for betraying his own family and his boss, Stefano Bontate, to the Corleonesi. He had already lost more than a dozen relatives in the war and they had tried to kill him too.

The Cosa Nostra, he maintained, had become a power-crazed gang of thugs and murderers, ruled by the military wing of the Corleonesi. Contorno made no bones about it. What had happened within the Cosa Nostra, and on a wider scale throughout the Mafia, had arisen through drugs. Every major Mafia family, he reckoned, became involved because there was huge money to be made.

It was far more profitable than bribing local officials for a cut of the construction industry, better than building houses, better than kidnapping, better than any business the Mafia had ever been involved in. A hundred million lire invested in morphine base was returned quickly, tenfold.

He explained how the morphine base came on to the island, in great loads. He and many of the witnesses who followed him to the stand described the system. It was delivered from several sources, via Turkey, where there were several major connections who had originally dealt with the Camorra in Naples. There were supplies imported from the east via Bulgaria which were linked to the arms deals with the 'Ndrangheta, through their northern stronghold discovered earlier by Judge Carlo Palermo.

These connections were vital, particularly in the early stages, but at the end of the day, said Contorno, it was the Sicilians, the Cosa Nostra itself, that controlled the drugs trade in its entirety. They answered to no one, not even the American Cosa Nostra: 'It started out from Palermo, and everything had to come back to Palermo. It was strictly controlled.'

There was plenty to go around. By 1980, the Cosa Nostra had tapped directly into the Golden Triangle. Massive supplies were brought in from Thailand via various side deals and agents, notably a particular dealer in Singapore whose first shipment in 1981 delivered 3,750 kilos of morphine base into Palermo on a devious route via Copenhagen. This single consignment was sufficient to make four tonnes of refined heroin, enough to keep more than half America's known addict population doped up for a year.

When a major shipment came in, said Contorno, everyone dived in for a share. 'If I wanted a hundred kilos, they'd give me a hundred kilos,' he said. 'They refined it in Palermo and everybody took what he wanted and sent it out to his own customers, dealt with whoever he wanted, anywhere. The money would come flowing back to us, and we had no difficulty in changing it. We had the bankers in our pockets – people who were inside the big banks, dealing for us. Cleaning it up. That's the way it operated.'

He had agreed to become a *pentito* because of what the Mafia had become since the Corleonesi took over. He had been on the losing side, but today there were no losers because 'they do not exist – they were all wiped out, murdered'.

The trial wore on day after day, with the parade of more than 1,300 witness coming forth to denounce the Mafia, some with the same devastating effect as Contorno and Buscetta; others, by then extremely nervous of the consequences, took part in a pantomime of evasiveness, changing their stories or backtracking on statements made earlier to the Falcone team. One man took the witness stand and appeared to have gone mad. Another, a youth who had been in the car of a mafioso when he was arrested, claimed he did not even know the man and was promptly arrested for perjury.

Another young *pentito* changed his story after bursting into tears and claimed he did not know any of those he had once accused. The judge ordered him to walk over to the cages and take a closer look. He did, and walked up and down, peering at the men who glared back. No, he said, on his return to the witness box, he did not know any of them. His new story, he assured the judge, had nothing to do with the fact that on that very morning, the father of another *pentito* giving evidence at a trial in Messina had been shot.

The familiar symptoms of Mafia trials, heart attacks, madness and loss of memory, began to come forth in profusion, much to the disdain and disappointment of the Falcone team. One who did not change his story was Vincenzo Sinagra, who gave a chilling account of events at the Cosa Nostra torture chamber and confessed that he himself had killed a man simply because he did not like his face.

His evidence and that of others slowly hardened the attitude of those in court. Early on, a judge vomited and the trial had to go into recess after a particularly gruesome description of one murder. Eventually, the court became desensitized to such things as the stories poured out about severed heads, dismembered genitals, gouged out eyes, appendanges left on car seats or sent to relatives through the post.

Sinagra was a *pentito* and like the rest had no particular deal for a reduced sentence for his own crime. He would eventually be sentenced to twenty-one years for murder, though in reality he might spend little more than ten years inside – if he survived, that is.

The killing had not stopped and another round of Mafia outrages was expected. It was not long in arriving and one incident, eight months after the trial opened, brought horrific confirmation of Buscetta's evidence that the present rulers had no qualms about killing children.

One afternoon in October, eleven-year-old Claudio Domino was walking home with a friend from his mother's bookshop in the San Lorenzo district of Palermo. They had just left when his mother, Graziella, heard a bang which she thought was a car backfiring until her son's friend ran back into the shop, screaming that Claudio had been shot. Graziella ran out and saw her boy lying there. 'He was lying in the road, unrecognizable. His face had been shot away and his body was covered in blood,' she recalled. 'He was already dead but I could not accept it. I can remember only screaming, "Why? Why?"'

The reasons would become all too apparent. Claudio's father ran a staff agency in Palermo and the company supplied cleaners for the Ucciardone prison cell blocks where the trial defendants were being held. At the beginning of October, someone in the company was approached by Mafia people, wanting to make use of this most convenient access to the prison. They were refused, and Claudio paid the price of that refusal.

The Mafia sent an assassin on a motorcycle to conduct the cruellest and most cowardly killing in Mafia history.

CHAPTER FOURTEEN

An Appeal Court Judge, His Handicapped Son and a Campaigning Journalist – Dead

As the maxi-trial moved on, grinding its way through the complexities of the system, if there was a moment at which the signal of trouble ahead could be identified, it was on 22 June 1987, when across the Atlantic the much publicized Pizza Connection trial ended in New York. Like the maxi-trial in Palermo, interest had diminished to the point of weariness long before then. The media had paid little attention to it for months and only revived their attendance in the closing stages to remind the public that the trial was actually still going on.

In Palermo, a more sinister undercurrent could be detected, even before the first of the maxi-trials came to a conclusion. Forces of persuasion were moving in mysterious ways and turning on the anti-Mafia crusade. The object, incredibly, was to discredit Falcone and his team. Ferraro explained:

> At the beginning, when we first started out on the maxi-trial adventure, we had every support; from government, from the newspapers, from public opinion, right across the board. But then as the trial wore on, we began to notice a very subtle change.
>
> It started with a kind of whispering campaign, with people saying, 'Well, the maxi-trial is going on, the Mafia

chiefs are in prison, perhaps the Mafia does not exist any more.' Initially, it was a very soft and as I said, subtle movement but day by day, we began to notice something more obvious was happening. I will give benefit of the doubt and say that certain people cannot always live with the pressure of the exceptionality of what was going on in Palermo and it was perhaps simpler, for whatever reason, for them to say that once we had a risk, once we were in danger, and now it is over – when it certainly was not.

As Falcone himself said, this was a most difficult period for us because the criminality continued. We had arrested many people and were going to secure prison sentences on many Mafia leaders but we had by no means cleaned out the Mafia. Absolutely not, and some people would not accept that and even went beyond this false view by attempting to establish in the eyes of the citizens that the war was over.

First of all, they began attacking the image and when that did not work, they resorted to violence. There was a sinister smear campaign launched against Falcone, ridiculously alleging that he had himself had intimate associations with the *pentito* Salvatore Contorno. For a time there were serious undertones appearing as a result of a softly promoted campaign against Falcone. Things began circulating in newspapers, planted in a surreptitious way. They were saying that Falcone had used Contorno for his own purposes which was a complete fabrication. Falcone, always a fighter, brushed it aside. But it was a very worrying time, and we all had to be on the alert for developments.

Those 'developments' were not long in arriving and the outside world was left incredulous, wondering if the Italian establishment had ever been serious about purging itself of the Mafia or, worse still, if it had ever truly intended to allow Falcone to sustain the battle against the criminals.

Across the Atlantic, the American prosecutors faced a similar backlash as the Pizza Connection trial ended with a flourish. Gaetano Badalamenti, the former boss of the Palermo *cupola*, was sentenced to forty-seven years for drug trafficking and other offences in spite the assertion of his pal Tommaso Buscetta –

the star witness in New York as in Palermo – that he had never had anything to do with drugs, at which point one of the defence counsel had asked, 'Would someone please tell me what we are all doing here?'

The jury, however, was prepared to accept the weight of other evidence whose volume in paperwork needed a truck to carry it. The judge, in turn, stipulated that Badalamenti should serve not less than thirty years. In all, twenty-two defendants stood trial. Badalamenti's son Vito was the only one cleared by the jury – but others faced punishment elsewhere. Badalamenti's nephew, Pietro Alfano, survived an assassination attempt during the trial. He was ambushed by Mafia gunmen while on bail and was left paralysed for life. The FBI believed his execution was ordered from within and may have been connected with other matters, such as an arms cache found at Alfano's house. His lawyer negotiated a plea bargain and he was given a lower sentence of fifteen years for conspiracy to supply drugs.

Gaetano 'Tommy' Mazzara, aged fifty, a key figure in the New York heroin distribution network and co-owner of a restaurant used as one of the outlets, did not survive to be sentenced. Mazzara, a member of the Noce family from Palermo, was sent to the US in 1978 as 'drugs ambassador' to oversee distribution and cash transfers on behalf of the Sicilians. He had been involved with various groups, providing the link between wholesale and retail deliveries and securing the cash in return.

On the day before his defence was due to put him on the witness stand in December 1986, Mazzara, also on bail, went missing. Two days later his body was found in a gutter in Brooklyn, wrapped in plastic sacks, but with his feet sticking out. His torso was badly mutilated, apparently from torture. Both his legs had been broken before he died, his tongue had marks which had been made by pliers, seemingly in an attempt to tear it out, and a X-shaped mark had been cut into the back of his head. Then he had been shot.

The trial judge was told that the task force agents were at a loss to explain the murder, suggesting that his death had been ordered by a fellow defendant for fear that he would crack on the witness stand. It seemed an unlikely motive.

Thirteen others originally sought by the task force had been indicted but never made it to the trial. Twelve went missing or had their charges dropped.

The thirteenth, Sicilian-born Cesare Bonventre, aged thirty-four, originally from Castellammare del Golfe who joined the Bonanno family in New York at the age of twenty-three and became its youngest *capo*, was murdered shortly before the trial began.

He went missing as the FBI task force began their round-up of Pizza Connection suspects. His dismembered body was found three days later in three barrels of glue in New Jersey – head and torso in one barrel, legs in another, arms in the third.

When the trial ended, the American Justice Department breathed a sigh of relief and then found itself in the middle of a huge controversy as soon as the verdicts were delivered and the media was able to re-examine the case. Everything about it had been 'big' – the mass of documentation, thousands upon thousands of pages of depositions and transcripts, hours upon hours of legal arguments.

When it was over, the lawyers and the press were at one in crying 'never again'. The case had been brought under the relatively new RICO law – the Racketeering-Influence and Corrupt Organizations Act – which allowed the state to charge that apparently unrelated criminals were working together for the benefit of an overall criminal enterprise – in this case the Cosa Nostra. It was indeed very similar to the Italian maxi-trial arrangement. Lawyers from both sides agreed that the trial had been too unwieldly and too costly. It had taken more than eighteen months, plus four years of investigation, to bring a relatively small, but vital, collection of Sicilians to book.

Soon afterwards, the Chief US District Court Judge, Jack Weistein, a leading federal jurist, ruled that mega-trials were dangerous to lawyers, judges, juries and defendants alike. How could a juror in a complicated case be expected to remember what happened in the trial eighteen months earlier? How could the State even expect the jurors to be available for that length of time? It was against all principles of humanity and justice. The next mega-trial that came up, involving sixteen organized crime suspects, was divided into six separate trials over a one-year period.

Another severe setback was suffered by the FBI task force in their fight against the Gambino family who had been one of the biggest franchisees of the Sicilian heroin. John Gotti, who had taken over as head of that family after the murder of 'Big Paul' Castellano by his own kind in December 1985, just as the Pizza trial was opening, had subsequently been arrested on a string of charges including murder. On 7 June 1987, he was acquitted on all counts and released.

Additionally, a highly critical article in the *New York Times* branded Ronald Reagan's war on drugs as 'a joke' and even critics in his own party denounced it as a sham that had done nothing to stem the flow of drugs. There was just as much heroin and much, much more cocaine on the streets of New York than when the so-called crusade began in 1982.

The Sicilian anti-Mafia forces had better success, although similar criticisms were about to be unleashed upon Falcone and his crusaders, for quite different reasons. Whereas in the US, the attacks had been launched at the lengthy judicial process and the failure of the Reagan administration's promise to crack organized crime once and for all, the undercurrents of dissent described at the beginning of this chapter by Ferraro were much more sinister. The slowly-building movement against the anti-Mafia brigade was orchestrated by the Mafia itself and spread slowly through political, business and social strata of public life.

The catch-all policy of mass arrests and mass trials had built-in difficulties, not least of which were the hidden political undertones.

Mayor Leoluca Orlando's avowed policy of cleaning up the construction industry had brought an unexpected reaction. Construction workers, thrown out of their jobs as several major projects were shut down during investigations, organized demonstrations, carrying posters proclaiming, 'Long live the Mafia – we want work.'

As to the trial itself, it had become, like the American equivalent, a monkey on the back of Palermo. Public opinion, long dulled by political inertia and local violence, began to ask, as news spread that a second and perhaps a third maxi-trial would follow in the wake of the first, 'When will it all end?'

The now familiar sight of the judges, jurors, lawyers and the police associated with the trial dashing around the city and causing heavy traffic jams with their motorcades of bodyguards with sirens wailing, had begun to test the nerves of even Falcone's supporters.

For the participants in this legal marathon themselves it was even worse: life in a bunker, with little daylight and days on end without contact with families or friends. Falcone recalled that he had been out to the cinema once in three years, accompanied by his wife and twenty-five bodyguards who, cleared three rows behind him and three rows in front before he entered. It was that kind of life; an absolute nightmare for the family, though one to which the judges themselves had become wearily resigned.

That aspect of the war on the Mafia was often overlooked. Little credit seemed to be given for the efforts of these men and women which extended well beyond the call of duty. Yet when the first signs of a public backlash against the inconvenience of the trials, and the volume of material that was being religiously reported, day after day, in the local newspapers, it was the heroes in the front line of the fight who were turned upon, criticized and blamed for all of Sicily's troubles and bad publicity. Suddenly, it was the victors of the fight upon whom stones were to be cast.

The first murmurings of disquiet began among the establishment in the political and business arenas, and extended into the Sicilian and Italian middle classes perhaps half-way through the hearings. A truculent impatience set in. However, the ending of the first maxi-trial on 17 December 1987, brought a temporary resurgence of euphoria, a feeling that the battle against the Mafia was being won: 338 defendants were convicted on a variety of charges from murder to simply associating with the Mafia and were collectively sentenced to more than 2,000 years in prison. Not all were available to commence their terms.

More than eighty had never been arrested, and had been sentenced in absentia. All twenty defendants sentenced in the US Pizza trial were also given jail sentences by the Palermo court with the proviso that the Italian authorities would seek their return to Italy as soon as the US sentences had been completed.

All the members of the Cosa Nostra *cupola* and leading personalities were sentenced bar one: the imprisoned leader of the Corleonesi himself, Luciano Liggio. He put up a convincing argument against charges of associating with the Mafia and ordering the murders of ninety-seven people: 'How could I do such a thing? I have been in prison for the last twelve years. Do you wish me to call my jailers to confirm that I have not been out, that I do not hold committee meetings in my cell? It is impossible that I should have committed such crimes.'

Of course, everyone knew that Liggio did run his business from prison, had done for years, continued to do so while he was on trial and would continue to do so in the future. But it was not a situation that the Italian judiciary wanted to highlight at that time. There were too many instances of lax security and bribed officials allowing 'seriously ill' prisoners to be housed in private nursing homes. Liggio was cleared on all counts.

The Sicilian maxi-trial could be viewed at that point as a major success and was applauded around the world for delivering such a massive blow to the Mafia. But had the world's media who returned to Palermo to listen to the verdict stayed around a little longer, they would have noticed, felt the change that was very promptly to emerge in the establishment attitudes to the trial.

As the first trial ended, Falcone made it clear that his focus would next switch to the most sensitive area of the long-running investigation; the financial power of the Mafia and the links between the criminals and the political establishment, in other words the Third Level.

In fact, he had already begun this quest. Charges of corruption and financial impropriety were pending against a number of local politicians. At that point, however, Falcone was pulled up sharp. The news from Rome was devastating. A promotion he had been expecting had gone to another judge.

In March 1988 the theoretically independent Supreme Council of Magistrates selected Mr Antonino Meli, aged sixty-eight, to become senior prosecutor in Palermo and it would fall to him, now, to oversee the work of the judiciary. The appointment caused uproar, because everyone in the Sicilian judiciary expected the job to go to Falcone, then forty-nine and the acclaimed expert on all matters to do with the Mafia. The smear campaign had had its first effect.

The council explained that Meli was older and more experienced and that in the tradition of promotion by age and seniority in the hierarchy, his appointment was inevitable. That was not true, because Meli was long past retiring age and if there was one style of judicial management that was not applicable to Palermo at that time, it was that of an ageing, fragile judge who might have difficulty dodging paper-clips, let alone bullets. At the time, Falcone accepted the decision with good grace and told Meli that he would have his full support and cooperation.

However, once Meli was installed, Falcone discovered that his ideas about the operations of the Sicilian judiciary were completely the opposite of his own, and of the rest of his team, for that matter. Obviously working to orders from on high, Meli ordered the immediate disbandment of the anti-Mafia Pool of judges and said that henceforth, the judges would be dispersed to cover all other aspects of criminal and civil law.

In that one act, Meli turned the pool system on its head, emasculated the Falcone team and with awesome echoes of the past when prosecutors were individually assigned to a particular case – and thus easily picked off by the Cosa Nostra assassins – judges would now find themselves transferred from a big Mafia investigation to routine cases, such as mugged tourists, domestic disturbance or traffic violations.

It would have been laughable if it had not been so tragic, and in many ways it was a terrible slight against the memory of those anti-Mafia heroes who had already lost their lives. Under the new system, judges who once worked on Mafia cases would lose their protection in these less serious roles, and their lives would be placed in jeopardy.

Politics had taken over. The gentlemen of the Palazzo were hovering in the background, giving the nod of approval to a demolition job on the anti-Mafia collective operating in Palermo. The then Prime Minister, Ciriaco De Mita, patron of Christian Democrat reformers like Leoluca Orlando, barely involved himself, diverted as he was by the demands of running a government which was clinging to power by the merest of margins, propped up by a tenuous five-party coalition plagued by self-interest, inter-party factions and external pressures.

There were few prepared to go to bat for Falcone. De Mita's Interior Minister, Antonino Gava, and his predecessor Amintore Fanfani, the veteran Christian Democrat, were both dismissive of the anti-Mafia Pool. Fanfani who after three decades leading a dominant faction of the Christian Democrats counted several political leaders in Sicily among his most ardent supporters, quite baldly stated on his recent visit to Palermo that he did not think the Mafia was 'a high priority'.

Interior Minister Gava meanwhile was insultingly light-hearted about a rumour that Falcone was planning to resign: 'Well, if that's what he wishes to do . . .'

There was much talk in high circles that accused Falcone of trading 'handcuffs for headlines' in pursuit of his career, suggesting that he enjoyed racing around Palermo with gun-cocked cowboys riding shotgun to satisfy his macho image, in short that he was a glory-hunter. Backbiting, backstabbing and innuendo spread.

Meanwhile, as Ferraro told me, a growing body among the Rome establishment were openly stating their opposition to the courtship and use of the *pentiti* on whom Falcone's team had relied for corroborative testimony. They ignored the *pentiti*'s pleas for safe passage and security after the trials, on the lines of the US Witness Protection programme. 'They'll kill us all,' said one.

The Falcone crisis drifted on.

By July, Falcone had had enough. 'Present conditions make it impossible to work effectively against the Mafia,' he declared and indicated that he would seek permission to hand in his letter of resignation. His opposite number in New York, Thomas Sheer, had already done the same, leaving his post as head of the New York office of the FBI to become risk management consultant with a company advising major multinational conglomerates on the potential terrorist threat to future overseas investments.

In an attempt to avert a public crisis of confidence, the Italian government announced it had appointed Judge Domenico Sica from Rome as the new anti-Mafia commissioner in Palermo. Sica was Rome's most trusted judge, having investigated the

P2 Masonic Lodge and the kidnapping by Israeli intelligence of Mordechai Vanunu, the nuclear technician. It only made matters worse.

Falcone resigned immediately. Seven members of the anti-Mafia Pool threatened to follow if he was allowed to go. The head of Palermo's detective squad, Inspector Antonino Nicchi, also quit.

Paolo Borsellino, Falcone's chief confidant, went public to confirm the anger of his colleagues: 'By dissolving the anti-Mafia Pool, the investigations will be split into a thousand pieces. Everything we have worked for during the past five years will simply be tipped out of the window. The police, even now, have no idea what is happening within the Cosa Nostra – because it is already reorganizing, regenerating itself, just as it always does.'

By August, the situation had developed into a political storm. Italian President Francesco Cossiga personally intervened and summoned the Ministers of Justice and the Interior to his palace. Soon afterwards, he ordered the leaders of the five coalition parties to return from their holidays for a conference, demanding action to halt the demise of the Sicilian initiative which he considered vital, if nothing else than for the credibility of the Rome administration.

Cossiga demanded that the Supreme Council of Magistrates re-examine the situation that existed between Falcone and Meli. The result was a depressing negative for the anti-Mafia people. By a narrow margin, Falcone supporters on the council were defeated and it issued a communique denying that the judiciary had gone soft on the Mafia.

Furious, Falcone responded by simply saying: 'We have lost.'

By then, it was becoming apparent that he was right. Lawyers representing the defendants sentenced in the Pizza Connection trial in the US launched an appeal against their sentences issued by the Palermo court in absentia.

The Italian Court of Appeal threw out the maxi-trial convictions against every one of them on the grounds of 'double jeopardy' under the terms of the Italian-American Treaty for Mutual Assistance on Criminal Matters signed in 1982. Judge Corrado Carnevale ruled that coded conversations between suspects, taped-recorded over the telephone in America by the FBI, were too cryptic to be admissible. It was impossible, he said, to be sure that the references were really about drugs.

He ruled that a defendant 'adhering to mafiosi methods . . . could not be considered a member of the organization'. Then he said that a money launderer in the Pizza case could reasonably claim to have been unaware he was handling drug money, although the dollars came in bundles of small-denomination notes, in substantial quantity passed to him by 'Sicilians in the strongest odor of the Mafia'. Every case was thrown out.

Next, dozens of appeals were launched by the convicted Sicilian mafiosi of the Falcone maxi-trials and elsewhere and the unwieldy Italian judicial system took its course. A large number of them would be released, their sentences quashed or with an appeal pending. Even Falcone's most prized defendant, Michele Greco, was cleared on appeal, though he was re-arrested as he walked from the court and charged with a new batch of murders.

These curious events were not restricted to Sicily, either. In Naples, the electoral heartland of Interior Minister Antonino Gava, Michele Zaza, the Camorra boss of bosses and close ally of the Cosa Nostra, had been given a ten-year sentence in 1987 for drug smuggling and an array of other Mafia-related crimes. His arrest was seen by the Neapolitan anti-Mafia unit as a major coup, on a par with the arrest of Michele Greco by the Palermo squad.

In the early summer of 1988, however, Zaza was back in court with his lawyers, having served less than nine months of his sentence. He was granted what is termed under Italian law 'provisional liberty' because of an alleged heart condition, confirmed by a collection of notes from his personal physician. Zaza walked free, and promptly caught a plane to Los Angeles.

By the autumn, several major personalities in the maxi-trials had been set free. Giuseppe Bono and his brother Alfredo, sentenced to forty-one years between them, were out on bail pending appeal and never went back. Antonino Salamone, sentenced to twenty-two years, was allowed home under house arrest by the Supreme Court because of poor health, and he too caught a plane to more peaceful climes.

More serious were the court decisions on appealed cases from the maxi-trial. One case after another was thrown out by the higher court, often at the behest of Judge Corrado Carnevale.

Many were rejected on simple technical grounds such as errors on forms or courtroom mistakes by lawyers, which was perhaps not unexpected in a trial of that magnitude. But to the outside observer all of this would be seen as a nit-picking response to an important list of cases. The final blow came in the autumn when Carnevale rejected the catchall premise on which the maxi-trial had largely been based – that of the defendants belonging to a single criminal entity.

The court ruled that the Mafia was composed of family units each with its own designated territory and with no vertical hierarchical structure. In effect, the court turned the clock back half a century and said the Mafia didn't exist.

Less than a year after the herd had been sentenced to that colossal 2,000 years inside, the cornerstone of the prosecution, the whole basis of the Falcone team's case, as set out by Buscetta, Contorno and the rest, was knocked away.

And so what had been heralded as a major triumph for the anti-Mafia brigade had turned into a bizarre mockery of a determined fight for justice. A supposedly enlightened Italian legal system in truth provided loopholes in abundance through which the defence lawyers could plot an escape route for their clients.

By the end of 1988, only 74 of the original 342 defendants convicted remained in prison. It was the same story elsewhere: 100 of the 120 convicted in Turin, where the judge had handed down 26 life sentences and 700 years of imprisonment, were set free.

As Paolo Borsellino said, it was a mirror of the old days, when mafiosi could be arrested, tried and convicted – and walk out of court.

Even for those who remained inside, the prospect of an early release now seemed a possibility. In 1986, a new law laid down a system of sentence reductions for model prisoners. Good behaviour earned a six-week holiday from prison each year plus a three-month reduction in sentence for every year in jail. Long-term prisoners who had served ten years without trouble would be given semi-liberty in prison near their homes, days outside and nights in. By the beginning of 1989, more than 4,000 prisoners out on release had not returned to complete their sentences. Many were mafiosi, largely from Sicily and the south, serving sentences for kidnapping, drug trafficking and even murder.

Another group yet to qualify for the prison discount system were listed as on sick leave from prison. Their doctors confirmed a number of ailments which required their immediate transfer to private wards in the Civico Hospital.

All of these ridiculous legal shenanigans gave the Mafia its signal – and it moved rapidly to demonstrate that it was neither dead nor buried, not even mortally wounded. It was alive, strong and capable of continuing in exactly the same vein as before. And why not? A good majority of those who had been taken off the streets two years earlier were already back in their old haunts, slick-suited, cocksure and as arrogant as ever.

At the end of September, the Mafia delivered its first message of reassurance to the judiciary and the carabinieri that it was alive and well, and that nothing had changed.

Judge Antonino Saetta, a presiding judge, was one of Sicily's most trusted and revered judges who had devoted his life to strenuously defending the principles of his profession, decrying and exposing corruption and having no truck whatsoever with attempts to influence his decisions. He was due to sit at several important appeals coming up in Palermo in the following few months, resulting from the maxi-trial. He was also a known anti-Mafia campaigner and a strong supporter of the idea that an anti-Mafia unit among the judiciary was the only way to combat the criminal force.

Early on the evening of Sunday, 25 September 1988, Judge Saetta was taking his handicapped son for a drive along quiet country roads outside Palermo. He had no bodyguards or protection. Inevitably, Mafia assassins were watching him. He had been selected as a target to send their message to the judiciary. The gunmen overtook him and pumped a hail of bullets into Saetta and his son, and left them lying dead. His murder was seen as a warning to the magistracy of Palermo who would soon be deciding upon important cases against Mafia people in the second and third maxi-trials already under way in the Palermo bunker courtroom, and the appeals against sentences handed down at the first maxi-trial.

Across the island, a second atrocity was committed the following day when Mauro Rostagno, aged forty-six, was shot dead. He was a left-wing journalist, a former student leader who had since founded a community project for the recuperation of young drug addicts near Trapani. He had regularly spoken out against the Mafia in his articles for newspapers and on television. He had consistently named and condemned local drug pushers and Mafia leaders in the Trapani province. His killing was taken as a warning to the local community: the code of *omertà* was being reinforced once again and anyone who broke it would get the same treatment. It did not need spelling out; everyone knew the reasons.

The three murders once again aroused anger among ordinary citizens. At the funeral service for Judge Saetta and his son, crowds shouted abuse at politicians. Claudio Martelli, deputy leader of the Socialist Party, was embarrassed to find himself in front of a throng of people waving fistfuls of banknotes, the implications of which were inescapable. The crowd had a particular message for Interior Minister Antonio Gava: 'Gava of the Camorra – get out of government.'

After the shooting of Saetta, one of his most senior colleagues, Judge Carmelo Conti, president of the Palermo Court of Appeal, announced his resignation. 'The war against the Mafia is lost,' he declared. 'There is no longer any hope.'

In fact, the shooting of Judge Saetta marked the beginning of another round of bloody killings, as Mafia killers next turned their guns back towards their rivals and the prophecy of the *pentito*, Salvatore Contorno – 'within weeks, you'll be picking up corpses on every street corner' – began to come true.

Within the week, there were seventeen murders and the battle lines of the 1981–3 Mafia wars were drawn again.

On Tuesday 27 September, Contorno's brother-in-law Giuseppe Lombardo, twenty-seven, and his friend Francesco Fricano, twenty-six, were found shot dead in their car in the village of Casteldaccia, on the fringes of Palermo.

The following day, 28 September, Giovanni 'the Lawyer' Bontate, brother of the murdered Stefano Bontate, was sipping espresso coffee with his beautiful wife Francesca in their luxurious villa in a select part of Palermo, opposite the site of an old heroin refinery, when he received visitors. He must have known the callers who had penetrated elaborate security systems at the villa, and it appeared he had been pouring coffee when he was shot in the back of the head by a pistol. His wife, still in a blue silk nightgown, was shot where she sat, reclining in an easy chair.

It was widely believed that Bontate, who was sentenced to eight years at the maxi-trial but had been freed pending appeal, was being repaid for leading the few remaining members of the Bontate clan into an alliance with the Corleonesi. He, according the informers, was the one who betrayed his brother Stefano to the Corleonesi in 1981.

Within hours, there were two more killings. Giuseppe Leone and Giuseppe Agrusa were shot dead by a Kalashnikov aimed from a passing car as they sat drinking coffee outside a bar in Cinisi, twelve miles from Palermo, the family seat of the Badalamentis. Agrusa was among the last surviving members of that family whose leader, Gaetano, had been tucked away in prison after the Pizza trial in the US.

And so it went on, yet in spite of the despair, there was still a burning hope and a dedication among the old anti-Mafia team in Palermo.

Falcone withdrew his resignation, and stayed on to pursue the next round of prosecutions. The feelings of them all were summed up by another his colleagues, Giuseppe Ayala, one of the leading prosecutors in the maxi-trials whose name, he was sure, was high on the hit list. Though he longed for the day when he could walk freely around the city of Palermo with his wife and three daughters, he knew it would never come. His life had been destined to become a security nightmare since he had joined the anti-Mafia initiative five years earlier.

CHAPTER FIFTEEN

A Bomb for Falcone and 400 More Mafiosi – Dead

When Giovanni Falcone agreed to stay on, the news was relayed to the Mafia in New York, and picked up on an FBI wiretap. As might be expected, they were not happy and having failed to dispose of him by rumours, smear tactics and innuendo in an underground campaign of black propoganda, the Sicilians now resorted to other means. Apart from the Mafia, he had also collected an abundance of enemies within the judiciary and among the gentlemen of the Palazzo. 'His critics,' Ferraro explained, 'were people who were unable to admit to themselves that Falcone was a real judge and remained so until he died, regardless of who he upset in the process.'

The campaign to discredit him in any way possible had had a severe effect, even in Palermo itself where the relationship between him and the man appointed by the Ministry of the Interior as Commissioner to combat the Mafia, Domenico Sica, had descended into a strained contact conducted by memo.

The two men barely spoke to each other. Falcone had been particularly angered by the comments of a senior figure in the Ministry who telephoned him from Rome and, incredibly, blamed him for the new outbreak of violence occurring in the badlands of Naples, Calabria and Sicily.

It was a fact that during the first five months of 1989, there were more than 400 murders of Mafia-linked people in those areas and there was obviously a view that Falcone, with his new round of maxi-trial revelations and supergrasses, had disturbed the hornets' nest to such a degree that they were fighting amongst themselves once again.

The year of 1989 was already bad enough for Falcone and the now disbanded anti-Mafia Pool. First, they had been forced to release all but a dozen of the 160 suspects arrested following confessions by a new supergrass, Antonino Calderone, who had turned himself in and began spilling the beans on the Catania Mafia, of which his family had been a major part. His brother, Giuseppe, was head of the regional *cupola* there until he was murdered by the Corleonesi in 1981.

Calderone was considered to rank alongside Buscetta in the quality of his information which, incidentally, included the confession that he had carried out seven murders himself, for which he was destined to receive a long prison sentence. But as important as Calderone was, the ebullience and sheer wanton enthusiasm that had gripped the anti-Mafia investigators in the mid-1980s was slowly ebbing away.

The last of the three maxi-trials ended in a humiliating collapse, largely because of the imminent introduction of new laws passed earlier in the year. The old law which had been part of Pio La Torre's original all-embracing charge of associating with the Mafia was to be replaced by one which required absolute proof of such membership. It had been originally designed to overcome the perpetual difficulty of lack of proof of Mafia crimes, due to the unwillingness of witnesses to give evidence.

Now they had the evidence, but parliament had moved the goalposts. The maxi-trials of 1987 and 1988 had heard the likes of Buscetta, Contorno and others monotonously reeling off the names of people whom they said were members of the Mafia. But, as we have seen, the Supreme Court or the Court of Appeal threw out case after case for lack of 'specific' proof which tied a particular defendant to a particular crime or proof of Mafia membership.

A ruling was even made that membership of the Mafia did not in itself prove criminal activity – in other words, even the theory of a Mafia collective had collapsed. The prosecution also had to prove, beyond doubt, that the suspect was a member of a criminal organization. As Falcone himself admitted, 'We are now placed in the position of having to actually prove the existence of the Cosa Nostra – and under the new system this will not be easy.'

His worst fears were realized on 16 April 1989 when the third and final maxi-trial ended in disarray. The verdicts were devastating for Falcone's team: forty convictions, eighty acquittals. Among the latter, once again, was Michele Greco and even he could not believe it.

'Me? Acquitted?' said the astounded Greco to his lawyer, having listened for the umpteenth time to the *pentiti* accusing him of ordering, as head of the Cosa Nostra *cupola*, some of the worst atrocities in Sicily over the past decade.

'Yes,' the lawyer replied. 'You are free to go.'

He was, at that particular moment. But there were still outstanding matters to be discussed and the police served new arrest warrants for another set of charges before he could disappear into the ether once again.

What made the outcome so controversial was the inconsistency with which the jury returned its verdicts – some men were acquitted, others found guilty on identical evidence. Above all they dismissed the existence of an overall criminal conspiracy – which was tantamount to saying that the Cosa Nostra, the Mafia, did not exist. Falcone was right. They had to go back to square one and prove that there was such a thing as the Mafia.

The dismay of the lawyers and the investigating judges, not to mention the police, was evident. The president of the Parliamentary Anti-Mafia Commission scribbled a note to the President of Italy: 'Dear Cossiga: the Mafia has won.'

In Palermo, the state prosecutor, Gianfranco Garofalo, declared: 'I just did not believe my ears. I truly cannot believe this is happening. This city just swallows up its dead and its scandals. You listen to the anti-Mafia fanfares, and they are followed by mass arrests and big trials. Then the State walks away, the citizens lose interest and you suddenly realize – nothing had changed. We are back to year zero.' The following month it became official, or as near as possible to an official declaration: an appeal court judge in Rome actually ruled that there was no proof the Mafia existed. The result of the Palermo trial was a crucial one because upon these decisions rested the future, by implication, of a host of other cases still in abeyance, either at Supreme Court level or at the Court of Appeal which had already been given its warning with the murder of Judge Saetta. Thereafter, a succession of cases were thrown out. The anti-Mafia movement was in deep gloom and in those darkest hours, they were saying quietly to themselves that the Mafia had beaten the system with the help of the system itself, aided by covert people in their pay.

In the wake of the collapse of the last trial, the blood-letting began again: eighteen murders in as many days and they included several who had just been acquitted.

The police then learned of an astonishing development. Salvatore Contorno had gone missing from his protective compound in the US. Just after the latest acquittal verdicts were announced, he had given the slip to his American minders in the Witness Protection Programme and apparently flown to Rome, then on to Palermo.

His arrival coincided with a fresh outbreak of killings, and soon it was being said that Contorno had launched a personal vendetta to avenge the murders of twenty members of his own family and friends. Smear tactics were quickly brought into play. An anonymous note to the Ministry of Justice suggested that Contorno had been given 'permission' to wage this private war by Falcone himself, on the basis that what the courts had failed to do, he could do himself as executioner and the law in Palermo would turn a blind eye and then allow him to return to the US without hindrance. It was one of many pieces of black propaganda that Falcone had to suffer.

Contorno was recaptured after a tip-off. Police raided a farmhouse twelve miles outside Palermo at dawn on 26 May 1989. They immediately tested him for forensic clues that might link him to the recent crop of murders, without success, and he was returned to his protective environment. Only he knows how many, if any, of the recent deaths were at his own hand. But he was angry, all right: 'I put my life at risk to testify against the Corleonesi and the rest, and now they are all being let free,' he told the police.

Though the events of the previous eight or nine months had represented a devastating reversal for Falcone's people, he and a close-knit group of colleagues did not give up. As Ferraro confirmed, they were in deep despair at the time having witnessed the attacks from within, as well as from the Mafia itself. The disbandment of the group, the court reversals of all they had worked for, the threats, the unending killings, were sufficient to excuse them for wanting to pack their bags and 'get the hell out of it'. Any one of them could have secured a far safer role in life in industry, just as several senior figures in the FBI had recently done.

But they did not. Caponetto, Falcone, Borsellino, Ferraro and the rest spoke passionately and dramatically of 'destiny' and the need to go on, continue the fight. It was, however, patently obvious to all close observers – and even more so now with the benefit of hindsight – that as soon as their attack against the Mafia looked to be succeeding, a new level of criminal influence became apparent and to some degree explained why, at that moment in history, it was impossible for the judiciary alone to even begin to eradicate the Mafia. The problem was not simply to wipe out the top men in a criminal syndicate.

By then, also, there was a new dimension. By the beginning of 1989, the production and distribution of cocaine from South America had shot off the graph. The cocaine explosion was creating even greater sums of black money, a fact which Falcone himself quite readily appreciated because a large portion of it was ending up in Italy. Heroin production remained the Mafia's principal source of revenue for the time being, but it had already made moves to corner the European market in cocaine. Even as the maxi-trials were going on, the CIA and the DEA had tracked continuing meetings between Mafia chiefs and the cocaine cartels of Columbia and Bolivia.

The fininacial implications were already becoming the subject of panic memos within the financial community. A decade of Sicilian drug trafficking had produced vast, secret stockpiles of money invested through the length and breath of Italy, in industry, property and government bonds. Other billions were afloat in the world currency markets. In 1989, a report produced for the European Parliament calculated staggering figures of narco-cash awash in the system. Top secret reports compiled earlier by the US National Security Agency for the Reagan Administration (carrying a note threatening 'criminal sanctions for unauthorised disclosure') sent Washington statisticians into a panic, estimated that the global narcotics industry produced revenue, from source to retail, of the barely believable figure of half a trillion US dollars.

This was the backdrop for the Sicilian battles. In 1989, the year Falcone sought to break through the mysteries of Mafia money, he was seeking information on specifics. The new laws demanded precise proof of accusations which might be made against a suspect. The word of the *pentiti* was no longer sufficient to secure a conviction and he had already begun talks with international banking authorities, notably the Swiss.

'Falcone by then,' said Ferraro, 'was determined to achieve greater levels of international cooperation. He talked about it endlessly and he was especially interested in trying to break the secrecy of the banks.'

The Swiss had readily responded, stating that they had every wish to assist in tracking suspected drug funds deposited in Switzerland. They provided chapter and verse on two accounts in which more than $200 million had been deposited and had been moving in and out, obviously being used for currency dealing as well as drug trafficking.

Falcone invited officials from Switzerland to Palermo for talks to attempt to unravel some of the complicated financial scenarios with which he was presented. He had planned the meeting around the time he rented a holiday villa at Addaura to spend a brief time with his family. His plans which he often kept vague for security reasons, were in this instance known in advance and were obviously leaked to the Mafia by a spy in his camp.

It presented an occasion when Falcone might be off guard, although the villa was carefully checked and was surrounded by bodyguards. Quite by chance, one of them caught sight of a coloured bag in the rocks, close to where Falcone would be sitting enjoying the view in a brief respite from the bunker in Palermo.

He went to investigate and discovered the bag contained a bomb: 45 kilos of dynamite, fitted with timer denonators set to go off within the hour. Since access to the villa by land was carefully monitored the only route in for the bombers was by sea, probably by a frogman using a boat during the previous night.

If Falcone ever doubted that the Mafia was intent on killing him at the earliest opportunity, he knew it now.

The setbacks Falcone experienced in 1989 were mirrored by events surrounding Palermo's other great anti-Mafia campaigner, the mayor of the city, Leoluca Orlando. 'It began as a struggle for power between conflicting factions of the Christian Democrats,' Orlando recalled in 1994. 'And as the months wore on, it became clear that I was on the wrong side.'

In what seemed to outsiders a complicated political structure, the contest for leadership of the Christian Democrats had developed over the years into a battle that was almost as important as a general election itself. As a party, the Christian Democrats had dominated Italian politics since the invading US forces gave them the route to power in 1944. Within the party, however, there were factions who had fallen in behind particular leaders, like Moro, Piccoli, Fanfani, Andreotti and De Mita. The power of each particular leader was dependent upon the number of members of parliament behind him.

The political power-base of Sicily had always been of vital importance in this leadership race and in shaping the national parliament. The Mafia had, since 1944, always held sway with its influence over voting patterns on the island. Its leaders openly, and truthfully, boasted that they could make or break a particular politician.

In Palermo, a city of 700,000, it was said the Mafia controlled 180,000 votes. For the province of Catania, it was said to be 200,000. As the *pentito* Antonino Calderone from Catania had explained to Falcone: 'In my area, there were eighteen voting districts and each one of them contained not less than three families, spreading out across the community. That's how important the Mafia was to the politicians.'

These figures barely hint at the web of political and economic patronage enjoyed by the Mafia since the war. As every DC leader knew, the Mafia could influence the colour of the government. Several times, in past elections, regional Christian Democrat MPs found themselves ousted if they had earned the displeasure of Mafia families who switched their alliance to the Socialists or the Republicans to teach them a lesson.

For years, the Sicilian CD vote had fallen in behind Giulio

Andreotti. In 1985, Ciriaco De Mita had taken the leadership of the Christian Democrats and guided his five-party coalition government through knife-edge diplomacy. In 1989, he lost the leadership and was succeeded as Prime Minister by Andreotti, the veteran prize-fighter of the Christian Democrat movement and a dominant figure for three decades.

Leoluca Orlando had lost his patron. De Mita was the man who had given him the quiet authority to hit the Mafia where it hurt: through their building contracts. Now, that support had gone and Orlando's own power in Palermo was swept away. He had stitched up his own political alliance to hang on to power, but without De Mita, it seemed a lost cause.

The crunch came in that year of 1989, when the Christian Democrats were nominating candidates for the European Parliament and wanted Orlando to stand with Salvo Lima, the so-called King of Palermo, a former mayor who led his successor, the disgraced Vito Ciancimino, into office. It was also a fact that when Falcone and his team went through their most recent reversals, when they were at their darkest hour, Lima gave no quarter. He openly warned Falcone to back off. He was finished.

At a swank reception at the Norman Palace in Palermo that year, attended by Andreotti and dignatories from the European parliament, Lima said in a coded speech, openly taunting Falcone: 'Do not look for skeletons in our wardrobes. You will find only evening suits.' And everyone laughed.

A few months later, in the Hotel President, the regional DC was to make its selection of candidates for the EC parliament. Orlando, knowing that Lima was locally termed as a 'polluted politician' refused to take part. 'I told them it was him or me,' Orlando said. 'I asked the party to choose – and they chose him, and so I resigned.'

Andreotti, who had flown in from Rome for the occasion, boasted of his man's success – in spite of murmurings of Lima's past and present association with leading Mafia figures. The Parliamentary Anti-Mafia Commission produced a 34-page report on Lima, voicing their suspicions about his connections, and noting his past favouritism to Mafia-linked companies.

Andreotti said, 'My friend is being unjustly slandered.' Lima was elected to the European parliament for the third time and remained within the circle of Andreotti's most trusted advisers.

For Leoluca Orlando it was, temporarily, the end of the road. Although the handsome, charismatic and courageous politician secured more votes than any other councillor in the new elections, his party rejected him as mayor for a second term. He wanted to form a coalition government for the region, taking account of all interests. The Christian Democrats insisted on a single-party administration – and Orlando resigned from the DC.

On 4 January 1990 he moved further towards his all-out campaign against the stink of political corruption and Mafia domination of his city, and throughout Italy. With thirty other like-minded individuals, he formed a new political party called La Rete (The Net) with a high moral and ethical theme, linked directly to an anti-Mafia stance. His co-founders included General Dalla Chiesa's son Nando in Milan and the son of the Catania newspaper editor murdered by the Mafia, Giuseppe Fava. Orlando was elected to the Sicilian regional parliament in La Rete colours in 1991 and to the national parliament in 1992. 'There exists in this country,' said Orlando, 'a crisis of impunity. It is the kind of impunity that exists in banana republics, for the friends of dictators. There is a risk that Italy will infect the rest of the Continent with its disease.'

CHAPTER SIXTEEN

A Supreme Court Judge, a Euro-MP and an Anti-Mafia Fighter – Dead

Ferraro had returned to the Ministry of Justice in Rome, where she continued to observe the mounting despair of Falcone and his team and to the surprise of everyone she would soon be joined there by Falcone himself. Months of legal wrangling in 1990 promised no end to the reversals suffered by the anti-Mafia group so widely acclaimed for its successes at the maxi-trials. 'Falcone was immensely disappointed by these developments,' she recalled. 'We all were, of course. He was a very fair and honest jurist, and in his view there was no question of the guilt of these men who were being released on technicalities. But we as jurists knew better than anyone that a court decision is one which must be accepted.'

Falcone, interviewed on television, was not ready to accept the developing situation without protest. He was angrily critical of the 'ulitilization of our laws' to the benefit of the criminal. He was especially bitter about the scenes in court when convicted killers were released. Lawyers representing them joined relatives and others in rushing to their cages to shake their hands and embrace them as if they were heroes. 'We will soon see the results of this folly,' Falcone predicted. 'The massacres and the murders are already starting up again. We are basically back to square one – it is no better than it was ten years ago.'

For all of them, it seemed that the years of confinement in the security bunkers, all the physical pressure and the mental strain of living under the constant threat of assassination had been an absolute waste. It was during this time that an additional code in Italian law came into being which had the direct effect of assisting the convicted mafiosi, rather than the judiciary.

It provided a mandatory twelve-month limit on the time between conviction and appeal. This along with other time-limits between arrest and charge, trial and conviction, had the effect of putting the overloaded judiciary in a strait-jacket. In October 1990, 100 magistrates in Sicily and the south of Italy threatened to resign en bloc unless the government in Rome did not do more to help them.

The Ministry of Justice responded by promising changes which would exclude defendants associated with organized crime, i.e. the Mafia, from the liberal early release clauses of the Italian penal system and create stronger measures to ensure the protection of informers. But the amendments to the law took months to pass through the system, and came too late. By the year's end what remained of the original pool of judges, now operating singly, had been overtaken by an air of dejection and rejection. Giovanni Falcone himself remained the object of vicious rumour campaigns and anonymous letters to his superiors.

In February 1991 what looked to be the final humiliation of the anti-Mafia team was delivered once again by the Supreme Court Judge Corrado Carnevale when he handed down his verdict on the remaining lower-court convictions of the reputed leaders and gangsters. He released a further twenty-eight previously convicted men and the judgement was made on the basis of a legal technicality – that which made it illegal to detain prisoners for more than twelve months between their conviction and appeal.

Carnevale ruled that it was his 'duty to apply the law even if it has unwelcome effects'. With his latest decision he had effectively overturned virtually every major verdict made by the lower courts in the previous four years. Once again, among those he released was the *cupola* leader Michele Greco, on the basis that the prosecution had missed a court appearance deadline. The man who was earlier convicted of eleven of the seventy-eight murders with which he was originally accused in 1987, walked free on the slender principle of a legal loophole rather than any new evidence in his defence.

Inevitably, Judge Carnevale was castigated by Falcone's supporters and investigated for possible Mafia connections. He maintained, however, that he had no choice – in his reading of it, the law had to be rigidly applied, whether to mafiosi or simple muggers. He could not differentiate.

Michele Greco was ordered to leave the province of Palermo and choose a town in Sicily of not more than 10,000 for his residence, and report daily to the police. However, in the outrage that again followed he was re-arrested. Other Mafia leaders released at the same time included Francesco Spadaro, nicknamed Little Franco, who had been described at his trial as 'the most ferocious killer in the service of the Mafia'. He stayed out. Similarly, another of the Cosa Nostra's reputed ambassadors to Naples, Stefano Fidanzati, who was said to 'control all business links between the Corleonesi and the Camorra' was freed, as was one of his associates in Naples, Umberto Ammaturo, a suave and handsome Camorrist serving fifteen years. He was in very poor health in prison, and was allowed to go out under house arrest to recuperate and made a miraculous recovery. He moved into a hotel in northern Italy where he submitted to the release system of 'house arrest' but was last seen driving away in a red Ferrari driven by a young woman. He turned up a few weeks later in Brazil, was arrested, escaped again and has not been seen since.

There was another curious anomaly which became known as the sick-note to freedom, where prisoners were allowed out for medical treatment. Pietro Vergengo, a Mafia leader from western Sicily serving a life sentence for murder, was admitted to the urology ward of a Palermo hospital for treatment without any proper guard and promptly vanished. There were simply insufficient police or prison warders to keep them in custody during these excursions. 'If they do not escape,' said Vittorio Aliquo, one of the Palermo prosecutors at the time, 'it is only thanks only to their own good will.'

The whole situation had developed into a farce, a chaotic mesmerizing of the law. Even Toto Riina, the external head of the Corleonesi who was sentenced in absentia to life imprisonment, was absolved. These and other rulings in the previous few months meant that most of the major criminals who had been sent to prison during the maxi-trials were now back on the streets and it now seemed that the whole expense of building the new courthouse, the twenty-one months of trial hearings, followed by months of appeals and Supreme Court sittings costing billions of lire, were all for nothing.

The outspokenness of Falcone was widely believed to have had a lot to do with the next development, although it was denied by himself and to me by Ferraro. In April 1991, he was summoned to the Ministry of Justice in Rome for talks with the Socialist Claudio Martelli who had been deputy prime minister to Giulio Andreotti in his five-party coalition government, and had taken over as Minister of Justice.

Other government changes at the time included the departure of the much criticized and taunted Minister of the Interior, Antonio Gaza, who had been replaced by Vincenzo Scotti who was, like Martelli and Falcone, publicly committed to ridding society 'of this cancer'. In that respect, the political balance seemed quite suddenly tilted towards the Falcone way of thinking, though it must be said that the politicians now in charge of subduing the nation's criminals were, by and large, reacting to public pressure and the demands of the media, the university professors and the sociologists. The time had come for change in Italy's whole approach to law and order and Falcone would figure prominently.

In April, after his meeting with the Justice Ministry, Falcone accepted the offer of a transfer to Rome to become Director of Penal Affairs, a wide-ranging brief which included not merely the administration of the judiciary and liaison with the security and police forces, but also had a say in the formulation and eventual execution of new laws.

Falcone took as his deputy in this task Liliana Ferraro who recalled the quite mixed reaction he received when he accepted the job. There was a good deal of sneering, she said, and lack of understanding about what Falcone intended. There were strong voices in Palermo who considered he had abandoned the fight, that he had been taken in by the government to be silenced, because he was too much of a nuisance on the outside. There were many such accusations. Even Palermo's most vociferous anti-Mafia public official, mayor Leoluca Orlando, questioned whether Falcone had been conned by the politicians. 'The fact that he had switched chairs,' said Ferraro, 'was a deliberate choice. He anguished about it and decided to take the job because he saw it as a natural extension to his work in discovering what more could be done against the Mafia. There were those who, for reasons I cannot fathom, could not understand this and so, really, understood nothing of Giovanni Falcone.'

Orlando had already been critical of the Sicilian judiciary, including Falcone, for what he described as 'half-hearted' investigations into political associations and politically motivated murders by the Mafia. Falcone swept aside the allegations. He had not changed sides, he said, and he was as determined as ever to pursue the Mafia in every quarter, political or otherwise. His commitment had not changed, and he saw his organizational role in Rome as important as his prosecutory one in Palermo had been. He had long conversations with Ferraro before accepting the job, and eventually decided that he could do more good on the inside, from the seat of government, from where he could make his opinions known directly to those who passed the laws. Ferraro was adamant; Falcone had no intention of giving up the fight. Far from it.

It could perhaps only happen within the context of the complicated relationships between Sicily and Rome that a judge taking up the second most important job in the Ministry of Justice could, paradoxically, be perceived as abandoning the fight against organized crime and allowing himself to be drawn into the web of the politicians. It was in many ways an alarming paradox. Falcone was plunged into the midst of the gentlemen of the Palazzo and in the eyes of many, the most potent investigative force of the anti-Mafia brigade on the island of Sicily, and indeed the whole of Italy, had been neutralized.

It was being said that the man who had become the symbol of anti-Mafia forces in Sicily had agreed to move after realizing that it would not be possible to make any further progress with his investigations into the higher reaches of the Mafia, where politics and organized crime were inextricably linked.

Falcone dismissed these criticisms through his positive response to the job and began working towards a legal solution to bringing back to the courts as many as possible of those men who had been freed over the past few months.

What he knew, from figures not generally available, was that when he went to Rome in April 1991 of the 374 people sent to prison during the maxi-trials, less than three dozen remained inside.

But this was no localized Sicilian problem. From the Minister of the Interior, Vincenzo Scotti, Falcone discovered figures which confirmed a terrifying national scandal: in the twelve months since July 1990, 100,000 dangerous criminals had been released from Italian jails. The majority were actually freed in accordance with the system of non-custodial sentences, which ranged from probation to house arrest, the latter having been introduced to make more room in Italy's overcrowded prisons. But of the total, 22,000 had been released on legal technicalities, such as the expiry of the time allowed between arrest and trial, or between conviction and appeal.

One other statistic from the Ministry of the Interior also confirmed in cold, hard figures the truth of Falcone's forecast of a further outbreak of mass murders and vendetta killings in the wake of the release from prison of so many ardent criminals.

They showed that to June 1991, Mafia-related murders nationally had run at the rate of three a day for the previous eighteen months: a total of 1,643 deaths. The majority were in the south and Sicily where death on the streets had once again become a daily occurrence. The region covered by the 'Ndrangheta was particularly bloody. In Calabria, the stronghold of this fierce band of Cosa Nostra cousins, the murder rate was put at 63 per 100,000 inhabitants – which per capita gave it a higher violence rating than New York. The murders had made little impact, coming in ones and twos, outside of their particular province or city. It was only when they were put together under one aggregate number of deaths for the nation as a whole that the sheer impact of the Mafia murder tally could be seen.

On their arrival in Rome in April, Falcone, Ferarro and liked-minded colleagues began working towards reversing the reversals, lobbying their way towards getting the maxi-trial verdicts reinstated, and the Mafia bosses put back inside. They succeeded in the early summer when the Palazzo itself approved an order to take back the forty Mafia bosses who had been released. It was the first time in Italian history, and perhaps in any constitutional state, that the executive overruled judicial power and signed a warrant of arrest.

The move produced a lively debate among the judiciary and a ferocious response from lawyers representing two of the re-arrested *capomafiosi*, the brothers Gaetano and Salvatore Greco, who represented a strong case challenging the constitutional legitimacy of the action.

Judge Antonio Scopelliti, in the Supreme Court, rejected their claim and confirmed the arrest. In June 1991, further applications were made to Scopelliti, asking him to ratify the result of the first maxi-trial and especially the most important decision that established the existence of the *cupola*, and in turn the uniqueness of the Mafia as a criminal organization.

On this decision would rest the future of bosses like Michele Greco, Pippo Calo and Pietro Vernengo, and perhaps even Luciano Liggio himself. According to the testimony of later *pentiti*, the *cupola* called an emergency meeting and decided that there was only one thing to do: kill Scopelliti. With his elimination, it would be necessary for a substitute judge to take over, and he would have to study once again the thousands of pages of documents gathered by Falcone for the maxi-trial. Many months would pass before they would be ready to proceed and in the meantime, the mandatory time factor would have expired, and all would go free.

On 8 August 1991 Judge Scopelliti drove to the villa in Calabria where he was born, for a brief stay to consider the forthcoming trial and reread his documentation. He was driving his BMW along a quiet country road on his way from the seaside when he was apparently stopped. Mafia assassins, probably from the 'Ndrangheta in view of the murder weapon used, were waiting for him, and hit him with two cartridges fired from a shotgun into the back of his neck, blowing off half his head.

They tried to make it look like a crime of passion. Scopelliti, a handsome 56-year-old, was divorced and had a reputation as a womanizer. The word was put out, and believed for a brief while, that it was a murder which had a romantic assignation as its cause.

Falcone scented the trick immediately and the misconception over the murder was quickly put right. Furthermore, Scopelliti was rapidly replaced by Judge Arnaldo Valente who began work immediately, round the clock, to read up on the cases he would take over, and on which the future liberty or otherwise of so many mafiosi rested.

Renewed public outrage was heightened when the Mafia followed the murder of Judge Scopelliti with a new atrocity. Two weeks later in a clear demonstration of their power, the Mafia moved against a man who woke up one morning and decided he was going to make a stand against them.

The story of Libero Grassi, a middle-aged Palermo businessman who had lived all his life in the city, had a loving wife and family and was a respected member of the local community, is a poignant one. Grassi, sixty-seven, was a successful industrialist making dressing gowns and nightwear. He had a thriving business which employed 100 people and had an annual turnover of seven billion lire ($5.5 million). This did not go unnoticed by the Cosa Nostra who in the mid-1980s demanded their share.

Grassi refused, and the first sign of trouble came when his guard dog was found bludgeoned to death and dumped outside his factory gates. Then the telephone calls began – day and night – whose continual message was that Grassi would suffer if he did not avail himself of the security of 'protection'. He didn't, and three masked men armed with shotguns held up his wages department and stole 60 million lire.

Soon afterwards, he was invited to contribute 30 million lire to help the defence of three 'friends in jail'. He refused again, and this time broke the Mafia rule of going public – he denounced the threat of violence towards him in the pages of the Palermo newspaper, *Il Giornale de Sicilia,* said he would not pay and became a national hero, as the media flocked to the city to tell his story.

There was, of course, nothing unusual about the Mafia's demands for *pizzo* (protection). It was, and still is, widely believed that as many as eight out of ten businesses in every Mafia stronghold have been paying out a percentage of turnover for *pizzo* to the Mafia for decades. There was nothing new in that; it was always regarded as one of the Mafia's traditional forms of income, and by local business as just another tax they had to pay.

What made Grassi different was that he refused, declared his refusal publicly and campaigned among his fellow businessman, trying to persuade them to join him in the boycott. 'The result was,' his son Davide recalled, 'we were isolated by the local business community. We were shunned by our friends who would turn away rather than be seen with us. Members at the yacht club refused to drink with him. My father could barely believe the reaction he received from others who he tried to get to join him. It was obscene, and of course the local chamber of trade always denied knowledge of any such payments.'

But now Grassi was a national figure, written about in the newspapers and interviewed on television, and in the villages, towns and cities where protection was a way of life, a reaction began to stir. At that point, the Mafia decided to act. In late August 1991, the Cosa Nostra assassins set out to make an example of Grassi and reassert their strength and their power, and let others know what would happen it they, like he, refused to pay the *pizzo*. Grassi was gunned down outside his house on the outskirts of Palermo in typical Mafia style, in a hail of bullets.

In the business community, Grassi's heroism was seen as an act of gross folly. Many sympathetic words were spoken, but few who would be publicly identified would speak in his support. His murder merely highlighted an element of Mafia activity which has been overshadowed in these pages by other atrocities more often connected with the drugs traffic. It showed once again that beneath this strata of high-profile activity, the Mafia continued its traditional forms of extortion, blackmail and kidnapping with as much vigour as ever.

Professor Franco Cazzola of Catania University carried out a study of the *pizzo* phenomenon and estimated that 90 per cent of businesses in the south of Italy and in Sicily were forced to pay, and a lesser percentage in the north were facing the same problem. Arson attacks and violence were the usual forms of vengeance against those who refused.

The National Federation of Small Businesses made a similar study and estimated that the Mafia collected $2.3 million a year from its members in extortion and groups of traders in Naples even petitioned the government to allow the *pizzo* to be tax deductible. Thousands of small business were going bust because of the Mafia's demands, and others who wished to start up were stifled by the fear of *pizzo*.

In Palermo itself, there was even a move to get the banks to arrange special low-cost loans for new businesses which categorically refused to become involved with the protection racketeers. It found little support.

And so Libero Grassi became the most famous of another smaller, but important list of Illustrious Corpses – those who had defied the extortionists and had been assassinated, now numbering eight in the previous ten years in Palermo alone.

The killing brought a new national outcry. Grassi was typified as the hero who stood out alone, and was cut down just as quickly. Even newspapers abroad carried the photograph of this courageous man. In Milan, where the Mafia's presence was increasingly evident, especially in the business and financial world, one of its daily newspapers, *Corriere della Sera*, attacked the slovenly attitude of successive governments to the problem of organized crime which had reached 'every corner, every nook and cranny of Italian life'.

It was a statement that had been heard repeatedly through modern Italian history, and each time the government had promised action. The newspaper produced a list of all the unfulfilled promises made by government in the wake of each Mafia atrocity in the past decade – and concluded that nothing had been achieved by these waves of sudden activity which usually faltered at the second hurdle, if not the first.

Interior Minister Scotti, goaded by Falcone, promised to bring swift government action to what he perceived as an emergency situation which required emergency laws similar to those brought in to help Dalla Chiesa fight the terrorists in the late 1970s.

He wanted suspected mafiosi to be held in custody until proven innocent, regardless of the time between trial and appeal, which Falcone had also campaigned for. There would be additional police and greater powers of co-ordination between the police and the judiciary. There would be renewed effort to arrest and keep inside all those Mafia bosses whose names had become famous through the maxi-trials and who were now languishing in their luxury villas by the seaside or in their penthouse apartments high above the city skylines. This was a political declaration, made by a man who was a member of the Christian Democrats. The message, it was said, ought to have been clear.

If it wasn't enough, the one from Judge Arnaldo Valente surely was. On 30 January 1992, presiding over the Supreme Court, he began reconfirming many of the sentences imposed by the first of the maxi-trials. The fight-back was in progress again. One by one, all those familiar names were called again, back to the cages and to prison. He confirmed what had become known as the Theory of Buscetta in the fight against the central controlling power of the *cupola*: that the bosses are caught, remain in prison for life and so the atrocious murders become useless.

Sure enough, the judgement is perceived among the mafiosi as the worst. Words, according to the *pentiti* of 1994, could not describe their fury. One of the foundations of the Cosa Nostra was its guarantee of impunity. The Men of Honour, in the past, have always known that they could rely upon help, legally or illegally, from the Third Level, the 'associates' in higher places. Now, it is no longer available. The door, it would seem, had been slammed shut in their face. The bosses were rampaging around Palermo, exclaiming that someone was going to pay for this – and how.

Forty-eight hours after one more series of damaging court decisions, the selection was made. A general election had been called for 5 April 1992 and the name of a most senior politician was put in the frame for a liquidation. He was Salvo Lima, seven times mayor of Palermo, the king of the property and building boom of the sixties and seventies, close friend of Prime Minister Giulio Andreotti since 1968, member of the European Parliament since 1978, close ally of the disgraced former mayor Vito Ciancimino who was sentenced to three years for Mafia association and was currently under house arrest.

Lima left home in Mondello, the wealthy seaside resort west

of Palermo, just after 10 a.m. on 12 March 1992. He drove his official car, a dark blue Opel, with two political aides as passengers. It was perhaps a sign of his feeling of security that he was one of the few public officials in Palermo who did not have a permanent bodyguard. He was said to have considered himself 'untouchable'.

As he headed out along the Viale delle Palme towards Palermo, a red Kawasaki motorcycle overtook him, drew level and slowed down. The pillion passenger raised a gun, sighted it and opened fire. Two bullets passed through the windcsreen on either side of the steering wheel. Lima skidded to a halt, got out of the car and began running along the road towards a nearby house. The motorcycle turned and roared back towards him. Lima had run about fifty metres and was within a few feet of an entrance to the Villa Blanca when they caught up with him.

The pillion rider fired twice. The bullets both hit a tree. Lima kept on running, and reached the gates of the villa when two more shots rang out in quick succession, hitting him in the head and neck. Then a whole magazine of bullets was emptied into his body. The red Kawasaki roared off, and was later found abandoned and set alight.

Lima had often been described as a 'polluted' politician, but this did not lessen the shock of the murder which brought the Mafia to the heart of European politics. The Christian Democrat Party put out a statement which said that the assassination of Lima 'put to shame those who have persistently accused him of being close to the Mafia. All those who consciously and unconsciously launched falsehood and calumny must feel the weight of things which were said unjustly.'

Others were more realistic in their appraisal of Lima's killing. It was exactly because of his association with the Mafia and his failure to prevent Falcone and the rest from continuing their attempts to have the maxi-trials' sentences ratified that Lima was murdered.

Antonio Caponetto, one of Sicily's most respected examining magistrates, founder of the Pool and spiritual mentor of Falcone and Paolo Borsellino, explained: 'Lima for years developed the role of intermediary between the Mafia and politics. He was without doubt one of the most senior links, though only one of several. He was killed when the Corleonesi realized that Lima could no longer guarantee them anything, not even his silence – and his death, twenty-five days from the general election, was a warning, that promises to the Mafia are sacred and have to be kept.'

Beyond that, Lima's assassination became the hot potato of the year for Prime Minister Andreotti. As Caponetto confirmed, Lima was a key man in Andreotti's circle as well as in his political machine in organization and electioneering. There was never much doubt that the Mafia was in the shadows of Lima's activities, though Andreotti himself denied any knowledge or even suspicion of these connections.

Even at the end, Andreotti maintained his stance, and after Lima's death, said, 'Slanderers are worse than assassins. My friend Lima was unfairly accused for years and when slander and hatred get together, an assassination is on its way. I always tried to investigate the insinuations against him but always found nothing.'

Even then, Andreotti must have known that he himself would face an inquisition about Mafia association. He was stepping out on a long and muddy trail. As Lima was buried, investigators were already on their way from Rome to the US to question the star *pentiti* about what they knew of Lima, Andreotti and the Mafia's political connections.

A new era in the fight had begun.

Even as Sicily swarmed with security forces after the killing of Lima, there was to be one more audacious act on the very eve of the general election – undoubtedly a killing designed to strike fear among voters and send the message that the Mafia was still in control in the villages and the towns, regardless of the show of force. On that day, Giuliano Guazzelli, a fifty-nine-year-old captain in the Carabinieri who was deeply involved in a judicial investigation against a mafia family in the province of Agrigento, was selected as the target. He was gunned down in the streets that were so familiar to himself and his family and, after a lifetime in the service of his country, became one more terrible statistic in the continuing horror of the Illustrious Corpses.

CHAPTER SEVENTEEN

Giovanni Falcone, his Wife and Four Bodyguards – Dead

In the confines of their office on the fourth floor of the Ministry of Justice in Rome, Falcone and Ferraro spent long days and nights plotting and planning the renewed attack from within. They were in the office early, six days a week, invariably lunched on sandwiches and were usually still in their offices well into the evening. Falcone's wife Francesca, herself a magistrate, would often join them. Security was as intense as ever.

Falcone and his wife lived in a tiny three-roomed flat inside police barracks. Ferraro lived close by. The need for protection had increased rather than diminished and to get to work each morning, a journey of a mere 400 yards, entailed the whole machinery of bomb-inspections of vehicles, look-outs for suspicious movements and travel by wailing bullet-proof cars into the Ministry of Justice compound, through the barrier manned by machine-gun carrying carabinieri.

Far from abandoning the fight, as he had been accused of doing by some of his former associates in Palermo, he had thrown himself in at the deep end with renewed passion. 'By now his contact with other countries was increasing all the time,' Ferraro recalled. 'So he did a great deal of travelling and was generally feted wherever he went. I used to tell him he was like a rock star. He did not like that because he was a very simple man, but it was how people were seeing him, in that kind of fame which is unfamiliar to those of us in this profession.'

Because of his experience, he knew how to establish his position and foster some important changes, predominantly to re-establish a pool of special anti-Mafia fighters. Ferraro recalls:

> Within one year there was a revolution going on at the Ministries of Justice and the Interior – a series of new measures came into effect which were part of a measured plan promoted by Falcone, not a haphazard reappraisal of existing laws that changed on the spur of the moment each time there was an emergency or an atrocity. From the beginning of Falcone's time in Rome, we introduced a new department specializing in Mafia affairs. We initiated new laws to protect the *pentiti*, who until then had no protection at all. We established a pool of twenty-six people and it was Falcone's idea to have a clear design and an organized attack against the Mafia and indeed all aspects of racketeering and corruption. It was the first time in Italian history that such laws had been submitted and approved and today [in 1994] the results of those laws have become very evident. Falcone always believed that collaboration between all parties, and other countries, was vital to any investigation. The judiciary, by disposing of the united effort, would become a divided force against the Mafia network, which is united. He did not, as some feared, intend to bypass the autonomy of the magistracy. He just wanted to be sure that they were all pulling together. From the Mafia's point of view, the risk was clear, that such a plan would allow the pool of knowledge to be reorganized and maintained.

Falcone achieved much of his success through an upsurge of public and media outcry in the wake of the recent assassinations. With the monotony of an old record stuck in a groove, people said that something was going to be done. That repetitive song of politicians and kings the world over had turned up over and over again. This time, wheels were turning, slowly and at times even going in reverse, but they were moving.

Falcone intended to keep them turning and though he did not appreciate it then, he had already sparked off the beginnings of a chain reaction of events that would go far beyond his imagined outcome.

He had never attempted to quantify the results of what he and the anti-Mafia team, along with all those the Mafia had killed off every time they came close, had set in motion. As far as he was concerned, and it is a philosophy reiterated by Ferraro herself, it was a fight against the Mafia and it would lead him to wherever the trail stopped. As the months wore on, however, he found himself immersed ever deeper in the world he had to some extent tried to avoid, that of politics and more particularly that mysterious Italian phenomenon, the so-called *sotto governo.*

This in literal terms meant 'the underneath government' – the subterranean machinations of the power game, the invisible side of political domination, exercised through electoral patronage and the apparatus of the state, such as the police, the security services, the bureaucrats and indirect control of the judiciary. For years, and it was still the case even after the 1994 general election, the group that controlled the *sotto governo* actually held greater power than the democratically elected executive, as represented by the Cabinet.

This, by and large, had been in the hands of the Christian Democrats until the 1992 election, when Giulio Andreotti departed the scene in the wake of scandalous allegations against him. In Milan, Judge Antonino Di Pietro had followed Falcone's lead and had just begun his controversial 'clean hands' investigations into corruption in Italian business and political life. That particular line of inquiry, coupled with Falcone's own efforts, led to the biggest explosion in Italian political history.

It was during this period that Falcone promoted changes in the law governing the *pentiti,* who had begun to come forward in increasing numbers. Falcone wanted to encourage more collaborators with new laws aimed at providing limited protection on the lines of the US programme and allowing for the previously barred facility of plea-bargaining.

But the most crucial element on the attacking front was the formation of the DIA (Directorate of Anti-Mafia Investigation), an elite force similar to the FBI whose principal aim was to coordinate all the efforts in a single attack on organized crime.

It was an idea which was floated by sociologist Pino Arlacchi, as consultant to the Anti-Mafia Commission, and was eventually given the go-ahead in December 1991.

It was supposed to be equipped with 2,500 men, chosen from the best investigators from the police, the carabinieri and the Guardia di Finanza (the finance police). It was set up, in the face of opposition from established security forces, within six months, which most concerned thought to be 'a miracle' although thereafter progress was slow. Six months further on, only 230 staff had been recruited but later it developed into a true attacking force.

The Ministry of the Interior also obtained government approval to strengthen the Sicilian police force with an additional 1,000 men and 530 more carabinieri. Changes were also made to give the judiciary more time to investigate Mafia-related cases – doubling the period from one to two years on a particular case, thus eliminating one of the key causes of the 'out of time' technicality on which so many mafiosi had been freed. The police would also be allowed to search property, or even an entire district without a warrant from the magistracy.

Other proposals included ending *omertà*, the conspiracy of silence, by making it an offence to remain silent; it would also become an offence to tell only part of the story, so that anyone who made less than a full confession would be subject to punishment if it was discovered that some facts had been held back.

There were also plans to allow DIA agents to infiltrate the Mafia, but perhaps the most important idea of all was the suggested appointment of a *superprocura* – an anti-Mafia supremo who would bring together all the elements of the battle. Falcone would have liked that role himself because it would have put him right back in the front line as the leader, rather than the manager of the fight.

All of these developments, along with Falcone's own pressure for more direct action against the enemy, took him ever closer to the very edge of the precipice and every move he made was being tracked by the Mafia and its allies. He was tailed when he went off on his trips abroad to forge closer links with the financial centres of the world and with the law enforcement agencies in a dozen countries.

He had commuted to the US and to Switzerland where at last he was receiving real cooperation in opening the books and bank accounts. He went to South America and travelled throughout the EC, where he was welcomed as a hero. Always, the Mafia was watching, waiting for the opportunity to kill him.

Ferraro said he knew that he was the prime target. He had often talked about death, and the threat to his own life, not to mention those around him, his colleagues and bodyguards who were in danger through mere proximity to him. He deliberately tried to avoid those situations he could not handle. He was always cautious but tried to bring a relaxed, almost sanguine approach to the situation by joking about it. 'After all,' he would say, 'you can die walking across a street or in an air crash or from cancer.'

He managed a dry wit to relieve even the most fraught situations and only resorted to sarcasm against himself. There was an open contract on his life. Any hood or gangster anywhere in the world had the permission, the instruction, of the *cupola* to take a shot at him. 'Only with death,' he admitted, 'will this threat be extinguished, natural or otherwise.'

The fatalistic approach did not, however, lead him to disregard security, not for himself or anyone he worked with. He constantly updated his movements, listing bogus appointments on his diary. Only those closest to him would know, at any given moment, where he was, what he would be doing and whom he would be meeting. 'I am not on some kamikaze mission,' he would say, 'but nor am I a trappist monk.'

What he was, however, what he had become and what he might yet become represented the biggest danger to the Mafia and its leadership. Nor could he escape becoming involved in the judicial campaign to expose corruption by then beginning to emerge in Italian political and business life. Though Mafia and the 'clean hands' corruption investigations were not generally linked except in a few specific cases, the culture of corruption, the stink of it as one politician noted, carried the odour of Mafia.

Falcone above all others had a unique understanding of that

culture. He would tell his colleagues that there was no point at all in solving a Mafia murder if the underlying elements that caused it remained secret. These elements could only be known by acquiring a complete understanding of the criminal organization, so that the whole of the picture could be set in place.

That was always his point in arguing the case for the Pool, and for a special unit of Mafia-fighting police. It was impossible for magistrates or policemen operating individually on a single case to pull all the strings together and arrive at a solution which produced an overall picture of Mafia operations.

In the case of the Lima murder, he would say that it was possible to run through the basic reconstruction and put most things in place: when he was killed, how he was killed, where he was killed and even by whom he was killed . . . but why?

The answer may be in the hands of a *pentiti* being interviewed by another magistrate or policeman who was not involved in the Lima case, thus that key question might not be asked and the information lost. That was just one example of why he was campaigning to reform the collective initiative and put a single coordinating figurehead at the top.

It was this aspect that worried the politicians and the bureaucrats, that Falcone or whoever was appointed to the role would have too much power, with indirect control over sections of the judiciary, the police and the military. He would also acquire more knowledge than a single person outside of government was entitled to have and it must be remembered that the Italian government itself was in a state of turmoil in the period before and after the 1992 general election, and so for the time being the appointment of the super-prosecutor and many of the reforms that Claudio Martelli was pressing for were in abeyance.

The Lima case, meantime, continued to fuel lively discussion. The backdrop to his murder was a multi-layered entanglement of interests. Falcone had not yet completely satisfied himself as to why he was murdered, but there was a good deal of speculation that the assassination was not merely a matter of his failure to accommodate the Cosa Nostra by stopping the judges reimposing prison sentences on several mafiosi already freed.

There was talk of other reasons, a secret agenda with

international implications, and that because of the possibility that Lima might one day talk to save his own neck, he had to be silenced, no matter how, to save a most important and strategic Mafia connection to the *sotto governo.*

Falcone positioned the crucial names around a circle drawn on his pad. There was Giulio Andreotti at the top, Lima's friend for almost three decades and veteran DC leader. Below him was the name of Stefano Bontate, the Mafia boss to whom Lima was closely associated before he was eliminated by the Corleonesi in 1981 in the war that took Liggio's 'beasts' Toto Riina and Bernardo Provenzano – named on the other side of Falcone's circle – to the summit of the organization. Next came Vito Ciancimino, born in Corleones and closely associated with that family and with Lima. Next to him came the tax-collecting Salvo cousins, Ignazio and Nino (who died in 1985) who were patrons of both Lima and Ciancimino as well as four other known politicians in the Catania and Trapani provinces, and heavy benefactors of the DC. Then, he drew in Luciano Liggio, the true boss of bosses to whom Ciancimino and the Salvos gave allegiance and whom Lima was forced to acknowledge in fear of his life after Bontate was killed.

To that circle could be added more names and the continuous line would link, via Lima and Ciancimino, the Mafia to the highest level of politics. There was also a question mark, one unnamed figure in this circular equation who may have been that of a senior officer within the secret service, to be questioned later.

Falcone's sister Maria believed it went deeper than anyone knew and other colleagues went so far as to indicate that Falcone was on the brink of naming the man who had replaced Lima as the Mafia's contact with the Palazzo.

In this, as in every case, that last piece of the jigsaw was the tantalizing one that would dominate Falcone's mind and he would not rest until he had pursued every channel, every witness, every piece of evidence from the *pentiti* for a resolution.

By May 1992, he was heading towards that goal and was reaching into the core of organized criminal activity and its political and financial ramifications, connecting as it did with the corruption scandals exposed by Judge Di Pietro and his colleagues in Milan.

Many of the reforms Falcone had battled for had been passed and others were ready for approval and awaiting final ratification from the incoming administration after the 1992 general election. The voters had shown their dissatisfaction with the Christian Democrats who polled only 29 per cent of the vote, but they were still the largest party again in a patchwork four-party coalition government under the Socialist prime minister Giuliano Amato.

Globally, the major institutions in the financial world were at last taking action to stem the flow of uncontrolled dirty money and cooperating, albeit on a limited basis, to expose the launderers. Vital parts of the Italian judicial system were being overhauled. The law agencies were being reinforced and the issue of appointing the super-prosecutor was awaiting approval by the new government.

Five days after his fifty-third birthday, Falcone set out his aims for the future. There was still a long way to go, he said in a newspaper interview, and there were many areas yet to be explored. The battle against the Mafia had been revitalized, but it was still in its infancy, in many respects.

That weekend, on 23 May 1992, Falcone decided to take his wife Francesca on a short break from Rome to their home in Palermo. Francesca was thirty-six and also a strong anti-Mafia campaigner. They had both been married before, and had no children. Francesca had shared his ups and downs over the dramas of the past decade, living with him for most of the time in the barracks and bunkers of the state security services while he went about his business.

Very few people knew of his plans that day although he had to alert his bodyguards and, at the last moment, the island security forces who would be meeting him with a motorcade at Punta Raisa airport.

He and his wife drove in his motorcade to a military airport in Rome for the hour-long flight to Sicily aboard a secret service plane. Someone, somewhere in the Ministry of Justice or the secret service had learned of his imminent departure and warned the Cosa Nostra. From past experience, they knew that if Falcone was to be liquidated, it could not be by the bullet or localized bomb. No one had been able to get close to him in five years, and they had certainly tried. Oh, how they had tried.

He was also particularly cautious about his visits to Sicily. Ferraro explained:

> The Mafia had sentenced him to death and what that organization decrees has to be kept. That is the logic of power assertion. Falcone was well aware of it. We talked about it often. He could not be murdered by a sniper or normal professional killer. It would have been difficult, for Giovanni was careful. In Rome it would have been doubly difficult to organize a slaughter. The Mafia is nowhere near having the same control over the territory there as in Sicily. Besides, Giovanni himself believed that since the Mafia had decreed his death, this had to take place in Sicily, otherwise the symbolic significance of the killing would be lost. It had to be on Sicilian soil, carried out by a Sicilian; it was part of the rite.

It seemed an almost impossible thing, even for the skilled killers of that organization, to set in place the enormous cache of explosives without being seen between the time his plans to fly to Sicily became known on the criminal grapevine and the time he actually arrived.

It was no small bomb they were planning.

The *pentito* Salvatore Cancemi of the Porta Nova family, who was arrested in 1993, would state that the planning had been done long in advance, following a meeting with Toto Riina and four other members of the *cupola* at a country house in the hills near Capaci, twelve miles from Palermo: 'I had called to the house for other matters and learned that the planning of Falcone's murder was already in hand. I did not know the precise point of the ambush, neither could I have imagined what they were planning. One of the *cupola* members told me that they had a man in Rome who was following Falcone's movements and would report everything to him.'

One ton of explosives were to be planted in a culvert under the main six-lane highway linking Punta Raisa airport to Palermo. It would need a truck to carry it, several men to unload it and plant it in a secure and unobtrusive position, because one ton of explosives is a very large pile. It would need at least two very skilled men to wire up the material and prepare it for a remote-controlled explosion and it was not the kind of device that the Mafia was used to dealing with. It was quite probable that experts were imported specifically for the purpose, kept in hiding until the job was done and then taken off the island by fast boat immediately afterwards.

Setting a bomb of that nature would take at least an hour or more. The site would have to have been scouted well in advance, and even the ground prepared so the explosives could be packed into the culvert.

Then on that day of 23 May, the alert was given from Rome and the Cosa Nostra military unit in Palermo swung into action. The pile of explosives must have been primed as Falcone's aircraft lifted into the sky from Rome. An hour later at Punta Raisa aiport the plane taxied to its usual position well away from the terminal.

A ring of carabinieri was in place with armoured cars ready to take Falcone and his wife to their home. Falcone acknowledged his friends, and held out his hand to take the keys of the armour-plated Alfa Romeo. He said he would drive himself, and the motorcade took off, just as it had done a hundred and one times before, racing along the highway towards Palermo with sirens blaring.

At the airport and along the route the Cosa Nostra had stationed look-outs with walkie-talkies to track the precise moment that the motorcade left the airport area. The approximate timing of its journey to the point at which the bomb was set must have been rehearsed in advance, to give as near as possible an accurate assessment of the moment the motorcade would arrive at the precise spot, at the turn-off to Capaci.

Speeding along at between 80 and 90 kilometres an hour, the motorcade reached the spot. Somewhere in the hills close by, the button was pressed: the ton of explosive went up and blew the motorcade to pieces.

The wreckage was hurled into the air like children's toys and strewn up to 200 yards away. The explosion was heard miles away in Palermo, and in the motorway a huge crater filled with the debris of shattered, twisted metal.

Falcone was killed instantly along with three of his bodyguards. His wife Francesca suffered terrible injuries and died five hours after admission to hospital. Twenty other people, bodyguards and innocent travellers along that busiest of Sicilian highways, were injured. But the Mafia cared nothing for the innocent, so long as their target was hit.

The adjectives to describe the shock and the sheer horror of this terrible act, after so many that have been called into use in these pages, now begin to become elusive. Perhaps it is best to recall that ten thousand filled the streets of Palermo that night to protest and hurl abuse at the Mafia. It was a death which left a deeper scar even than that of the national hero General Dalla Chiesa and in terms of modern Italian history, could only be compared in its gravity to the murder of Aldo Moro.

Commentators were very quick to condemn not just the Mafia, but the corrupt state machinery, the weakness of government that had allowed such an atrocity to happen, the ineffective judicial system that had set all but 48 of the 374 convicted mafiosi from the maxi-trials back on the street to continue their murders.

The killing of Falcone did the Republic of Italy enormous harm, not merely because it had lost one of its most determined servants and greatest heroes, but because in the eyes of many nations the dire condition of public order coupled with economic crises and with sinister dealings, presented a disconcerting image. The loss of Falcone represented a tragic admission that the State, seemingly powerless to curtail Mafia violence, could not even protect the one man known to be most at risk and whose murder had not only been predicted but promised.

Ironically, Falcone had discussed this issue on the very last page of the book he had written with the French journalist Marcelle Padovani, *Men of Honour: The Truth About the Mafia*, published in 1991. He said he was often amazed at the ignorance of the subject of the Mafia and its links with Sicilian politicians. Few seemed to have grasped that apparently innocuous statements, certain behaviours, which were part of normal Italian political life, took on a special meaning in Sicily.

On that island, nothing could be considered from the outset

as innocent, not a visit to the bank manager, not an argument between policitians or an ideological conflict within a political party. He believed it to be incontrovertible that politicians murdered by the Mafia, like Mattarella, Reina and La Torre, had become isolated because of the political battles they had undertaken, and thus certain behaviours served to identify the future victim without that victim himself realizing it.

Falcone himself knew he was a potential future victim and the last two sentences of his book were tragically prophetic: 'One usually dies because one is alone or because one has gone in over one's head. One often dies because one does not have the right alliances, because one is not given support. In Sicily, the Mafia kills the servants of the State that the State has not been able to protect.'

In the final analysis, the State was unable to give Falcone that absolute protection. The Mafia, in broad daylight, packed its bomb into a very public place without hindrance, without anyone apparently seeing. And according to testimony received later from the *pentito* Salvatore Cancemi, the Mafia's military commander Toto Riina, in hiding, threw a party for his Corleonesi brethren and toasted Falcone's demise in champagne. 'It has gone very well,' he said, raising his glass in the air.

CHAPTER EIGHTEEN

Paolo Borsellino, Five Bodyguards and Salvo the Tax Collector – Dead

As troops and police reinforcements flooded onto the island of Sicily to bolt the stable door and put up another almost fatuous show of strength to calm the fear of its people, Giovanni Falcone was laid to rest with all the well-deserved trappings of a national hero. Tributes came from around the world. Those who had worked with Falcone poured out their grief. Politicians recited their platitudes and Oscar Luigi Scalfaro, speaker of the Chamber of deputies, pleaded with members of the electoral college in Rome to set aside their differences. 'Democracy appears painfully defeated by this atrocious act,' he said. 'Let us give the people the perception of a responsible political world that feels the urgency of unity.'

He was certainly right. At the time of Falcone's death, the Palazzo was locked in battle for a new president, following April's general election, and it had that very week descended into an unseemly brawl, literally, when two MPs came to blows amid allegations of cheating and corruption among the candidates for this highest of Italian offices.

Mere words would not calm the feelings of the people of Sicily. When acting President of the Republic, Giovanni Spandolini, led a state delegation to Palermo to pay homage to the dead hero, thousands of furious Sicilians lining the streets wept openly and hurled abuse at the politicians. They vented their rage with banners and verbal insults, and contemptuously pelted the delegation with coins and waved banknotes, calling out, 'Assassins!' and, 'Go Back to Rome!'

Pino Arlacchi, the Mafia expert and sociologist, wrote a strongly worded attack:

> The assassination of Falcone is not a challenge to the State. It is an indisputable victory over the State and its laws. It is a defeat for everyone working for the moral and political renewal of Italy. If Cosa Nostra had eliminated a politician or even a prime minister it would not have had the same effect. The devastating effects of this crime will be felt for years.

Falcone's colleagues turned out in force, wearing their black robes which seemed to signify a deadly office, led by his dedicated partner and dearest friend, Paolo Borsellino, who was one of the pallbearers, and his deputy who would now inherit his mantle, Liliana Ferraro. At the burial service, Borsellino laid his hands on his friend's coffin and gave a grim warning to those remaining in the fight: 'Those who want to leave should do so now, because this is our destiny.'

Destiny is the word that keeps arising. It was used to me by Ferraro when she described her feelings when she was called in to be invited to take over Falcone's role as Director for Penal Affairs for Italy. At the time, she said, she was in black despair, and had wept uncontrollably when news of the tragedy reached her. However much a person may steel themselves towards the knowledge that a particular event may happen, it is impossible to overcome the feelings that well up inside when that event occurs. She had worked with Falcone for almost a decade, they had travelled through some of the most tortuous, dangerous minefields that exist anywhere in the netherworld of organized crime. When the moment of his death came, and when knowledge of how it was perpetrated was revealed, there were, as we have said, few words that could truly express the feelings of horror.

She could rely on memories, and accept the mantle with some pride though with very great apprehension and not a small amount of fear. She had always been in danger, just as they all were. Now, Ferraro herself was a prime target. But again she is quick to remind her interviewer that there were always others in greater danger than herself though, as Leoluca Orlando, another of those in the front line, told me, 'It could be any one of us, at any time. Ferraro like all of us could never be sure that around the next corner, or beyond the next hill, there would not be a bomb or a bullet waiting.'

One other such person, as Ferraro and Orlando well knew, was Paolo Borsellino, the chief prosecutor of Palermo and Falcone's greatest friend. They had worked closely together since the first beginnings of the anti-Mafia Pool back in 1981, but their friendship went back to their Sicilian childhood. Ferraro recalled that they used to joke about death, and Borsellino told how he once visited Falcone's home and said, 'Look, Giovanni, I think you had better give me the combination of your safe. Otherwise, how will we open it when they kill you?'

They kept up their spirits with such banter, but the reality was felt as much by their families. Back in 1984, when Falcone led them towards the maxi-trials, the danger was such that he and Borsellino took their immediate families into impenetrable accommodation at a high security prison on the island of Asinara while they prepared the trial documents. It was there that one of Borsellino's two daughters, Lucia, began showing signs of the nervous tension that engulfed them all, and which eventually developed into anorexia nervosa.

It was a reaction, undoubtedly, to the life she and her family led, surrounded by bodyguards, listening to her father returning home or leaving for work in the siren-wailing motorcades, not knowing if he would ever return. Like all those involved in the anti-Mafia crusade, Borsellino and his wife tried their best to surround their children with love and affection, and live as near normal a life as possible. But it was not possible.

Borsellino was the second name on the Mafia's hit-list. He knew it, and his family knew it. They lived with it day in and day out. Borsellino and Falcone were from the same era. Borsellino was born in 1940 to a middle-class family in Piazza Magione, in the heart of the old city. As a youth, he and Falcone used to play football together in the Albergheria quarter along with – as both used to point out later – other youths who would become the Mafia chiefs against whom they would subsequently pit themselves. They both studied law and passed the state examination to become magistrates at around the same time and they both married the daughters of their legal mentors. Borsellino's wife, Angela Piraino Leto, was the daughter of a presiding judge.

Borsellino went to Sicilian towns liks Enna, Mazara del Vallo and Monreale before returning to Palermo in 1975 where, four years later, he found himself once again alongside Falcone. Borsellino worked under Rocco Chinnici in the public prosecutor's office and formed the unit that became the scourge of the Mafia in the early eighties.

After the near-collapse of the maxi-trials through reverses suffered in higher courts, Borsellino had moved to the town of Marsala as chief prosecutor in 1987. He returned to Palermo to take over from Falcone as the Sicilian standard-bearer of the anti-Mafia crusade, when his friend moved to Rome. After Falcone's death, Borsellino was seen as the most likely heir to the role of super-prosecutor that would almost certainly have gone to Falcone had he lived. The job would have entailed him heading a new team specifically assigned to renewing the attack on the Mafia, though the decision on the creation of that role was still held up by political in-fighting.

But even as he stood, filled with grief, at Falcone's funeral, Borsellino was already under sentence of death and before long the Italian secret police would become aware of exactly how imminent that threat would be. Three weeks after the funeral, intelligence on this possibility was placed in the hands of Antonio Subranni, head of the Italian special operations police force in Rome.

He in turn telegraphed a most secret message to the senior officer in command of police at Palermo, warning that there were plans to murder Borsellino 'in the very near future'. The message stated that the assassination had been 'commissioned' after Borsellino had signed warrants for a new wave of arrests. The source even named the Mafia groups who were likely to undertake the killing.

Others besides Borsellino were also named, including two politicians, another judge and two police officers who were working in close collaboration with him. The secret service intelligence reported that the Mafia believed that the murder of Borsellino would finally halt the anti-Mafia investigations, or at least seriously curtail them.

Whether this message was relayed to Borsellino is not known. However, he knew that the 'explosives to kill me have arrived'. Like Falcone, Ferraro, Orlando and the rest Borsellino viewed this constant threat with a fatalistic resignation, though always tried to keep his security in place. Questions would be asked later why, if this information was available to the highest of ranks in the Italian security services, Borsellino and his family were not taken away to the security of a police barracks until the additional troops and police by then active throughout Sicily had tracked down suspected assassins. It is a question that remains unanswered.

An interesting observation could be made about the ability of Italy to secure the safety of its most threatened officials. Borsellino travelled to Mannheim in July to discuss German links with Mafia figures, and the continual problem of drugs. As soon as he arrived, Borsellino was surrounded by a close circle of fifteen guards, and was driven in a eight-car motorcade, whereas in his home city he had five guards and two outrider cars.

Borsellino had boldly pledged to continue undeterred, and that the memory of his good and close friend Falcone would not be marred by a discontinuation of the effort. Already, the new gentlemen of the Palazzo had been jolted into action by Falcone's death and were promising to rush through parliament the remaining measures which Falcone, Ferraro and their friends in the Ministries of Justice and the Interior had been campaigning for to tackle organized crime.

Prime Minister Giuliano Amato revealed in mid-July that the new measures had been approved by his cabinet, but parliament had 'not yet got around to passing a decree for them to become law'. Even so, new laws were not necessarily an answer to the problem.

Since 1982, when the Pio La Torre demands were put before parliament in the wake of his own and Dalla Chiesa's assassination, there had been 113 new laws and decrees passed specifically to fight organized crime. The laws that Falcone had pressed for to combat money laundering and to reveal the source of wealth of suddenly rich people, were still bogged down by ministerial disputes. As ever, progress inched forward at a snail's pace and on 16 July Borsellino actually warned Prime Minister Amato that he was 'fighting against time'.

On 19 July his time ran out. That day, Borsellino turned up unexpectedly (pre-arranged appointments were seldom possible) at the house of his friend, Giuseppe Tricoli, a professor of law at the University of Palermo, with his wife and son Manfredi. They talked about death, out of his wife's earshot. It was to Tricoli that Borsellino said, 'They are preparing to kill me. The dynamite has already arrived. It came last Monday.'

Tricoli asked him how he managed to go on. He replied, 'I'm a Catholic. It is my duty to believe in humanity.'

After lunch, Borsellino decided to visit his mother, leaving his wife and son at the villa. There were never set times for these impromptu calls and this one certainly was not planned. But the Cosa Nostra was tailing him, day and night, as they had with Falcone. They knew that Sunday was the most likely day that Borsellino would make this visit. The killer was already in place. He had been selected by Toto Riina, a psychopath named Lorenzo Tinnirello with a reputed 100 murders to his name. On 18 July, Tinnirello and an accomplice named Natale Gambino took a tiny Fiat 126 to a car repair shop in the back streets of Palermo and filled it with 270 kilos of explosives. At 6.30 a.m. the following day, Tinnirello drove the car to Via D'Amelia and parked it close to the apartment house where Borsellino's mother lived. He then walked to another car parked nearby carrying the remote control device that on the push of a button would explode the car bomb; he and two others waited nine hours and eventually the moment arrived.

Borsellino's motorcade drove cautiously down Via D'Amelia in the centre of Palermo, his own armoured-plated car sandwiched between two cars carrying his bodyguards. They stood outside while he went into the building. The street was filled with Sunday morning activity and people. It ought to have carried a government health warning as one of the most at risk areas of Palermo. Everyone who lived nearby knew of the possibility that when Borsellino and his bodyguards arrived, there might one day be trouble.

That day was upon them. As Borsellino went to his mother's house, the street outside was crammed with cars, some double parked. As he came out, at precisely 4.45 p.m., Tinirello, parked well away, pushed the button.

Paolo Borsellino and five of his bodyguards were killed. One of them, a woman, was thrown 200 feet away. The gruesome but now familiar task of scraping up pieces of human remains took three days. Twenty other people in the street at the time were injured. A dozen cars were wrecked. Windows were blown out along the entire street; property was damaged, some beyond repair.

Sicily and the whole of Italy went into a state of shock. Television programmes were interrupted to announce the murder. Crowds began to gather on the streets of Palermo. There were simply no words left in the Italian vocabulary to describe the shock, but there was panic and unbridled fear.

There should have been one other killing on that day – Leoluca Orlando was visiting the 'Ndrangheta stronghold of Calabria for an anti-Mafia meeting on behalf of his party, La Rete, and somewhere, unseen and unknown, was a group of assassins waiting for the chance to take aim. Suddenly, the security men closed in on him. A police helicopter landed nearby and he was bundled away and flown to the airport. There, he was put on board a mail plane, sitting uncomfortably among the sacks of letters all the way to Rome. On route, he learned that his friend Paolo Borsellino had just been blown up. Orlando was driven to his bunker in the centre of Rome, a small apartment with sleeping quarters and kitchen, around which workmen had just installed steel walls, where he remained until the danger had passed.

That week, he returned to Palermo for succession of constrasting events. The funeral of the bodyguards was on Tuesday 21 July, and the state delegation appeared from Rome, this time led by the new President of Italy, Oscar Scalfaro. Crowds of anti-Mafia supporters jostled government leaders and the widow of one of the dead bodyguards ran to the altar and reprimanded Cardinal Salvatore Pappalardo, Archbishop of Palermo, for his comments that the Mafia should be allowed to repent and be forgiven.

The funeral of the five was a noisy contrast to the quiet

and dignified mourning for Borsellino at the parish church of Santa Louisa di Marillac. The family had refused President Scalfaro's offer of a state funeral at Palermo Cathedral, and initially refused to allow any government officials to attend their service. His widow later had a change of heart and invited the president to attend. As the head of national police, Vincenzo Parisi, arrived the crowd yelled, 'Buffoon.'

By then, Palermo and other major towns and cities on the island were being flooded with troops and additional police. More than 3,000 reinforcements had been flown in since Borsellino was killed. The national parliament was finally shamed into action and passed without opposition all of the new, strong measures that Falcone and the Ministry of the Interior had submitted a year before.

Armed with that new authority, Liliana Ferraro began to fight back with a vengeance. A combined army, carabinieri and police operation swooped down upon the town of Corleone on the very day of Borsellino's burial, in a pre-planned, top secret mission. Swooped was the word to describe the operation. Armoured troop carriers and dozens of military jeeps carrying soldiers swung into the town from both ends of the main road that runs through it. Suddenly the skies were filled with helicopters and aircraft from which a crack unit of Army parachutists dropped down into the surrounding fields and began to move in. Section by section, the town was taken apart. Startled officials ran from the town hall and innocently began to ask: 'Who are you looking for?'

Of course they were searching for Salvatore Toto Riina and his sidekick Bernardo Provenzano, who had reputedly not been seen for twenty-two years. Riina was the most famous name in Corleone, more famous now than the old master himself, Luciano Liggio.

The townspeople, until recently ruled exclusively by the Christian Democrats since 1945, would be at one in claiming that they were prisoners of its own name, since *The Godfather* movie made Corleone famous. The menace, however, swirls around those little concrete houses like a biting wind.

The troops combed the town, street by street, house by house and found nothing and no one of particular criminal interest, save for a few minor law breakers. Elsewhere, similar operations were being conducted against Cosa Nostra strongholds in Palermo and the nearest they got to any arrest was at the house of the former drug dealer and killer Paolo Alfano, sentenced to seventeen years at the maxi-trials, released in 1989, and who had already fled before they arrived.

In the afternoon, the troops combed regions along the coast and areas of traditonally high Mafia density. 'The aim of this operation,' said Giuseppe de Constanzo, head of criminal investigations in western Sicily, 'is to put pressure on entire areas where fugitives are hiding.'

It was a show of strength which seemed to have more to do with quelling the fears of the people than making any serious arrests. Palermo was filled with police and troops looking mystified and lost and with little to guard but themselves.

In spite of the massive presence of security forces all summer long, however, the Cosa Nostra was unperturbed and perhaps even pushed into reasserting its own arrogance and strength. If it wanted to kill, it would kill – and did so again in spectacular fashion.

Their target would be considered by many to be one of their own, though he had always denied it: Ingnazio Salvo, one of the cousins from Trapani who had become multi-millionaires on the backs of the tax-collecting franchise they held of behalf of the government for almost three decades.

Salvo had been sentenced to three years' imprisonment at the maxi-trial in 1986 and had since been released. Though he and his now dead cousin had long ago been stripped of $30 million worth of assets and their international trading conglomerate put in the hands of receivers, Ignazio still lived a luxurious life-style.

His connections with the Mafia, first with the doomed faction led by Stefano Bontate, and a forced allegiance with the Corleonesi, had earned him millions as a money changer for the Mafia drugs billionaires. He had built his business on the backs of the people through the taxes he and his cousin collected, then from the bribery and corruption that secured him a huge stake in property and real estate development.

An Anti-Mafia Commission report on his activities had branded him the controlling force behind 'an unlawful centre of power capable of influencing every corner of Sicilian politics . . . he has been long associated with some of the most infamous of Mafia chieftains.' The Salvos were in turn heavily linked to Salvo Lima and other politicians within the Christian Democrats.

But his usefulness to the Corleonesi had expired. He had been outcast by the politicians and had no influence in the business arena of banking, finance and laundering. The *pentiti* who came forward in the wake of new laws which granted them protection, would give testimony that Toto Riina was fearful that Salvo might talk to save his own skin. He knew too many secrets, particularly in the area of the Mafia's high finance. He knew where the secret bank accounts were and who controlled them.

On 17 September, Ignazio Salvo had just got out of his Mercedes to walk into his villa at Santa Flavia, twelve miles from Palermo, when he was ambushed in traditional style – with a shotgun pushed into the back of his neck. Three shots were fired, and Salvo, the baron of taxes, lay dead with his brains scattered on the pathway to his house: one more statistic, and one more death of a man who knew too much.

Even then, with the whole of Italy supposedly now alerted to Mafia activity, and with the concurrent corruption investigations turning up new scandals almost daily – by the end of 1992 more than 400 people had been arrested on the mainland, mostly politicians and businessmen – the Mafia showed no sign whatsoever of being subdued. There was every sign that it was regenerating, returning in force to the bad ways of drug trafficking which many had not even bothered to give up; but above all it continued to laugh in the face of authority and to demonstrate to those left in the anti-Mafia crusade that it cared nothing for them, and did not fear the thousands of extra police swarming every Mafia stronghold from the far north of Italy to the very tip of Sicily.

This was demonstrated again when the judiciary began to move in on a gang allied to the Corleonesi, centred on Catania. Police and Italian secret service were already getting close to arrests, and on 27 July, less than two weeks after the killing of Borsellino, Giovanni Lizzio, a 36-year-old police inspector and family man working in Catania, was ambushed on the outskirts of the city and shot. He died later in hospital.

Lizzio had been involved in a nationwide investigation, led by Judge Antonino Ferrara of Catania, into a major arms and cocaine smuggling operation from which the Italian secret service had gleaned some remarkable intelligence. Undeterred by the killing of Lizzio, Ferrara pressed on. His own assassination had already been ordered and in early October, 1992, the Mafia launched their attempt to blow him up.

Ferrara was due to fly to Milan in a police aircraft, and then travel by armoured car to Linate, in the north of Italy, where the gang had based its warehousing operation.

He and his guards were to have been blown up on their way to Catania airport in Sicily in October 1992, but they changed their route at the very last minute and were saved. The story behind his escape from death was like a mini-thriller and demonstrated, if proof were needed by those in authority, that the Mafia was as unperturbed as ever by the threats of politicians and the law and the massive police presence.

Ferrara's investigation had highlighted a developing trend among the Sicilians, that many had switched from heroin into arms dealing and cocaine, the latter transported in their own ships from South America and landed in various ports, most popularly in Spain, for onward transmission to retail outlets across Europe.

The presence of the Mafia in northern Italy was never a secret and one of the *pentiti* had explained the strategic importance of its base at Linate, outside of Milan, to both Falcone and Judge Ferrara. It was a major staging post which served the most important drug markets in the north, and the lucrative market in Germany – which Borsellino had discussed in Mannheim only a few days before he was murdered.

The territorial command was in the hands of Giacomo Riina, an ageing uncle of Toto Riina. He ran the operation from his house at Budrio, near Bologna. The Italian DIA had discovered the presence of another major Mafia boss, Giuseppe Madonia, and surveillance on him led them to the operational base at Linate, in a massive warehouse near the football ground which also had dry storage and a cold room, as well as loading facilities to serve a fleet of lorries.

Giuseppe Nicolossi, a magistrate from Florence, was placed in charge of this inquiry, linking up with Ferrara in whose district it had originated. In mid-June, a month after Falcone's assassination, and in consultation with Liliana Ferraro in Rome, Ferrara in Catania and Borsellino in Palermo, Nicolossi ordered a round-the-clock surveillance on the warehouse by the GICO, a special division of the Italian internal revenue department.

An undercover unit secured a listening post 350 metres away from the warehouse and filmed every movement day and night and, with the help of the Italian secret service who installed micro-spy equipment in the building, eavesdropped on everything that took place inside. The information obtained through this remarkable operation confirmed the importance of the warehouse in the drug network which the Catanesi (a group of families from Catania) operated in conjunction with the Corleonesi, represented by Toto Riina's uncle.

They were buying and selling a huge range of merchandise including small arms, drugs and heavy weapons, some acquired within Italy and others imported from the former Soviet bloc countries. Through the micro-surveillance devices, the agents listened in to mafiosi conversations in which deals were being discussed, along with talk of vengeance against the *pentiti*, the elimination of rivals and the rooting out of unreliable connections.

A fountain of information flowed during the weeks of the surveillance. Not least of interest were the discussions on finance which revealed a daily turnover of around one billion Italian lire ($624,000).

Plans for the future were being discussed as were development plans for the warehouse itself. The gang was planning to build itself a bunker, apparently fearing attacks not from the police but from rivals. From intercepted telephone calls, the police discovered that a multi-million dollar consignment of 1,000 kilos of cocaine would be delivered to the warehouse for onward transmission to Germany on 21 October.

Nicolossi decided to move, knowing that the bosses would have to meet at the warehouse for the division of the cargo and the finances. But by then, Mafia spies had learned of Nicolossi's intention. Two days before the shipment was due, the Linate group received a hand-delivered letter which came from a Mafia boss in prison.

His message was relayed over the telephone to the Cosa Nostra operational centre in Catania, ordering them to proceed immediately against Judge Ferrara, in other words, to kill him. The imprisoned Mafia chieftain provided graphic detail of the judge's movements and ordered: 'You must blow him up as soon as possible. Do it as he goes to Mass on Sunday, which he does every week.'

He said, specifically, that Judge Ferrara would be leaving the airport at Catania after Mass to fly to Milan, proving once again that the Mafia – even those in prison – still had access to highly sensitive information that could only have come from within the security service. Explosives were to be planted somewhere along the route. The men of the GICO managed to film the mafioso who was telephoning these instructions, first with the letter in his hand and then when he had finished the conversation, burning it. At that point Nicolossi decided upon prompt action. To hell with the 1,000 kilos of cocaine, he said. A judge's life was a stake.

A security ring was thrown around all of the judges of Catania and on the night of 18 October 150 men of the GICO moved on the warehouse at Linate where they arrested 20 people.

They discovered a great deal of documentary evidence and obtained a list of telephone numbers the Mafia boss at the warehouse had dialled from his mobile phone. They included calls to highly placed people in the Italian Ministry of Defence in Rome, and others in customs and airports. One of the most-dialled numbers was to a contact in the Defence Ministry, obviously of great importance, and concerned with the securing of weapons from Italian sources.

The Linate experience was one of the more successful operations against the Mafia, and in the end it saved the life of at least one judge.

CHAPTER NINETEEN

Father Giuseppe Puglisi and Padre Diana, Two Parish Priests – Dead

The office was left unchanged. Liliana Ferraro moved into one of the hottest seats in the Italian civil service as Director of Penal Affairs and left the room exactly as it was when Falcone walked out. It had a comfortable feel about it. The desk was modest, the furniture simple. There were no flashy glass and chrome adornments that are available in the furnishing stores to senior legal executives. He had the Italian flag on a pole behind his desk, and a television set permanently switched to the teletext news until he wanted to watch a particular programme or bulletin. Over in the far corner was a display of ornamental porcelain ducks which he collected. Ferraro kept them for old times' sake, a touch of unusual sentimentality.

She was shaking as she walked in. She does not mind admitting it. She recalled that in the beginning, at the time of her appointment, it was with considerable trepidation that she sat in Falcone's chair, even though she had been working with him for so long and knew pretty well everything there was to know about the mechanics of the job. She admitted to me that on the day she was appointed, her mind was a turmoil of thoughts, from pride to anguish, and yes, fear.

Above all, she faced the prospect of succeeding the man who had become a national, if not international hero, an acknowledged expert and a walking encyclopaedia on the Mafia. That knowledge was undoubtedly the cause of his death and had a depth which few could attempt to match. For the first time in her life, she experienced sleeplessness:

> I felt honoured that I had been chosen for the job, mainly because it was Giovanni's. At the same time, I felt the weight of that inheritance on my shoulders. Falcone, Borsellino and all the others were gone; so many deaths. But I had to shake off the gloom of these tragedies. I knew I would have to outperform myself and I decided that I should try to be guided by my memory of his words, his general demeanour and his superior organizing abilities. From the beginning, we both understood that we shared a similarity in our working methods. We did not waste words; eye contact was often sufficient. His approach was to work hard, long hours, starting with a situation at its most basic level and proceeding step by step until he reached its conclusion.
>
> He was a great detective and a master of prosecution. In this respect, I would find him impossible to match. He also had a considerable ability in bringing together the various factions of our State machinery and ultimately received great support in Rome.

Ferraro knew she would be stepping into very large shoes and after the shock and sympathy for her assassinated colleague had faded, she would attract her own critics, anxious to point out that those shoes were several sizes too large. That is the way of Italian politics in which the cut and thrust of the business can be brutal. There was also the other age-old confrontation that faces career women all over the world, and it is especially so in the male-dominated bastions of Italian business and political life: the problems of a woman doing what was considered by men to be a man's job. Ferraro told me:

> That, of course, was very true. It is probable to the outsider that the Italian male may seem very chauvinistic, and perhaps in the area in which I was working it was especially

> so. Nowadays, in our enlightened age, there ought to be no problems for women, none at all. But is it case in practicality? No. Women must have credit cards. And by that I mean they must demonstrate that they are capable of doing the job. There is still a mentality that women must show what they can do, to a degree that is greater than that which may be expected of men. Day by day, we are still faced with having to prove our credibility.

Regardless of the apprehension of some, not least some senior members of the judiciary, the courage and determination of Ferraro could not be denied. The cordon of protective steel, which I have described elsewhere in these chapters and which had long become the norm for most involved at such high level, was as tight and effective as the security forces could make it. It would not be long before she presided over some spectacular successes.

She quickly picked up the reins and pursued the goals set out by Falcone. It involved the first use of the new laws aimed at organized crime. Internationally, she was continuing Falcone's working relationship with the FBI, the DEA and the world banking authorities over money laundering, in conjunction with other security chiefs and especially with Gianni De Gennaro, head of the Italian Anti-Mafia Department (DIA) who was regarded by many as the police's equivalent to Falcone.

There was also a particular ambition of Falcone's that Ferraro took up:

> When Falcone was killed, I decided that the whole strategy he had envisioned for our fight should be pursued by myself and the few of us who remained. He had, at that time, been discussing the possibilities of far greater international cooperation and following a conference in Versailles, he had formed a strong view a global effort was becoming essential. There were so many aspects which were arising that he felt we would no longer rely on bilateral agreements with countries affected, notably the United States. Organized crime today has no borders and to beat it, there had to be a much greater level

> of transnational contact. We could all see quite clearly from our own evidence that the Mafia and other criminal groups had formed into multinational conglomerates. We needed to focus the minds of countries across the world, not just in police matters, but at ministerial level. There were many easily identifiable problem areas, especially in Third World countries where drugs and weapons trading was rife. We were also on the threshold of an explosion of criminal groups throughout the former Soviet Union, where powerful and dangerous entities were linking up with more established groups like the Mafia and the Triads. It was a problem, we believed, that should be dealt at the level of the United Nations.

In December 1992, Ferraro pursued Falcone's aim, and persuaded the then Minister of Justice, Claudio Martelli, to approach the UN with the idea. The response was immediate. She and Martelli were invited to meet the UN Secretariat, and the result was that she herself would be charged with organizing a major conference under the auspicies of the United Nations, to declare war on international organized crime. That lay in the future, and will be dealt with in later chapters. For the time being, however, Ferraro and her colleagues faced more pressing problems in what was a period of frenetic activity.

She was liaising with and coordinating the work of twenty-six separate offices from which prosecutors were conducting the fight against the Mafia. The organization, crossing the whole spectrum of the Italian law effort, focused upon the strategy that Falcone had developed. It hinged, basically, on the original idea of a pool, except that now it had been expanded to embrace a top-level professional corps of investigators, police and judges working from a centralized control, which had the benefit of the computerized database that Ferraro herself had helped originate. No longer could the Mafia simply kill off a judge, and put the investigative effort back to its beginnings.

With extra troops and police already seconded to Sicily, the next phase in the field was Operation Leopard, masterminded by the special anti-Mafia operations group, the DIA, in conjunction with the Italian secret service, the carabinieri and police. It was a top-secret operation aimed at an all-out attack on Mafia heartlands.

An undercover task force had spent weeks on intelligence work, pursuing leads, tapping telephones, interviewing the increasing number of *pentiti*, until they were ready to move. There were several strikes but the ultimate target was, as ever, the arrest of the military leader of the Mafia, Salvatore 'Toto' Riina. In November 1992, they were given the order to move in.

Wave after wave of raids, carried out by hundreds of heavily armed police and military, saw the arrest of more than 250 people throughout Italy and Sicily itself. The round-up included many Mafia soldiers, several important figures in the hierarchy, politicians and businessman as the investigation spilled over into the more general area of Italian malaise known simply as 'corruption'.

Simultaneously, but quite separately, the Milan judges under the direction of Antonio Di Pietro were pursuing their own judicial revolution against corruption in high places and their latest round of arrest warrants included those for three MPs, a former under-secretary to the Justice Ministry, several leading politicians, businessmen, builders and property dealers. The net was now being cast across the whole spectrum of Italian political and business life.

Old ground was being re-examined. In the autumn of 1992, the supergrass Buscetta who had previously refused to discuss politics and confined his testimony largely to Mafia activities, was brought back temporarily from his hideaway in America to begin a new round of 'consultations' with judges investigating the political alliances of the Mafia.

Yet another prong of attack was set in motion by the finance police. Under the new laws of confiscation of property and possessions obtained through illegal means, they began to round up the assets of the criminals. Within a few days they had taken control of $1 billion-worth of property suspected of criminal origins. The haul made an incredible list: 160 villas and apartments; 62 companies which were put in the hands of administrators; 200 bank accounts frozen or possessed; 202 cars, including Porches, Ferraris, Mercedes; and six boats.

Meanwhile, the task force assigned to Operation Leopard

continued its forays and in December arrested one of the most senior of Mafia *cupola* figures, Giuseppe Madonia, ally of Toto Riina who was himself still proving elusive.

The police had put together a complete run-down of his history, his known associates, his whereabouts, gleaned from the most up-to-date intelligence available. They knew his two henchmen, Bernardo Provenzano and his brother-in-law Leoluca Bargarella, were his two most strident enforcers. They knew that he was living with his wife, Antonietta, scion of the Bargarella family, whom he had courted since she was fourteen. They married in 1966 in a ceremony conducted by a Mafia priest, a member of the Coppola family, and they honeymooned in Venice. She was an exceptionally intelligent girl who graduated from college as a teacher. They knew that the Riina children were born at a Palermo maternity clinic, that three of the births were registered in Palermo and that the children had for a time gone to school there.

The only evidence of Riina and Antonietta's existence was a photograph taken on their honeymoon in Venice which had come into the possession of the police. They sent a copy of that photograph to the FBI to be put through their new computerized machine which would 'age' the image of Riina and Antonietta to give a present-day likeness of the couple. It was published in the newspapers and, in the event, it was remarkably accurate.

The special operations force continued their blanket observations in Palermo and Corleone, though they did not know whether the Riinas were still on the island of Sicily. Searches were made in sections, patiently hoping that finally they would discover a clue. If there was a tip-off, the police are not saying, but success finally smiled upon the hunters.

In the second week of January, the police began to take an interest in a smart suburban house in Palermo. There, it was reported, lived a woman who looked remarkably like the picture of Antonietta. From the command headquarters in Rome under the control of the carabinieri colonel, Mario Mori, the officers of the task force were ordered to keep watch on her and the house day and night.

At 8.30 on the morning of 15 January 1993, there was movement. A silver Citroen drew up outside the house and a thickset man, grey-haired, small, came out and got into the passenger seat. In that brief glimpse, no one could be sure if it was Riina, but as eight unmarked police cars fell in behind in pursuit as the Citroen proceeded on its way, the order was received over the car radio: 'Take him.'

As the Citroen slowed down and then stopped in traffic, the police made their move. In seconds, the Citroen was surrounded by gun-wielding policeman. 'Riina,' the senior officer yelled. 'Get out of the car with your hands in the air.' It was a cliché, but seemed to fit the moment. Riina, looking like a venerable grandfather, nondescript, unremarkable in every way, got out of the car and said, 'You are making a mistake. My name is Vincenzo Bellomo.'

But he wasn't. This was Riina and at last the police had him. News of his capture was relayed to a jubilant Liliana Ferraro and made headline news around the world. He was charged with two specific murders, of two Mafia brothers Vincenzo and Pietro Puccio in 1989, and later with dozens more. It was the biggest coup for the police since Luciano Liggio was put away in 1974.

Riina was taken to a secret location in a top security prison far from Sicily but the anti-Mafia forces were under no illusion as to his continuing power. Liggio himself had continued to run the Cosa Nostra *cupola* from his cell for years and it could be expected that Riina's influence would not be neutralized by his mere imprisonment. Not at all. Much more was yet to be heard of the man who had been described as controlling the most ruthless killing machine in the history of the Mafia.

There were, of course, those who would say with jubilant optimism that now, at last, the Mafia was finished. Without Riina on the outside it could not longer challenge the authorities, no longer muster the power to fight the law. As events would show, that was cloud cuckoo land. 'The aftermath of such a major development is always a difficult time,' said Ferraro. 'The illusion that the Mafia is defeated creates a false sense of well-being. The Mafia was not defeated and if we relaxed our impetus they would be very quick to take the advantage.'

Over the next eighteen months or more, Riina would be brought before various courts in the Italian judicial system to answer the accusations against him, evidence made possible through the testimony of that other modern phenomenon of

Italian life, the *pentiti* who by the spring of 1993 were being counted in their hundreds; there were almost 700 informers by mid-1994. They had come forth in ever-increasing numbers to take advantage of the new law which Falcone and Ferraro had outlined which would give a *pentito* limited protection and an income, though the Italians did not have the resources of the American FBI to provide security and the life-style enjoyed by several of the more senior supergrasses, like Buscetta and Contorno.

The issue of the *pentiti* would draw much criticism, and naturally from the accused men themselves. During the numerous court appearances Riina made in the following eighteen months, he sat passively in his courtroom cage, listening to the informers giving evidence. There would be many accusations. In the first hearing, it would be said that he had ordered the killings of Luigi Impastato, killed in Palermo in 1981, of Salvatore Badalamenti, killed in hospital in Carini in 1983, of Agonstini Badalamenti, killed in Germany in 1984. The list went on, and finally Riina lost his cool, an aspect of his demeanour which had received a good deal of press attention.

'The *pentiti* are being paid to say these things,' he fumed at the judge. 'They are crazy, mad.' His rantings caused the president of the court, Judge Gioacchino Agnello to turn off Riina's microphone. At a later hearing, when the issue of the *pentiti* become a matter for continual public debate and criticism, Riina chose his moment to take advantage.

From a courtroom in Reggio Calabria in May 1994, he managed to give a press conference to reporters, declaring that the accusations against him, and the use of the *pentiti*, was a 'Communist plot' engineered by influential forces, naming specifically the sociologist and author Pino Arlaachi, former president of the Anti-Mafia Commission, and the pro-*pentiti* chief prosecutor for Palermo, Giancarlo Caselli.

By naming these men, Riina was also publicly declaring that they had been 'marked'. They were already in danger; now the risk to their continued survival was even greater.

Riina's ability to hold such a press conference in the middle of one of the most important criminal trials ever staged, caused outrage and the Italian President, Scalfaro, sent what was described to me as a 'hot telegram' to the Ministry of Justice, insisting that Riina should not be allowed to make such public statements again unless in evidence for his own defence.

As the furore over Riina mounted, the anti-Mafia forces secured another major success. On 17 May 1993, Bennedetto 'Nitto' Santapaolo, the most wanted man on their list after Riina, was arrested. As we have seen from previous chapters, he had supposedly been in hiding for almost eleven years, though in fact was living out his luxurious life-style, entertaining important people at his villa outside Catania.

According to the anti-Mafia police, Santapaolo was head of the Catania Mafia and was Riina's 'most ferocious ally'. The *pentiti* had already given chapter and verse on his activities, showing that he controlled many seemingly respectable businesses and real estate investments worth billions of lire in the Catania region which were fronts for his money-laundering and criminal activities.

For years, he had controlled protection rackets and extortion. But one of the most horrifying accusations against him, made by the high-level *pentito* Antonino Calderone, involved the murder of four small boys who had snatched the handbag of Santapaolo's mother. The boys were found, taken into the countryside and kept without food for two days. Other more moderate Mafia soldiers tried to persuade their boss to let the boys go. He refused. According to Calderone, Santapaolo ordered his men to strangle the boys and throw their bodies into a well.

When the carabinieri finally arrested him and searched his hide-out they found a greetings card signed by a Socialist MP for the region. He was just one of several local VIPs, according to the police, who were afforded the voting protection of the Santapaolo family.

By the summer of 1993, the investigators were also adding to the list of politicians and businessmen caught in the corruption trap. There were cases arising throughout Italy, with judges in Milan, Naples, Florence, Rome and elsewhere independently conducting their own particular inquiries and virtually queuing up to make scandalous revelations of corruption.

The so-called 'clean hands' investigations had turned up more links between the Mafia and much more generalized corruption, but by and large the two aspects were considered to be separate – it was seen that corruption per se was endemic in Italian business life, where kick-backs and bribes were expected in both state-owned business and private enterprise.

The political alliances of the Mafia had been brought into focus once again with the evidence of another new *pentito*, Salvatore Cancemi, who was arrested and charged with complicity in the murder of Salvo Lima in 1992, for which he was subsequently sentenced to six-and-a-half years.

Cancemi, who also collaborated with the anti-Mafia forces investigating the murders of Falcone and Borsellino, gave long statements concerning the activities of Riina, Bernardo Brusca, and other leading Mafia bosses. He renewed the allegations that Lima had been the Cosa Nostra's passive link with Rome and, like the others, he noted that Lima was the viceroy in Sicily of Giuliano Andreotti.

Slowly, the judiciary had been building its file on Andreotti, along with several other leading politicians of the past several decades, and these files were scattered among judges who were independently interviewing the *pentiti*, often without knowledge of what others might be saying.

The investigation of Andreotti, however, was placed in the charge of one of Italy's most senior and respected judges, Dr Vittorio Mele who, by the summer of 1993, had amassed a considerable dossier on the former prime minister.

It was a delicate investigation, as Dr Mele himself later described to me when I interviewed him in 1994. Andreotti, then seventy-three, was more than any other living political figure in Italy the embodiment of a political system and administration that had existed since the Christian Democrats were effectively placed in power by the CIA back in 1948.

He became an MP at the age of twenty-seven and had risen quickly through the ranks of power, and was an undersecretary at the office of Prime Minister Alcide de Gasperi by the time he was twenty-nine. He served in office at virtually every one of the major ministries during Italy's fifty or so post-war administrations. His record spoke for itself: prime minister seven times, defence minister eight times, foreign minister five times, treasury minister once, interior minister once.

He had been a dominant figure at every level of Italy's domestic and international political scene for more than forty years and at the time of his final fall from power in 1992, he still commanded the support of 20 per cent of the Christian Democrats, which was sufficient to ensure his supreme power in a party which still held the majority in the Italian parliament in 1993. Though he was personally out of office, and elevated to the role of life senator, the Andreotti faction within the DC remained a force.

His continued presence at the helm had become the topic of national debate, and Andreotti's most famous quip would be recalled: 'Power wears out only those who do not have it.'

The power was still potent, but as Leoluca Orlando, head of La Rete, the anti-Mafia party, pointedly remarked for my benefit that summer: 'Andreotti may have been ousted from the mainstream of government, but he is not yet harmless.'

The weight of material being acquired by Dr Vittorio Mele would, in the fullness of time, neutralize that power once and for all. Andreotti himself was interviewed in regard to allegations made by various informers as to his links with the Mafia through several families on the island of Sicily, and specifically through Salvo Lima.

Andreotti denied such connections, denied that Lima was ever a point of reference between himself and the families mentioned, denied that he associated in any way whatsoever with the Mafia and accused the *pentiti* of terrible calumnies against his Lima and himself, and claimed further that if anyone was a target of the Mafia it was himself.

In August 1993, however, Dr Mele received information which if correct would represent a most damaging allegation against Andreotti, and indeed his party, because scandal would filter all the way back through the DC's years of power.

Dr Mele told me: 'I had been given information which concerned the murder of the journalist Mino Pecorelli, who was killed in 1978 [after publishing an article suggesting that the death of Dalla Chiesa had been ordered because he knew too much about Aldo Moro's murder]. It was suggested by a *pentito* that Signor Andreotti had knowledge of the murder and of its perpetrators and, by implication, a complicity in its execution.'

These allegations came from a particular source in Sicily and soon afterwards Dr Mele flew to America to interview Tommaso Buscetta in his hideaway, to obtain what further information he could. Buscetta confirmed that the murder of Pecorelli was ordered by Stefano Bontate and Gaetano Badalamenti, to ensure that Pecorelli did not publish information which, said Dr Mele, would have been damaging to all concerned.

There now existed a very real prospect of Andreotti being arrested and charged with a number of most serious offences and this in turn brought about a crisis within the government. The national government, consisting of a faltering four-party alliance, collapsed after a left-wing group, the DLP, withdrew its support for the coalition when the government refused to cancel a ruling which granted Giulio Andreotti immunity from prosecution.

By the autumn of 1993, the nation was preparing itself for yet another general election, and the first major change in its electoral system since the days of Mussolini. After a national referendum in April 1993, members of parliament would be elected by a somewhat complicated system of proportional representation.

With the taint of corruption already bubbling through the ranks of Christian Democrats and to a lesser degree in the Socialist Party whose former leader and ex-prime minister, Bettino Craxi, was under investigation for having a secret bank account in Switzerland, Italian politics was already assured of a complete change of face and character.

No less than one third of the members of the Italian parliament, prior to the general election, was under investigation for corruption. Most belonged to the two dominant parties, the DC and the Socialists.

Now a new battle had emerged, with new people, new thinking and, possibly, new connections. On the left stood an alliance of progressives which included the former Communists, college professors, literati and young professionals. On the right, the media tycoon turned politician Silvio Berlusconi who staged a political miracle in forming and promoting a new political party, Forza Italia – 'Come on, Italy' – from nothing in just five months.

He used the power and the weight of his media machine of magazines, newspapers and television stations in a manner unprecedented anywhere in the world where free democracy reigns. He marketed his policies like soap powder and promised tax cuts, higher employment, higher pensions and so on.

Equally on public view even as the election campaign proceeded was the drama of corruption, bribery and greed unfolding almost daily on television. Nearly 1,500 businessmen, politicians and civil servants had been arrested and were moving through Italy's long and often tortuous legal processes. More than 3,000 others had received warrants calling them in for questioning.

When you spoke with some of these older politicians they would say that they were merely victims of the system, that they had simply continued to operate under what had become an all-pervasive Italian culture. In some cases, ministers had been coerced by threats of violence to themselves or their families, or blackmailed into criminality.

But to the exasperated Italian public, it was all too much. The words on everybody's lips were critical of government at a time when Italy's economy was on the rack, more so that in most other European countries. The sight of ministers being accused of graft at a time when so many were thrown out of work or forced to accept lower pay for longer hours, was simply too much. Italy wanted a change, and the worried, lined portrait of Giulio Andreotti, appearing on magazine covers as news of his troubles broke, suddenly became the classic embodiment of a party, a system, even a nation in terrible trouble.

Almost overnight, the ruling elite disappeared from view and office. In their place were new parties, new alliances, new men and with more than half the previous elected representatives out of the running, the new Italian parliament would be assured – whoever won – of a massive injection of new blood and inexperience.

The Mafia was by no means a major issue. Tax, unemployment and the economy all took precedence over law and order, in spite of the attack the judges were making on the establishment through the clean hands policy.

Even as the electioneering began to take off, the Mafia displayed once again its traditional arrogance, showing that it was not scared of the policemen standing on every street corner in Palermo or of the politicians, and that it would have its say, by demonstrating its capacity for violence.

The shock factor was raised even higher.

On a sultry evening in September 1993, Father Giuseppe Puglisi walked out of his church in the heart of Brancaccio, a district on the south-western fringe of Palermo. It was around 8:15 and the priest was tired after a long day – his birthday, in fact.

Puglisi was an unassuming man, a typical parish priest, admired and respected by his community but virtually unknown outside of Brancaccio, a district which is no different to many such poor, unattractive metropolitan quarters in the Sicilian cities. It is a labyrinth of narrow streets, an area where housing is modest and children have nowhere to play but outside, on the cobblestones. Old men sit at their doors or gather in groups, occasionally playing cards.

The women hang their washing from the balconies and most have a basket which they lower down for the postman to drop in their mail. The Mafia is never seen, apparent only from the occasional murder, but it is exactly the kind of area where it thrives, and recruits its youngest members into criminality. The locals never discuss the Cosa Nostra openly, but its members are there amongst them, and the street kids of Brancaccio are natural targets for Mafia membership when they grow older.

Puglisi was, like most priests who serve these areas, deeply involved in parish life but he was different in one single respect. In 1991, he formed a centre, a shelter for the children of his community and for others from outside. His idea was to offer an alternative to the street life, provide a place to play, meet others and join the modest programme of educational activities that Puglisi arranged. Nuns often came by to help, and gradually he was attracting a creditable collection of youngsters.

In that place where the Mafia knows everything, he was always careful, and had not made waves by joining in any of the public anti-Mafia activity that periodically goes on in Palermo. In fact, he kept himself pretty much to himself. He did, however, make one personal stand against the criminals in his midst – he refused to give communion to anyone known to be a mafioso. He also banned a local building firm, known to have Mafia associates, from tendering for a small contract for repairs to the tiny little church of San Gaetano. And, of course, during his educational sessions with the children in his shelter he would gently suggest that the Mafia was an evil in which none of them should become involved, thus robbing the local family of raw recruits. He would say to his colleagues that if he could divert even one potential 'little Riina' then it would be worthwhile.

Puglisi knew that his actions would upset the local Mafia families. The church remains a focal point of Sicilian family life, Mafia or not, but in recent years those who are at the ground level of the church, people like Father Puglisi, have shown an increasing disquiet about continuing to ignore the presence of killers and drug dealers in their midst. They have to be careful and colleagues had warned Puglisi to beware, especially in the area where he worked. The priest would shrug off the warnings: 'What can they do to an unimportant man like myself? Kill me? It is ridiculous.'

That night in September, Father Puglisi got into his battered old car and drove off to his house a mile away in Piazza Anita Garibaldi. He locked the car, and walked to his front door. As he was putting the key in the lock, he heard a noise. Suddenly, two men appeared behind him. One held a 7.65 calibre gun in the back of his neck and fired. An anonymous telephone call to the police – a male voice saying simply there had been a murder – sent paramedics to find him. Father Puglisi was lying in a pool of blood. He was still alive, but died soon after reaching hospital.

The police cordoned off the area around his house. They began asking for witnesses, but no one saw anything or heard anything. Two days later, 8,000 people lined the streets of Brancaccio, weeping and with heads bowed. Many personalities from the anti-Mafia organization came to pay their respects and denounce, over one more tragic coffin, the murderous, heartless band of criminals in their midst.

Today, Father Mario Golesano, who replaced Puglisi in Brancaccio, is keeping up his work with the shelter, though not without some personal fear. He says:

> You cannot help having fear. It haunts us all, everyone who lives here. Visitors who pass through may not experience it, they may not even sense it among us. But we live with an atmosphere of great tension, especially in these areas like Brancaccio. We know now, by this terrible act of murder, this incredible cruelty to a kind and gentle man who was no harm, really, to any living soul, that the Mafia has no heart, that it will if it so decides, punish us without regard for age or status. That is what we live with here. The Mafia is a closed circle and anyone who invades that circle is under fire.

Puglisi's murder was another first for the Mafia – the first priest to be murdered on the island of Sicily. Priests have been killed before, but in vendettas, family matters. Puglisi's was an out and out murder, an example to the public. It strikes a new terror into the hearts of these communities where the Mafia is still patently in control, regardless of the number of troops, the thousands of carabinieri who are occasionally flown in to pursue the perpetrators of atrocities, and then when the outrage has died down, leave again.

Even this 'first' was soon to be overtaken. In March 1994, Padre Giuseppe Diana, a parish priest in the town of Caserta, twenty miles northeast of Naples, was murdered by two gunmen from the Camorra. Like Puglisi, Padre Diana was always prominent in the community, an organizer of what church and social life could be mustered in a poor neighbourhood. He was a totally anonymous priest, known only among his parishioners. He too favoured the education of children against the Mafia, and for that he was murdered.

The murders of churchmen brought into debate the position of the church in regard to the Mafia and it had always been an area of controversy. For many years, senior churchmen in Sicily and in the Neapolitan regions refused to denounce the Mafia and indeed were seen to be in collusion with the Mafia in many areas until comparatively modern times. They saw the atheism of Communism and the liberal views of modernists who wanted the legalization of abortion, who pressed for easier divorce laws and birth control as a far greater danger. Even the Vatican did not begin to recognize the existence of the Mafia until the late 1970s and until quite recently church denunciations of the Mafia were less than emphatic.

Today, there is a groundswell of anti-Mafia feeling among the clergy but in small communities it is left to isolated individuals like Father Puglisi and Padre Diana to take them on – almost eyeball to eyeball. 'It is these atrocities,' said Ferraro, 'that finally make the people turn, and turning they are.'

BOOK THREE

Views from the Front Line

Yes, I know they intend to kill me, that is why I am not allowed for safety reasons to remain with my family and we seldom sleep in the same house . . . it would be far too dangerous for them . . . If one of my bodyguards rings the doorbell, my daughters will ignore him completely as if he weren't there. It is not bad manners . . . they just block out what they do not like . . . they pretend we are living a normal life.

Leoluca Orlando, Mayor of Palermo
to the author, April, 1994

CHAPTER TWENTY

Drugs and Arms as 'Wise Old Members' Guide the Mafia to Recovery

During these months of frenetic activity, one problem area disappeared from the caseload of Liliana Ferraro and the anti-Mafia fighters. Luciano Liggio, undisputed boss of the Corleonesi for almost forty years, de facto head of the Sicilian Cosa Nostra since 1981, when he had the opposition killed, dictator of the criminal network that had spread throughout the world and the man whom even the American factions feared and defied at their peril, died peacefully in his cell in the top security prison on the island of Sardinia in November 1993, at the age of sixty-eight. He was a man to whom could be attributed at the very least 1,000 murders, and probably many more, some of which he carried out personally but most of which were committed at his bidding.

The obituaries were curiously restrained, many ridiculously focusing upon the fact that while in prison he had undergone a rather touching transformation into a man of culture. He wrote poetry and an anthology of letters to his son who had refused to recognize him as his father.

He had become an artist of some renown and a collection of sixty of his landscapes of Corleone and other Sicilian scenes, along with portraits and etchings, attracted queues of thousands when they were displayed in an exhibition at the Marino Gallery in Palermo. Immediately, galleries in New York began to jostle for the opportunity to show his works, which were fetching up to $30,000 a time.

The American interest was understandable, in a commercially voyeuristic way, because his exhibition might show something of the man and offer some explanation of the despicable violence that he had meted out during his life; in other words, a psychiatrist's dream subject. It seemed an ironic notion that this man, who had presided over some of the worst atrocities that had befallen the island of his birth, should be paid the tribute of having people look at his paintings.

It had always been his hope that he would be allowed to attend the exhibition and discuss his work with his 'admirers' but sense prevailed in the Ministry of Justice and he was refused an exit visa from his prison cell to accept these accolades. Instead, he appointed his ageing sister from Corleone, Maria-Antonietta, to be his representative and collect the proceeds of his sales which he donated to provide a kidney machine at Corleone hospital – the hospital where, it will be recalled, his predecessor as head of the Corleonesi, Dr Michele Navarra, had given the young shepherd boy a lethal injection of poison to stop him telling the police about Liggio's murder of the trade unionist Placido Rizzotto in 1948.

Not long before he died, he was also given the opportunity to garner some decent PR when he gave a television interview from prison. He had dressed himself immaculately, sat smoking a cigar, and exuded great opulence, with the air of a feted tycoon holding forth on the problems of the world. He had all the arrogance that had been noted by his past adversaries, like Judge Cesare Terranova, General Dalla Chiesa, Rocco Chinnici, Giovanni Falcone and Paolo Borsellino. Unlike them, he had survived to die a natural death.

He had spent the last nineteen years of his life in prison, but it had not affected his ability to control and run his empire through his aides, lieutenants, and associates like the Grecos, Riina, Madonia, Santapaolo and others. Now these men too – the biggest of Mafia bosses – were in prison and the people of Sicily might have given a sigh of relief that in one year all this had come to pass, that at last those headlines about the Mafia being defeated, repeated down the years for a century or more, might finally have a ring of truth.

Defeat? It is not a word that is in the Mafia vocabulary. And without exception, every single person I interviewed for this book during 1993 and 1994 would not contemplate the use of the word either. The Mafia may have lost, temporarily, some of its most strident leaders to far off prison cells. But, as Liggio himself had proved for the previous twenty years, merely being in prison does not put them out of action. Liggio, I would be reminded time and time again, was in prison at the time of the Corleonesi's rise to domination of the Cosa Nostra, and the Mafia's of international crime.

In the late seventies, during that blight of kidnappings carried out by the organization he had formed, Kidnappers Anonymous, he was in prison. During the mass murders of the early 1980s when the Bontate, Inzerillo, Badalamenti and Riccobono families were virtually wiped out, he was in prison. When in 1981 he informed the American families that the Corleonesi had taken over as the controlling partner in the drug trafficking empire and thereafter they became the largest exporter of heroin and cocaine in the world, he was in prison. And, eventually, when he came before the maxi-trial accused of these crimes, he had the perfect defence. He was in prison. Now so were half a dozen of the other big bosses and in Sicily it does not mean a thing. Nothing changes. The Mafia is as present as ever, nowhere and everywhere, buried deep in Sicily's culture and indelibly marked upon its social and business life.

That very aspect of the Mafia, the cultural and social impact of its existence upon Sicilian life – not to mention the criminal – was still being debated when I returned to Palermo and its surrounds in April 1994, in the wake of the general election which had seen the modern political miracle of Silvio Berlusconi claiming power.

His Forza Italia movement had formed a government with the help of an uneasy alliance with the Northern League and the re-styled neo-Fascists, leaving the Christian Democrat party, which had for so long relied upon Sicily for its vote, which was delivered by the Mafia, shattered.

I travelled first to Corleone, that unlovely little town straddling the hillside on a road which winds out of Palermo and across the Plain of the Albanians and into Sicily's rugged interior. Many writers have tried to give an impression of menace, and true enough it looks a shabbily forlorn assembly of ugly dwellings, but no more forlorn than a thousand such towns in the south of Italy. More is perhaps expected of a place of such notoriety. Visitors with knowledge of criminal associations might expect its streets to be paved with gold plate, the piazzas filled with swank restaurants, the roads cluttered with Mercedes and BMWs and the hillsides jammed with luxurious mansions. Of course, no such trappings of wealth exist. Corleone is just a typical, slightly sleepy, slightly menacing little Sicilian town, home to 12,000 largely struggling inhabitants.

The most famous sons of the most famous criminal clan in the world have evidently not invested much of their ill-gotten billions in the the town from which they takes their name. But it does have a certain charm. Its architecture is crumbling, which as any traveller to southern Italy knows is fairly typical, there are few civic facilities, and the cobbled streets shake your bones in the small rented Fiats that are used by most visitors. Such cars are easily spotted, and attract inquisitive gazes and occasionally the attention of young criminals. The local population is used to the tourist visitors, eager to put a face to the town of Corleone that the *Godfather* trilogy made famous.

There is an air of menace but it only becomes apparent when you ask the wrong questions. 'Can you direct me to the Riina house?' I inquired several times before I managed to elicit a reply from a young man, looking this way and then that, who finally signalled the way Rua Del Piano.

There will be discovered a two-storey villa with the name Riina handwritten underneath the bell. Antonietta and her children returned to the town after Toto Riina was arrested. There was no need to hide any longer. I knocked on the door, and heard shouts from within, but no one responded.

A boy of ten or eleven passing by nonchalantly says, 'They will not answer.'

'The Riinas?' I asked.

'You are a stranger,' he replied and walked on. Nor would anyone in that street answer my inquiries as to the whereabouts of Signora Riina.

Back in the town, officials will talk openly about Corleone

being an industrious little town and hasten to add, and do so repeatedly to all inquisitive callers, that the Mafia does not reside there any more. They are trying desperately to live down the image. One official told me:

> We have been hostages to the name of the Corleonesi for years. That is why the carabinieri always pick on us. They come here first. When the helicopters and the tanks came last year, it caused great discomfort and fear to our people. But what was the point of it? To show off? To tell the world that the anti-Mafia is doing something, and of course it is attacking Corleone. What did they expect to find – a gang of mafiosi drinking vino in the town square? Ridiculous! The truth is that most of our people have nothing to do with the Mafia. The majority have rejected old influences and despise what has happened just as much as people in Milan might. We did not blow up Falcone or Borsellino. It was nothing to do with us, and we have great sympathy with those who have suffered.

But then, talking later to a young man who, like most, refused to be identified, it was apparent that fear remains a very strong element of life in Corleone.

> Young people here do not wish to become criminals. Like every town, we have our element of tearaways. You can see them, some of them sitting around here. I can point out two or three young men who will become mafiosi, of that I am quite sure. The Mafia is still here, but you will never hear the name mentioned. Nobody says 'Mafia' or 'Cosa Nostra' in this town. Nobody says it, but their presence is known to those of us who live our lives here. Mafia people live there pointing up on the hill, and there in the big villa behind you, and so on. Now, I must go . . .'

Back in Palermo, that bustling city where attempting to negotiate a set of traffic lights represents a far greater danger to tourists than the guns of the mafiosi, I began my task of attempting to put some answers to many pressing questions which anyone with the slightest knowledge of the Mafia activity of the last half century and more would wish to ask. For a mere visitor to the island and to the country, observations can only be descriptions of what is apparent on the surface, allied to factual history. It would be presumptuous in the extreme to begin to expound on what lies beneath, and so I wanted this to come from the people themselves. Thus I set out here the responses to a number of interviews I conducted in Palermo during April and May 1994 from which I believe the reader may glean something of the underlying feelings of the people who have lived their lives in this atmosphere of crime and crisis, where they may wake up on any day and find bodies in the streets or a thug on the doorstep demanding his piece of the action.

What very quickly became apparent is that just as the chronicles of Mafia criminality are unending, so is the anguish among the Sicilian people. Listening to them attempt to explain to the listener the cancer in their midst, it is, in the end, as if they are really trying to explain it to themselves, and thus expiate what appears to be an underlying guilt that the Mafia has been allowed to exist all these years because in Sicily there is a culture of consent.

Franco Nicastro, the brilliant investigative journalist who during his career had reported on most of Palermo's most outstanding cases, is now an executive: Presidenze, Ufficio Stampa (Press Officer), Palermo. A charming man, he greeted me with a welcoming handshake and a glass of thick blood-red Sicilian orange juice to wash away the dust. He talked at length and fearlessly. We had a long discussion, and I give below a tape-recorded extract with the interruption of my questions deleted:

> The problem of dealing with the Mafia has really moved on from a technical, legal aspect to a political one. We see the emotional reaction of the people and the politicians following each of the terrible atrocities. First there are tears from the public and a show of force from the State, and then after a period of time has elapsed we return to where we were before. We have new laws and more police, but the Mafia is still here.

In recent times, we have been seeing some stronger reactions from the people themselves, even from that part of the population geographically and traditionally linked to the Mafia. This is new, and it goes along with the new political climate. But I am not at all sure that it will be sustained.

Some alarming signals have come precisely from the general election in the declarations, statements and political projections of the new majority [headed by Silvio Berlusconi]. It leads me to think that they are looking for an easy consensus in all sectors of Italian life, setting aside the Mafia and the criminal problem in favour of other situations – important ones no doubt, such as the economy, unemployment and productivity. But this in turn will have the effect of helping a new Mafia strategy although in actual fact it is an old strategy.

The Mafia bosses will now be regrouping after the onslaught of the judges and the police of recent years. Its wise old members will counsel the movement towards recovery. The political line the Mafia has always conserved is never to enter into conflict with the dominating political regime. That's the way this old and ancient institution has survived so long.

Very important results have been obtained. Many Mafia members have decided to disassociate from Toto Riina and his leading group which has become a true dictatorship that not even the Mafia tolerate in the end. They got to the point of wanting to destroy Riina's power over the *cupola* and allowed his arrest. They knew that by following Riina's policy, the Mafia risked destruction from within itself. Riina's power was destablizing.

The public, even those in Mafia areas, began to show solidarity with the judges, especially in the most difficult times that we have recently experienced. Unfortunately, it does not last. This is due to the attitudes of both the working classes and the middle classes. The middle class do not believe strongly enough in the possibility of retreating from long-existing economical and environmental relationships with the Mafia in Sicily's history. The lower class, meanwhile, continues to become a breeding ground for criminality because of the economic situation.

There has been an under-estimation, a setting aside, in the past, of this problem and now it is returning. It is classic cause and effect. A poor public spending policy encouraged a system of patronage and public assistance. There has traditionally been a lack of investment in social and structural problems in the regions of Italy to the south of Naples.

Successive ruling administrations preferred a scattergun approach, dispersing public funds at a whim and without particular planning. In this way many more people were tied to the political system, so it was easier to obtain political consent. And more so, because of the Mafia's historical involvement in public works contracts. This attitude of government proved very useful indeed to people who live by obtaining public money for their projects.

Some time ago, I was more optimistic that progress was being made against the Mafia, now less so. I look at the middle class of Palermo as lacking in culture and it is directing itself, as a whole, towards television, surrendering most of all to the image of the strong personality, like Berlusconi. It is spreading throughout Italian life.

The attitude towards the Mafia also swings through its various stages and is present in all manifestations of social, business and political life. What I am saying is far too obvious, too common for those of us who live with it daily. It is clear that this situation strikes and astonishes the people who don't live here and it is only when we are confronted by the questions of visitors, that it reminds us of the enormity of what is happening. You have told me you notice a certain disregard for basic rules. There is a natural aversion to authority among Sicilians, which is born out of centuries of oppression and it is also out of that oppression that the Mafia was born, and became the oppressors.

The system of patronage, as another example, has existed for so long here that it is a way of life. People are always giving gifts, continuously seeking favours. In the end, the simplest favour is considered an exchange of interests between the two parties. This culture based on favours is more widespread than one thinks because it derives from a vicious origin that in some ways involves the entire life of a man from birth to death and intervenes in the most important movements of one's life, such as getting a job, or finding a house. Even work might be considered a favour, a privilege.

So at its most basic level, work, employment, which is normally a right that you achieve on the basis of qualifications, skills and professional ability, becomes part of the patronage system, and transforms itself into a favour granted by those who make you the offer, and a dependence is established. Your rights as an individual have made you a recipient of a favour.

This exchange of favours is the basis of corruption. It has deep socio-political roots and surely has resulted in the serious consequences that we have seen materializing recently.

The rules of the game have been long established here in Palermo, dating back to the early part of this century. The famous murder of Notarbartolo, for example, which is still a matter for discussion here, was a trial that ended negatively because politics violated the rules. The killers were acquitted and everything returned to the status quo. It is perhaps possible to identify that moment in our history as the point from which there could be no return – it is still happening today.

Then in 1926 and beyond, people believed that the Mafia would be defeated by Mussolini's Iron Man, Cesare Mori, when the regime had to put on a show of tranquillity, security, order, demonstrating the existence of a solid State. But we know how it finished. Mori thought that after the arrest of some Mafia bosses, he had done his job. He could have looked deeper, into the relationship between high officials of the regime and the Mafia, but he did not. They boasted that the Mafia was beaten, and it was not.

The undoubtedly decisive factor in the resurgence of the Mafia, and all that it later entailed, was the allied invasion of 1943. The alliance between the Americans and the Mafia chieftains actually provided the Mafia with its launching pad for all that came in the future – legitimizing the socio-political role of the Mafia; this was one of the single most important factors in the development of the Mafia from then on.

The political influences became widely established, and we have seen quite recently that the all of these things, political or social patronage, corruption, state violation of the rules, were brought into play than during the maxi-trials. Through devious means, the process of law was slowed down and all the work of the anti-Mafia forces became undermined by clandestine intervention at some point or other which led initially to so many acquittals. Someone, somewhere had ordered that to happen, or ensured the necessary delays so that time ran out for the prosecutions under our law. And the Mafia walked free.

That is our burden in Sicily. It is not just the Mafia. It is politics, too. The old political philosophy enabled the Mafia to work within the State; it had been going on for so long there was never any opposition. Even so, I am unsure that the new majority will not necessarily focus strongly on the Mafia. We must wait and see . . .

The cultural aspect of the Mafia allied to Sicilian and Italian life was the main thrust of the conference I attended at the Pedro Arrupe Institute for Political Education in Palermo in April 1994. It attracted eminent local speakers and the hall where it was held was packed to overflowing. The venue was important. The centre was founded in 1961 and run by Jesuit priests whose traditional outspokeness against the Mafia has in itself been of heroic proportions. In 1992 the centre received a $1 million grant from the Japanese Sasakawa Foundation, which links it to the resources of fifty other universities around the world.

It was one of several conferences organized in the run-up to the second anniversary of the murder of Giovanni Falcone. What struck me, as a visitor, was the interest which these conferences attracted among local people. Audiences were made up of a fairly diverse cross-section, from young students to elderly folk of average background. The common reaction to the speeches of the professors was: Why do we allow the Mafia survive and thrive?

It seemed to me curious that the Sicilians – and presumably the Neapolitans faced with the Camorrists and the Calabrians confronted by the 'Ndrangheta – should gather in such numbers for a kind of mass contemplation, as if it was necessary to confirm to one another that they had to do something, but quite what should be done was a matter for discussion. Demonstrations, political lobbying and even education in schools had taken them towards a goal but then, as Leoluca Orlando described, there would be sudden reverses.

Francesco Renda, professor emeritus of history at the University of Palermo, agreed:

> I would underline the fact that whereas here in public and at universities, we can openly speak about the Mafia, in Corleone and other places where the Mafia is strong, they can't. They have different clandestine names – in my village mafiosi are called *code piatte* [flat tails]. There is an element of fear in this, but there is also another reason, that simply speaking of the Mafia was a way of offending Sicilian people and they feel the need to react quite violently against the accusations.
>
> This is probably because the rules of behaviour have changed. Once, the Mafia would not kill women and children. Now they do. Once, the Mafia meant protection and it had the ability to prevail with a certain kind of 'justice'; today, we have to distinguish between the roles and functions of the Mafia, between the military wing and the families who still maintain their hold over community life, in this role as protectors.

What was apparent from these discussions was the knowledge among those taking part that the Mafia actually could not exist without some kind of support from elements of the population itself – the people themselves had not shut the door on the Mafia, because its influence still permeated down from the head of each Mafia family, through to street level, especially in the rural communities and townships.

Professor Bartolomeo Sorge, director of the university and a spiritual mentor of Leoluca Orlando, organized the conference. He has lived for nine years with threats to his own life because of his constant condemnation of the Mafia. He has a permanent bodyguard. He spoke at length on the culture of Sicilian life as one of the three most important aspects of the Mafia problem. The other two were political and economic, and all three in his opinion were more fundamental than the criminal aspect. He quoted the example of an intelligent professional young woman in the town where Madonia was the Godfather. 'Who will look after us now?' she asked after he was arrested. Sorge went on:

> It's illuminating, isn't it, that such a question should be asked in the 1990s. The Mafia phenomenon is a many-headed complexity. In many ways, it is specific to the Sicilian way of thinking, which has traditionally fostered the Mafia with a conspiracy of silence initiated through fear or because the Mafia is accepted as an essential element of our lives, ensuring jobs, protection and so on. Fortunately, this attitude is changing, but the new political system we have cannot fight it alone.
>
> There are widely held views on the relationship between politics and the Mafia – that the Mafia could not exist without politics. This may have been true in the past, but equally, the State had to be present in the fight against the Mafia, through the police, the army and the magistrature, and it has been. But I would compare its attitude to mowing the grass: the State has been cutting the grass, continually, but has never tackled the roots. So the grass grows again and the illusion that the Mafia is defeated soon fades because the roots were untouched.
>
> The complexity of Sicilian culture that favours the Mafia has been analysed by some of our finest writers. They conclude that Sicilians generally are more shrewd than prudent, more acute than honest. They love innovations, they are quarrelsome and envious by nature. They are subtle critics of authority, they believe that they know the answers to the problems of government. And yet on the other hand they are obedient, faithful to their rulers,

always ready to help, affectionate to strangers and loyal to their friends.

Their nature is complicated by two extremes: they are extremely shy and extremely bold. They are shy when they are dealing with their own business since they have a devotion to their personal interests and want to be successful. But they can transform themselves – like Proteus, the pagan god who would change his form continuously to avoid being recognized. They will submit to anyone who can help them and appear as if they were born precisely to serve, and then they will become totally the opposite, temerarious to the extreme.

Beyond these personality traits, there are additional factors which come into play, such as Sicily's historical insecurity, its geographical location and Mediterranean nature all of which have combined to create a vision of life which contains elements of fear, apprehension, suspicion, passions and difficulties in formal external relationships.

Insecurity and fear led the Sicilians to believe that there was privilege to be obtained through violence, whereas actually it has merely led to cowardice, weakness and arrogance. Psychologically, all of these aspects are crucial in examining how the Mafia has developed.

We must remember that it derived originally from an agricultural base, and passed on into an urban culture. The Mafia changed from its control of the fields to the urban rackets that we are all familiar with, the contracts, the building works, eventually adopting its international profile. Even now, it is still changing, undergoing financial reconstruction. We know that, but we find ourselves first and foremost dealing with an inherent cultural phenomenon which has to be understood before it can be tackled effectively.

The Sicilian culture itself is also changing, to bring itself more in line with national trends. Modern ways are cutting into the Sicilian way of life and the unconditional sense of feudal obedience, say, to the Godfather of a family which is typical of the culture of the whole of Sicily, may well be fading. The sense of friendship, so deep rooted and so nice in Sicily, which has degenerated into the system of patronage in business and politics and from which *omertà* is born, is an old value which is being challenged.

The 700 *pentiti*, for example, who have come forward to speak against the Mafia bosses have revolutionized the concept of servility, of *omertà* and of the slavery which was deeply rooted in Mafia traditions. Today, loyalty to a pact which was previously controlled by fear or revenge, or vendetta, is being rejected by men previously loyal to the conspiracy. So the Mafia is looking for a new legitimacy. This is what people like Toto Riina are after, and what frightens me is that a new form of legitimacy is already appearing which may even be a greater threat than the death and oppression upon which the Mafia feeds.

Only the cultural commitment, an effort by the people themselves, can attack the Mafia at its roots.

Umberto Santino and his wife Anna Puglisi have devoted their lives to the crusade of fighting the Mafia, and anyone in search of heroes of the fight could do no better than to seek out this unassuming couple whose lives are under constant threat but who have no bodyguards or State security cordons to protect them. They receive no state support, and rely on their lecture tours, writings and occasional funding from external agencies like the United Nations for their income.

Umberto Santino is the director of the Giuseppe Impastato Sicilian Centre of Documentation, the largest private archive on the Mafia anywhere in the world, and Santino himself is one of the world's foremost experts on organized crime, and specifically the Mafia. Santino knows about Sicilian culture and traditions; he has been observing them and recording them in all their gory detail these past twenty years or more.

He has listened to all the arguments of the psychologists and the sociologists, but he tends to wave them aside. To him, Mafia means criminality: gangsters, smugglers, extortionists, blackmailers, kidnappers, torturers, dope-dealers, killers. He has no time for niceties.

A tough, fast-talking man, Santino has lectured all over the world, is called upon regularly by universities, and by national and internationally-sponsored conferences on organized crime. He has written histories of international drug trafficking and has recently focused on the world black money market, which is clearly causing the international finance community considerably more anguish than they publicly care to admit.

Santino's documentation centre, which was a source of much background material for this book, was founded by himself and his wife in 1977 following the assassination of Giuseppe Impastato, an outspoken left-wing opponent of the Mafia from Cinisi. Since then, the Santinos have built up their huge library which now covers virtually every move made by the Mafia this century. Santino and some daring presses have courageously published strong articles and exposés dating from a time long before Falcone was prominent in the anti-Mafia crusade, when the Mafia's associates in politics and business would willingly sue.

The Santinos are to be discovered in an ordinary apartment building in the centre of Palermo. Their apartment is distinguishable only by its heavy entrance door, with its multi-lock system which would be adequate for the gold room door at Fort Knox. To anyone interested in the Mafia, the contents of this apartment are probably just as valuable. The rooms are lined with bookshelves, with row upon row of box files, books, a collection of oral histories, legal files, often clandestinely obtained, statements from 'deep throat' contacts inside the military and the police, reports from spies within the Camorra and the 'Ndrangheta, intelligence from all round Europe, the United States, Canada and South America.

Santino currently has two objectives in his battle, where the odds against success are as long as the commitment of he and his wife is undaunted: to target both the activities of criminal organizations in the traffic of drugs and weapons, and the global financial complex which allows the accumulation of capital and its reinvestment by criminal groups.

Santino deals in stark, hard statistics. He can quote drug totals exported into Europe, the US or anywhere else on the globe. He can tell you how much cocaine was produced last year in Columbia, or how many billions of narco-dollars were estimated to have been transmitted through the world money markets. His theses are often complicated but he speaks without fear:

There has been some suggestion recently that the Sicilian Mafia has been downgraded in the international traffic of drugs and criminality in general. I think this view should be treated with great caution. Drugs still form a great part of the revenue of the Cosa Nostra families but I do not think we should talk in terms of who is Number One or Number Two in the world in terms of criminal groupings.

The criminal market, to use a commercial term, is very complex. There are periods when it is possible to speak about which group is leading in, say, the international cocaine market and which is leading in the arms trade. In Europe, the Sicilian Mafia has negotiated agreements with other groups, particularly those who operate in what was the Soviet Union.

The Cosa Nostra retains primary control, in other words they have established agreements which ensure that nothing happens in their territories without their involvement at some level, whether it is the financing of, say, a drugs operation or the purchase and resale of arms.

The Cosa Nostra has a particular involvement in the prime ports where cocaine is imported into Europe from South America. This is in some ways a reversal of the origins of the Sicilian Mafia's drugs connections. They are more concerned with ensuring their involvement in the cocaine market, and this to a large extent involves traffic in the opposite direction, incoming as well as outgoing. But that is not to say they are out of the heroin business, either. Perhaps a third of the heroin imported into the US annually is of Mafia origin.

From the mid-1980s, Spain became the established country of entry of cocaine into Europe; there are now several points of entry and there is usually Mafia involvement at virtually every level.

The drugs trade is far more complex than it was before because where once it was dominated by the Italian Mafia, Europe has a much more diverse spread of criminal groups which have emerged in the past five years, notably the so-called Russian Mafia, the Triads, the Japanese Mafia and the Afro-Caribbean groups; there are many more.

Today there is a modern Mafia which, to me, is a configuration of criminal groups based in style and operation on the historical dealings of the Sicilian Cosa Nostra. There are a lot of new relationships and inter-activity. There is competition and there is war.

The arms trade which has always been part of Mafia business is now more important to them, and it has entered a highly dangerous area, embracing nuclear arms. Thus, they have found it convenient to trade with other groups, from Russia and Asia and even Germany. But in reality, there is nothing new in that. The Mafia has always been adept at negotiating alliances, so long as it remains in control.

In the past, it has been able to operate within the State because of its insidious connections in Italian politics and only recently have commentators from outside focused upon this aspect of the Mafia, as if it were something new. The judicial attack on corruption that existed in Italian political and business life has attracted international attention, but it has existed for many years. As far as the Mafia is concerned, I do not believe these recent investigations and prosecutions will curtail their activities. Why should it? It never has in the past and in any event, the climate is now perhaps more conducive to their prosperity.

The fall of Christian Democracy in this country has seen the emergence of the new political alliance of the right and the focus of the new government will be deflected away from the Mafia for some years to come. This will allow Cosa Nostra to flourish and the future for the Mafia is very good, because in Italy now, we have a form of criminocracy. There are criminals among those in power, even under the new alliance.

Also, we now have the possibility of having ministers in the government who are neo-Fascists who have no particular interest in fighting the Mafia, and we have in that same alliance the Northern League who would prefer to see Sicily floated off from mainland Italy. This is good news for the Mafia.

Another interesting fact is that there is a reaction against magistrates because of what has happened in Sicily in the past few years and ultimately, what will transpire is the revival of Mafia violence against the judiciary. Historically the Mafia utilizes its old experiences and merges them with new. What is happening in Italian politics will not detract from their continued operations.

They keep abreast of developments, do not go into conflict with politics and they take on board new operations and opportunities as they occur, but never let go of the old. They are updating all the time, like a multinational conglomerate. It is difficult to identify exactly which source is the cornerstone of their revenue. Extortion or protection, for example, has become a most lucrative activity in recent years – because of the extent of it in our towns and cities – and was identified in 1991 as still very important to traditional Mafia families. The frauds on the EC in which the Mafia is involved have similarly produced big revenues. Under every heading of traditional Mafia activity, it is possible to list very substantial figures, whether it is drugs, weapons, smuggling, prostitution, gambling, blackmail, frauds, public works.

The control of the Mafia is totalitarian, in many ways, and it has the ability to overcome setbacks. The trend, for those of us who live with it, is familiar: you have the beginnings of a major investigation, a new clamp-down on the Mafia; then comes a big assassination; followed by the reaction of the State and by the people; then the reaction simply fades away.

The anti-Mafia people try to keep the impetus alive, but it is often difficult and now, after the election, we have a situation where the prognosis under the new political alliance is very bad for us, very good for the Mafia. Neither is the culture of mediation between politics, business and the Mafia simply going to vanish. We now have direct involvement of government with business. The culture of Berlusconi and the political leadership is very anti-democratic, populist and arrogant. And we know from experience here that the combination of criminal activity with political power and social power is very dangerous.

If confirmation were ever required that the Mafia is still very much in business, as outlined by Santino, it came in September 1994 when a series of arrests were made in a joint operation between Italian and American police following an investigation codenamed Operation Onig which had lasted several months, centring once again on drugs activity in New York and the revival of the Pizza Connection.

It had been widely believed that the Pizza chain was back in operation for the distribution of heroin and cocaine. But this time, there was an added twist – the use of the United States as a staging post. While the Sicilians were once again bringing in the heroin, they were also returning with heavy loads of cocaine, bought in by the American Mafia and sold on to the Sicilians who could make very substantial profits in the European and former Soviet bloc countries.

This reversal of the old trafficking routes – as correctly identified by Santino long ago – was possible because as the Columbians and other South American cartels flooded the American market with cocaine, the price dropped. In Europe, however, a kilo of cocaine, in the autumn of 1994, was fetching $60,000 – three times its price in New York.

The investigation had taken three years to come to fruition, after the FBI had identified a Sicilian emigré running a New York pizza parlour with two of his brothers as a linchpin in the operation. A breakthrough occurred in May 1993 when the FBI intercepted a package containing three kilos of cocaine which the gang had attempted to mail from New York to Italy. The customary wiretaps were set in place, and the coded messages once again were passing back and forth.

By then, the FBI had tracked the routes of the cocaine and heroin drops, and had set up police surveillance in Mexico, Switzerland, Greece, France and Italy. In November 1993 there was another breakthrough: 168 kilos of cocaine worth more than $10 million wholesale and $30 million retail was seized as it was about to be smuggled aboard an Alitalia airliner in Bogatà.

As the network was watched and tracked, the FBI held conferences with the Italian police and decided to move in on 19 September 1994. Two hundred FBI agents arrested twenty-seven people in New York, while simultaneously, the Italians arrested fifty-six – diversely scattered in Cosa Nostra, Camorra and 'Ndrangheta territory.

It was one more set of arrests – but, as Santino insists, the Mafia goes on. Between the summer and autumn of 1994, the Italian and American agencies were in close contact, once again, along with other drugs agencies of other countries, some in South America. It had become clear, by then, that the Italian Mafia had moved back heavily into the drugs trade, deeply involving itself in every corner of the trade – processing and wholesaling heroin and taking on huge cocaine shipments for the European market and all points east.

As I write, predictions made to me by several Italian crime experts and officers involved in the fight, that the European drugs scene was on the point of an explosion similar to that which occurred in America in the early 1980s, were already proving entirely accurate. Although, as Santino rightly identified, there were now many more criminal groups vying for the business, the Mafia was in control of a large slice of the market.

Some very senior mafiosi had been in place since the end of 1993, notably in Germany, France and Scandinavian countries, to establish the routes and build up the connections. Among them was Toto Riina's brother-in-law Leoluca Bargarella, fifty, who was believed to have entered Britain through an east coast ferry port in the late summer of 1993 to establish an import network. Bargarella, like Riina's other main lieutenant in the Corleonesi, Bernardo Provenzano, has continued to elude police in Italy and throughout Europe.

The continued presence on the scene of Provenzano was arrogantly confirmed in the spring of 1994, when he had his lawyers in Palermo issue a statement denying allegations of his involvement in a particular Mafia atrocity.

Meanwhile, the British National Criminal Intelligence Service, in cooperation with their counterparts in Italy, established the presence in Britain of several known Mafia fugitives. One, who was the subject of an extradition order, had moved to Manchester, while an associate was living at a house in Rochdale. Another, linked to a Camorra family, was operating from an Italian restaurant in Scotland. The Mafia figures were identified soon after an abortive attempt to smuggle 230 kilos of cocaine by lorry through the port of Felixstowe, Suffolk. As the NCIS have repeatedly pointed out to the Home Office, Britain

– along with other EC countries – is proving to be a haven for mafiosi, because of the recent relaxation of entry checks by immigration and customs officers on EC nationals. The scale of the new drugs explosion is best signposted by the amount of drugs confiscated. In Britain during 1993, the amount was worth $3.6 billion, including more than 2,500 kilos of cocaine. If this is the amount captured, the figures for the drugs that managed to reach the market must be touching new heights, not just in Britain but across Europe, the eastern bloc and down to Australasia.

The move towards easier cross-border access as the EC moves towards the goals of the Maastricht treaty will, as Liliana Ferraro told me, eventually make it easier for the criminals, too. This problem is already at the forefront of EC discussion on organized crime, and Britain, now aware through continual warnings from criminal intelligence of the mounting drugs traffic into the country, launched its own anti-drugs campaign in October 1994.

Education at street level, however, is in itself merely toying with the problem. Almost at the same time as Britain's John Major launched his anti-drugs campaign, another of his government departments right at the forefront of the drugs war was being cut back. In October 1994, the week after the anti-drugs campaign began, it was revealed that one in five Customs and Excise staff were to be made redundant, including 600 front-line drugs officers.

The news came as the Italians were among those pressing for high-level joint EC and international action to stem the flow. The need for a strong European combative force with a base in all major EC countries to fight all aspects of organized crime, from drugs to money-laundering, was already apparent. Yet conflicting actions from inter-related government departments across Europe once again seem more likely to aid the Mafia rather than hinder it.

CHAPTER TWENTY-ONE

A Scare for the 'Walking Corpse' as Homes of Seventeen Mayors Are Bombed

In May 1994 Ferraro visited Sicily where she would be attending church services and public meetings in Palermo for the second anniversary of Falcone's death. Once more, as she passed the turn-off to Capaci on the road into the city from Punta Raisa airport, her stomach churned. Later, in the city itself, she found that already the anti-Mafia crusade which had flared with such public outrage in the wake of Falcone's death had itself suffered setbacks.

In the 1994 election, the anti-Mafia party, La Rete, headed by Leoluca Orlando, the mayor of Palermo, who has variously been described as the people's hero and a walking corpse, fared badly. Having achieved an unprecedented 70 per cent of the vote for the Mayoral election in 1993, Orlando's party did not take one of Sicily's fifty-three parliamentary seats.

They were virtually all won by the right-wing parties of Berlusconi and the neo-Fascist National Alliance. Perhaps the most significant outcome was the humbling of one of the great anti-Mafia heroes, the courageous former chief magistrate Antonio Caponetto who originated the anti-Mafia Pool back in the early eighties with Chinnici, Falcone and Borsellino.

Elected to the city council the previous year in the wake of the

Falcone and Borsellino murders, he scored the highest number of votes, with 40,000.

In the space of a year, attitudes towards the anti-Mafia brigade had altered significantly. In the general election, he was heavily defeated by a neo-Fascist candidate. A similar fate was suffered in Milan by Nando Dalla Chiesa, the general's son, and by the La Rete candidate in Catania where the film director Franco Zeffirelli was elected on the Forza Italia ticket.

Caponetto immediately resigned from the city council to devote more time to the anti-Mafia fight and commented bitterly: 'The vote has shown the patent determination by the majority of voters to exclude from parliament the most prominent people in a struggle that has to be carried on more intensely than ever.'

Mafia experts afterwards tracked a particular pattern in the voting, and suggested that the Cosa Nostra families had thrown their weight behind Neo-Fascists and Forza Italia. Whether they wanted it or not, the new majority had the backing of the Mafia.

Leoluca Orlando, the mayor of Palermo, was feeling more isolated than ever. In April 1994, local building workers went on strike to protest at the closing down of a large number of building projects suspected of having been under Mafia control. Orlando's name was mud, and he was once again being criticized by a section of the electorate who had put him in office to clean up the city. People who had once crowded around him and sung out his praises had clearly deserted his party, and all that it stood for, i.e. fighting the Mafia. It was a predictable sign of the times, following the pattern predicted by Franco Nicastro – outrage, emotion, apathy.

Orlando had in recent months put up with a long-running campaign against him by the building workers following his announcement precluding Sicilian firms from tendering for public works contracts unless they could prove categorically to be untainted by the Mafia. He faced taunts of: 'Orlando OUT. Mafia IN.'

He was warned specifically by one of the new *pentiti* in 1994 that he had been moved to the top of the Mafia hit list along with Liliana Ferraro. They would kill him at the earliest opportunity. His wife, Molly, and their two teenage daughters

Eleonora and Lena, are under constant guard, often living in police barracks or in hideaway villas.

Orlando himself lives almost permanently in bunker conditions, surrounded by a contingent of fifteen armed guards working on a shift rota. He is extremely careful about his security, although as a politician he cannot help putting himself constantly in front of the public.

He varies his movements and calendar and often makes two appointments for the same time in different places, so that no one knows until the last minute where he is likely to be.

Interviewed for this book, he spoke frankly, and occasionally with some very considerable emotion, of his feelings:

> I have not had what you might term a private life, a comfortable existence with my wife and two daughters for nine years now. It hurts me and it hurts them but we never speak of it when we are together, although my family often, very often, notice that I am afraid, that I do have fear. When I am in Palermo, I am not allowed for safety reasons to stay in our house for long. It would be too dangerous for my family. But we always try to spend some time together in our home even if it is only a brief period. Maybe we still fool ourselves that we have a normal life, because my wife and children live as normally as possible.
>
> The house where we, or more specifically they, live is super-protected. My office is Rome is similarly protected with metal walls. We travel in bombproof cars with permanent guard. My family lives anonymously, as far as possible. We are never photographed together and there are no official pictures of them because they could be too easily identified. My daughters try to avoid having a security escort. Who wants to go to a disco with an escort? How do they meet their friends with a guard in their shadow?
>
> When we are together, we try to be absolutely normal with each other, as if this other world did not exist. This is only possible with the love we feel for one another. But they do have a strange way of showing me their love and resentment at the same time. They behave with me as if I were 'normal'; they never speak about politics or what I do. They don't show the slightest interest in my beliefs

or interviews, newspaper articles, etc, and if at any time I happen to speak about what I am doing at that moment in time, or what I am planning, they simply go out of the room or change the subject very quickly.

If one of my bodyguards rings the doorbell, they will open the door without saying hello, and act as if he weren't there at all. I know exactly why they do this, of course. It is not a display of bad manners, or even stress. It is simply that they block out what they do not want to know or do not like – those precious hours we spend together are so important to them that they pretend we are living a normal life.

I must tell you that however unnatural and difficult it is, you can get used to anything. The evidence is that I go on doing it, with the support of my family.

Of course, it is at a price. I cannot do what other fathers do, which is to enjoy life and see my daughters going through their adolescence. That is the highest price. I suppose the ultimate price will be death. Yet to me the real question is not whether I feel worried about being killed but what I feel for living this kind of life which doesn't allow me to be a normal father for my daughters. This is a question which sometimes makes me think I'm wasting my days, my weeks, months and years – and they will never come back. But for what? You will have seen, they have been decrying me of late.

Our present situation is that nobody can say who is really in danger or not. The economic-business core of the Mafia, which has been hit during these last months by confiscation of property and arrests, is busily reorganizing itself. It is unlikely that this complex organization which is desperately trying to guarantee its own future, will attempt anything immediately. But we simply cannot predict what will happen.

One might get killed just because the central control of the Mafia needs to put on a show of strength. Any one of us might get killed on a whim, or almost accidentally. That is the paradox of the situation, and I wouldn't like to sound cynical but sharing the risk, knowing that I am not the only one and that there are others – the judges, the police, the prosecutors – makes it more bearable.

What is certain, to me and my colleagues in similar positions, is that the risk remains undiminished. The Mafia is still very much alive. The old political alliances may have been swept away but the Mafia isn't done for; certainly not. They have obviously reassessed their political situation and even if Berlusconi and the Neo-Fascists did not wish for the support of the Mafia, they've got it anyway.

The moral issue is no longer the main problem of the government. I am not saying that Berlusconi would not have won, or had not had an effect on our people – he had, right across Italy. It was an incredible success, coming from where he did – which was nowhere. But I will say this, that in the last days of the political campaign you could feel fear on the streets of Palermo and when you can feel fear, you know that the Mafia is playing its part.

There are other ways of winning votes, too. Franco Zeffirelli's tactic in the well-known Mafia stronghold of Catania was to play down the present significance of the Mafia in that region. So he ends up becoming the best candidate for the mafiosi and that, these days, counts for an awful lot of votes. So Zeffirelli wins as a candidate for Berlusconi's party.

The new system of proportional representation combined with directly elected seats strengthens the power of those who can control votes – and that brings us back to the Mafia.

That is the root of our fight. The engagement of the anti-Mafia forces cannot be just against the armed hand of it – the Riina faction. We cannot defeat the Mafia simply by sending Toto Riina to prison. It is the connotation of power that we must attack, the financial and political brains behind the Mafia which sadly have not yet been brought out; there is a group handling all their funds and investments and doing their business. Toto Riina alone would not have the power he had; it is impossible.

We have registered good successes in arresting the military commanders but we haven't begun to tackle the financial and political brains. I myself, with the size of my vote in the last elections, was given a mandate to fight corruption in the area of public works. Only when we bring the inner circle to court will we be able to begin to approach the possibility of defeating the Mafia.

At the moment, these are crucial times for the Mafia and its financial brains. They have to plan a strategy to protect its estates, interests and investments and expand into virgin territory. This is why I believe it essential for the assets of criminals and corrupt politicians to be identified and confiscated. Even though numerous bosses have been arrested, many politicians and corrupt officers of the State, nationally and regionally, are still in place. It may seem strange to the outsider that in Milan we are investigating bribery and corruption under the clean hands policy and in Sicily we are investigating the Mafia as if they were two totally different subjects. They are linked, sometimes criminally with the Mafia, sometimes in the sense of the culture of corrupt practice. Our inquiries have shown it.

If the Mafia is a connotation of power it is also a connotation of economical, political, criminal and – also – cultural power. The cultural aspect is important, especially in Sicily. The Mafia has traditionally fed upon the exasperation of a community which feels isolated from the State. In fact, I would like to warn against portraying Sicily as a 'different' people or that the island is 'a separate continent'.

Our culture, our philosophy, our way of living, even our cuisine are often described as something special or different, especially by those from the north of Italy. We are in fact no different to other regional communities, such as the Lombards, or the Neapolitans. Continual overstressing of this 'difference' has caused Sicilian people to create a sort of defence mechanism, a shield to their identity which has become a real prison. Because of it, the honest Sicilian has felt himself compelled to defend the dishonest in the name of the Sicilian brotherhood.

Even as Orlando spoke, the Cosa Nostra were preparing a spectacular to show that they were still in business, and as strong as ever. There had been much publicity concerning the activities of the anti-Mafia group. As the second anniversary of Giovanni Falcone's murder approached, his sister Maria

Falcone, president of a new foundation which bears her brother's name, was organizing a series of meetings to draw attention to current feelings among those in the community who felt that there was still much more that could be done in the fight against the Mafia.

A number of leading government figures from Rome had already signified their intention to attend the Falcone Foundation events, including the heir to the job he had held at the time of his murder, Liliana Ferraro. But even as these meetings and events were about to take place, the Cosa Nostra chillingly organized its own remorseless response.

It bombed the homes of seventeen mayors in western Sicily. One by one, their country houses were attacked with the use of car bombs and other explosive devices. Though there was no loss of life, it was sufficient to engender public outrage. It was as if the Mafia were demonstrating to all those who were wavering, all those mafiosi who had considered joining the growing band of *pentiti*, all those public officials who had by the culture of consent fostered Mafia activity, that they were still a force to be reckoned with. The fear factor remains a crucial weapon.

There were many issues discussed at the conference during May 1994 in Palermo, not least the willingness of the new administration in Rome to return to the fight. Berlusconi's new Minister of the Interior, Roberto Maroni, flew to Palermo to meet the mayors who had been bombed and announced his government's resolve for a 'strong engagement against the Mafia' but added that 'Sicily must play its part'.

He promised revisions in the system of administration to give Sicily a stronger voice, but said that there would have to be a review of the 'law of the *pentiti*' which had created a major controversy as more and more Mafia soldiers became informers and received protection and an income from the State.

Following the courtroom outburst of Toto Riina when he shouted to reporters, 'The *pentiti* are being paid to speak. It is madness,' it was widely believed that Riina had instructed the Mafia to send in some 'plants' – informers whose evidence would subsequently be discredited. Maroni insisted: 'The *pentiti* law has to be revised in order to avoid dangerous manipulations.'

Giancarlo Caselli, chief prosecutor of Palermo, argued: 'The *pentiti* are irreplaceable in our fight. There are already many safeguards and the judges who interrogate the informers are well aware of the dangers, and act accordingly.'

It was no coincidence, said Caselli, that the the first major success against the Mafia came with the first two *pentiti*, Buscetta and Contorno, and that a 'phase of stagnation' had accompanied a dispute over polemics. As I write, the debate continues but a revision of the law of the *pentiti* seems a certainty.

Passions ran high on that day of memorial; there were many arguments, many conflicting views and even Liliana Ferraro herself came under attack at a public meeting in which she and others in civil administration were accused of failing to 'furnish the imposing skyscraper built by Falcone and Borsellino, of which only a skeleton is left'.

Meanwhile, on the day of the anniversary itself, thousands of people joined demonstrations and marches through the centre of Palermo, which ended outside the apartment building in Via Notarbartolo – named after the banker who was murdered at the beginning of the century – where Falcone had lived. Guards with machine guns still patrol outside, and there is a large tree at the entrance to which hundreds of messages have been pinned, applauding Falcone's courage and mourning his killing.

Maria Falcone, principal organizer of the events, was heartened by the strength of the demonstration. 'They told me Palermo had gone back to sleep. Today proves otherwise.'

Maria, a teacher for more than fifteen years, is now leading a subtle fight against the Mafia's presence in Sicilian communities, and indeed has put herself in danger. The two priests murdered 1993 were killed for exactly that reason; for trying to instil into community life a reaction against Mafia control. Maria told me:

> My life has changed completely. Giovanni had always been at risk, but his death in such horrific circumstances is an experience that marks you for ever. At that very moment I also realized that I could no longer go on teaching in the same way.
>
> Although I had always tried to get my students to think

about social problems and their role in society, to educate them to respect the State, its laws and its officers, since Giovanni's death, I realized I had to take a step forward. It was not enough to do it on my own, I had to speak out, and make more teachers do this kind of job, and involve parents, too, with the goal of trying to make young people see the Mafia for what it really is.

Many people have said that Sicily has been for so many years outside of the State, that our culture actually lacks true values. And so in an almost unconscious way our children learn, from their very first years, a sort of behavioural code which, by the time they grow up, has become diffidence and hostility towards the State and its officers. We see all those things come into play: indiscriminate acceptance of privileges, asking for favours as if they were rights, the conspiracy of silence, arrogance and overbearing actions. In most cases families share these values and transmit them to their children for generations. If school fails to break this chain at a very early stage, it has failed its task.

And this is why I now promote the crucial role of education in the fight against the Mafia in secondary schools. It might be too late, that the learning should begin earlier, but we cannot ignore any opportunity. Some primary schools, teaching children from the ages of five to eleven, already work very hard on these problems and the colourful, naive, yet moving mobilization of so many young pupils on the occasion of the Capaci massacre's anniversary is an evidence of it. For too long, however, it has been left to individual teachers to organize their own tutorials. It requires promoting and official support.

There is a growing awareness of our problem, but at the same time less protest; more proposals and fewer complaints. Probably our losses have not been in vain. People are really beginning to awaken from their secular sleep, the traditional Sicilian laziness is changing into engagement.

We can see positive action all around us. The meeting about the role of '*Collaboratori di giustizia*' [collaborators with justice] which I have organized as president of

Fondazione Falcone was intended to be, and it has really been, a qualified contribution to the great debate on the *pentiti* law which is taking place in Italy at the moment. It is very crucial and years of painful work is being threatened by by useless polemics. So I thought we had to give a signal.

The meeting in Palermo at the Palazzo dei Normanni, seat of the regional Parliament, has seen the participation of all the most qualified magistrates, lawyers, state officers, journalists and of the new Italian Minister of Justice. What was really comforting, in my opinion, was that everybody, from different political sides, agreed on one point: it is a good law. Perhaps it can be improved but we cannot do without it and it has allowed us to strike many serious blows against the Mafia. My brother didn't like the word *pentiti*, according to him it gave a negative connotation which didn't help the public to understand the new phenomenon, he preferred to use the words *Collaboratori di giustizia* which carried a more positive meaning . . . he was foreseeing the risks that eventually emerged, that people would turn against the law of the *pentiti*.

Now we have the debate, and we see the new government's intentions are to foster decentralization of power from Rome and strengthen the Sicilian constitution. I only hope that Roberto Maroni's intentions are also to strengthen the fight, not to make it less effective. Prejudicial polemics are dangerous . . . let's have solid action. That's what we really need.

Maria Falcone was cautiously optimistic that at last there was a grass-roots reaction stirring in Sicily to coincide with the latest pronouncements of government, to 'strengthen our resolve and our engagement of the Mafia'.

Others remain less sure.

CHAPTER TWENTY-TWO

'They Just Keep On Coming . . . and Now They Are Into Nuclear Arms'

In the months after Liliana Ferraro took over from Falcone, the anti-Mafia effort had made considerable strides on several fronts. Her own department had proved to be an effective liaison unit, linking State offices with a much broader-based front-line attack being waged by the magistrates, the judges and the various forces of the Italian security services and police. She insists modestly that she was only a very small cog in what has developed into the most efficient anti-Mafia machine Italy has ever known.

Like Ferraro herself, the State had pursued the policies and tactics Falcone had set in motion and which burgeoned into activity largely after his death. New laws that had teeth and sectors within the police and carabinieri working exclusively on organized crime finally achieved a pooling of the investigative effort which at one stage looked as if it might be abandoned, but was now making great strides, cutting deep into the Mafia heartlands.

Since its formation in January 1992 the DIA, the Italian Anti-Mafia Investigation Department, had achieved a string of spectacular successes in cracking a number of top Mafia gangs, rounding up top Mafia bosses and making serious inroads into Mafia cash and assets. Up to October 1994, the

DIA had conducted 65 specific gang-busting operations and served 2,413 arrest warrants across Italy.

Another tough unit known as the ROS, the Special Operations Department of the carabinieri, which came into being at the beginning of 1991, had almost 900 staff operating in Anti-Mafia district offices spread across the country. Though it had scored successes in combating various kinds of criminal activity, including kidnapping and extortion, its activities in the drugs field hit the Mafia hard and for the first time, it began infiltrating the crime groups with undercover agents. Tons of cocaine were seized and many gang leaders caught. One group, arrested in 1993, consisted of ninety-five people, eventually charged with a multitude of crimes, including forty murders.

Then came the Central Cooperative Department of the State police, which scored a number of major hits on local Mafia leaders. All these efforts, unprecedented in Italian history, were coordinated with the DNA, the last of the special anti-Mafia units. The DNA was based upon the original concept of the Sicilian magistrates' pool and was set up in January 1992, with nineteen public prosecutors from across the country operating effectively as a team, thus going some way to neutralizing that well-established practice of killing the investigating judge.

Ferrarro remained, however, under no illusion that the Mafia was on the run. Its operations were so diverse and widespread that the arrests and sequestering of assets, though damaging, had in reality hardly touched Italy's river of crime. By the middle of 1994, the Italian Mafia as a whole was estimated to have an annual turnover of $70 billion, almost double its take even at the height of the eighties drugs boom.

The Italian law officers were beginning to see rewards from the process set in motion by the likes of Dalla Chiesa, Chinnici, Falcone and Borsellino, all of which came to a head under the regime of Ferraro. And at last, there were encouraging signs that the people of Italy, and especially the Sicilians, were not only supporting the anti-Mafia crusade but demanding to be told the truth about the past misdemeanours of important people.

Working days had been long and hectic. Staff in the ministry knew Ferraro to be a demanding but caring chief. She was, by and large, ensconced in her security enclave in the Ministry of Justice building but had increasingly been giving her *scorta*, who have become close and trusted friends, palpitations by insisting on becoming more visible, escaping from the *vita blindata*, going to schools and public meetings to help stir the positive force of reaction among young people. In the ministry, she was nick-named the Volcano and apparently Ferraro in anger was someone to be reckoned with.

The security aspects of her life continued to dictate a restricted social calendar which, like that of Leoluca Orlando and the others who live in that enviroment of 24-hour-a-day protection, could not change. She could never make scheduled appearances in public. Occasionally, she would slip into the theatre or a restaurant only after the most stringent precautions had been completed. More often she was to be found late at night in her room on the Ministry's fourth floor, usually working but occasionally relaxing in her secure apartment, listening to *Carmen*. She had not had a weekend off for many months.

All of that, however, was about to change, drastically.

Not long after Ferraro appeared with some of Berlusconi's new ministers at the memorial events for Falcone in Palermo in May 1994, the rumblings of change under the new administration began to sweep through the corridors of State offices in Rome. The coalition that had enabled Berlusconi to form a government was a patchwork of several colours, drawing ministerial appointments from his own Forza Italia party, the Northern League and the Neo-Facists.

In the months after he came to power on a ticket of attacking the corruption so endemic in Italian society, the group of judges in Milan continued their own clean hands investigations with ever increasing, headline-hitting vigour and for a while, Antonio Di Pietro's televised trial held millions of Italian viewers riveted nightly. Among the many famous names in Italian business and political life whom the judges brought in for questioning was Berlusconi's own brother Paolo, who subsequently admitted paying bribes to secure a favourable tax assessment on a company within the Berlusconi media empire, for which he served a brief prison sentence. There were strong predictions that Prime

Minister Berlusconi himself might be invited to appear before the Milanese judges.

By the early summer of 1994, it seemed that Berlusconi was heading for a showdown with the judiciary and there was considerable media speculation that once again, and in spite of the new government's promise of a clean-up, the new gentlemen of the Palazzo were going to intervene, and attempt to find a constitutional solution to bring a halt to the investigations. In other words, it was feared that the government would revert to the policy of *sotto* intervention.

In the meantime, the new Ministers of Justice and the Interior were shuffling the pack among civil servants. It was to be expected, of course, that a change of government would affect several key positions in the powerful offices of state and among those who fell victim was Liliana Ferraro herself.

It was headlined as 'Maroni's Revolution' – a major reshuffle at the top by Interior Minister Roberto Maroni, in conjunction with the Justice Minister Alfredo Biondi. At the end of May, there was a change-around of personnel at the helm of Italy's fight against organized crime, which caused several surprises among the higher echelons of the security forces. Not least among the moves was that of Gianni De Gennaro, who had become the first head of the DIA in December 1991, a man who had been at the forefront of the attack since the days of the maxi-trials. De Gennaro became deputy head of the State police's Central Operations department. Next to go was Luciano Violante, head of the Anti-Mafia Commission. 'The heirs of Fascism have taken over,' he said bitterly.

As for Ferraro, the Mafia hadn't managed to get her – but politics had. She was out of a job after almost two decades in the forefront of activity at the Ministry of Justice. The Ministry told me that she had been relieved of her post in order to coordinate the planned transnational conference on organized crime; the event, it will be recalled that Ferraro began promoting following the death of Falcone.

The new Italian government viewed the conference as a major effort in the fight against global crime. It had also been enthusiastically taken up by the secretary general of the United Nations, Boutros Boutros-Ghali, and now Berlusconi himself strongly supported it.

Indeed, at this point Ferraro was at an advanced stage with arrangements for the multinational effort which had been extended considerably in its scope since she and the then Minister of Justice took the idea to the UN. It aimed for participation at ministerial level and was to be staged in Naples in November 1994. She was the co-ordinating organizer, along with another of Italy's renowned anti-Mafia crusaders, Francesco Di Maggio, a former magistrate who had become Italy's permanent representative to the UN's crime commission in Vienna.

Ferraro was summoned to the offices of her superiors and given the news that she was being replaced. When I spoke to her later, she was predictably calm about what had happened and if she was angry, she would not let it show. 'Look,' she said choosing her words with care, 'I am a civil servant, an employee of the State and I must accept whatever decisions are made by ministers.'

It was always denied that it was a political decision, or that the changes were in any way related to the clean hands investigation. However, one close to the hub of the wheel of government in Rome told me:

> You must consider that Ferraro had in previous months aligned herself publicly to the inquiries by the judges in Milan. She had given a newspaper interview in which she had commented that the judiciary was setting an example, that what was happening was an excellent example of democracy beginning to work properly after years of cynicism, not to mention disgust. I think it would be correct to say that because many consider the Milan people to be anti-Berlusconi, she too might have been tarred with the same brush, regardless of the rights or wrongs of such an assessment. I think she was viewed as being the wrong colour politically.

With some emotion, Ferraro quietly packed her things and moved out of the office in which she and Falcone had spent so many hours, to devote herself to the final arrangements for the UN conference, and all that it would entail. I contacted her successor, Dr Vittorio Mele, the former chief prosecutor for

Rome, and was invited to Rome to meet him and Berlusconi. We set an appointment for September and when I arrived, Berlusconi's government was in deep trouble. As I walked down Via Del Corso towards his seat of power, the Palazzo Chigi, there were riots. Truncheon-wielding police charged crowds of angry protesters, trade unionists and militants demonstrating at Italy's economic plight, unemployment and cuts in pension spending. On the Italian Stock Exchange, shares were plunging and so was the lira.

Berlusconi was also being accused of attempting to seek a political solution to the corruption scandals which had dominated the headlines for two-and-a-half years in his efforts to bring the whole business to a speedy conclusion by suggesting a form of amnesty for all those who confess their sins and repay any bribes they may have taken.

His Minister of Justice, Alfredo Biondi, threatened to resign following criticism against the administration by Judge Saverio Borelli, the chief prosecutor in Milan. In an interview with the *Corriere della Sera*, Judge Borelli had indicated that some of Berlusconi's business interests might be investigated. This in turn brought a sharp response from a government spokesman who accused the judges of 'seditious acts' designed to interrupt democratic life and which had nothing to do with the 'impartial administration of penal justice'. There was no doubt that the Berlusconi administration was being laid low by the seemingly never-ending scandals.

The troubles rumbled on. Fighting broke out in the Italian parliament as passions rose and Berlusconi's only consolation was that France, and to a lesser to degree Britain, was also dogged by what has become known as the Euro-sleaze factor.

There had already been some spectacular verdicts. More than 400 well-known figures in establishment circles had been given prison sentences for accepting bribes, among them the former Socialist Prime Minister Bettino Craxi who was one of Berlusconi's closest friends in government at the time the prime minister was building his media and television empire.

Craxi, and thirty-two other VIP defendants, were accused of complicity in the payment of bribes totalling $90 million by a major industrial company which were said to have been distributed among the main political parties. Craxi was given a four-year sentence in absentia. Shortly before the Milan judges ordered the surrender of his passport, he left for his luxury villa in Tunisia from where he despatched a sick note. He is still there as I write, maintaining his innocence. Like many of his colleagues in the same position, Craxi denies the charges and accuses the judges who were the catalyst in the Italian political revolution of political bias and publicity-seeking.

Amid this background of traumatic developments I returned to the Ministry of Justice, proceeded through the same security precautions, through the armed guard at the entrance, back into the lift to the fourth floor, accompanied by a security guard, and past the cameras monitoring arrivals and departures, through the computerized locking system that controls doors to the inner sanctum of the Director of Penal Affairs.

Falcone's furniture and his collection of ornamental porcelain ducks had been removed. New modern furniture had been installed for Dr Mele, one of Italy's most senior judges who, as chief prosecutor for Rome, had handled the initial investigations into the alleged Mafia connections of former Prime Minister Giulio Andreotti, who was by then facing momentous accusations from the *pentiti* of his alleged associations with the Mafia.

Dr Mele explained that he had succeeded Liliana Ferraro in July. Her days at the forefront of the attack on crime were over for the time being, he said, though her life remained one which was 'by necessity' controlled by security precautions against any possible attempt on her life. Gradually, it was hoped these would be scaled down as the threat decreased and Ferraro disengaged from the front line.

Dr Mele himself is a small, retiring man, quietly spoken, exceedingly polite though a trifle apprehensive of my questions in view of the political events going on all around. He has an impressive record which has included appointment to the highest legal positions in Italy, and was for five years a senior judge at the Supreme Court. He served on the Higher Council of Magistrates, an independent body which controls the nation's magistrates and judges and was, until his move to the Ministry of Justice, public prosecutor for Rome for two years.

In his first year in that role he investigated 507 people accused of corruption. But the investigations into alleged links between Andreotti and the Mafia took him to America where he personally re-interviewed the supergrass Tommaso Buscetta. He was particularly interested to discover if Buscetta had any information on the murder of the journalist Mino Pecorelli in 1978 – the man, it will be recalled, who predicted the assassination of Dalla Chiesa. Buscetta would allege that Pecorelli was murdered by the Mafia, as a favour for the Salvo cousins who knew that Andreotti wanted him out of the way. 'Under Italian law,' Mele insisted, 'these allegations have to be investigated. We know that many people wanted Pecorelli silenced.'

Andreotti denied any knowledge of such matters and insisted, as he always has, that these allegations were the fanciful invention of the *pentiti* and others who wished to damage his reputation. The Pecorelli case was taken over by another investigating magistrate who had other associated matters to deal with and, as I write, the investigations are proceeding. Meanwhile, the chief public prosecutor in Palermo, Giancarlo Caselli, was compiling his own dossier against Andreotti and in February, 1995, he laid 96 formal charges against Andreotti alleging he was associated with the Mafia. The indictments and pre-trial submissions of evidence from witnesses ran to some 90,000 pages and was presented to an investigation judge in March 1995. He concluded that Andreotti should stand trial, and the date was set for September 1995.

The most damaging of the allegations in the submissions to the court include evidence from two separate witnesses who claim that Andreotti held secret meetings with the Mafia boss Toto Riina, in the 1980s. One of the *pentito*, Valdesare DiMaggio, claimed that he was present in the room in an apartment house on the edge of Palermo when Andreotti and his political aide Salvo Lima came to the meeting with Riina. 'Andreotti greeted him with a kiss on both cheeks,' the *pentito* claimed.

'A ridiculous story,' Andreotti countered. The Judge in Palermo, however, decided he should stand trial and, if convicted, could go to prison. At the time of writing, he was 76.

* * *

Dr Mele does not reflect upon these matters with any great satisfaction because of the damage it causes to the reputation of Italy. He is also anxious to draw a distinction between the corruption trials and the Mafia. There were undoubtedly overlapping interests, and some which still dated back to Falcone's own investigations but unlike Leoluca Orlando and Umberto Santino, in Palermo, who saw them as rolled up into one major problem stemming from an inherent culture of criminality born out of political expediancy, the Ministry of Justice maintains they are separate issues. It is in many instances a very fine line that divides them.

Dr Mele himself has inherited all the elaborate security that goes with the job. Like most other judges of his calibre, it has been a fact of life he has long ago attuned to; today he is given the ultimate protection, largely away from his wife and two children. His lodgings are at the nearby police barracks and he spends much of his time inside the Ministry building.

Like his predecessors in this office it is a destiny to which he devotes most of living hours. 'I live apart from my family for most of the time. I was here until 10 p.m. last night,' he explained with the same resignation and devotion that Ferraro and others in these pages have shown. 'That is not unusual. It is not a pleasant life and obviously one must have commitment, dedication and, anyway, I feel I owe it to the friendship that existed between Falcone and myself. And, as Falcone himself said, he who is scared dies every day.'

He knew Falcone well, from the early 1970s when they were both climbing the career ladder. He said:

> I think it is a mistake to personalize the fight against the Mafia. Men like Falcone and Borsellino are irreplacable but I believe it should be regarded as a general fight, by all of us, and not by individuals. It was through Falcone's insistence that we have now established a national coordination of effort, much on the lines of the original anti-Mafia Pool, which now encompasses every major city and region across the country. We also have an international division which deals specifically with crimes in other countries and liaison with foreign law enforcement agencies. And of course it is not merely the Mafia we are

dealing with. The whole spectrum of organized crime falls within this facility.

Even though he adopts a lower profile, Dr Mele has put himself in the front of the attack. He told me that only a few days before our meeting he had returned from visiting the FBI headquarters in Washington to continue the contact which Falcone established and which had, so recently, resulted in a large round-up of drug dealers, as outlined above.

The Mafia remains, as ever, a major contributor to organized crime across the globe and continues its links with the American criminal families. We may have Riina and Greco in prison, but we are under no misapprehension about their power. We do not believe we have actually halted their contact with the outside world, or with the criminal groups of which they are leaders. Bernardo Provenzano and Leoluca Bargarella remain free, at this time, and are the most powerful of Riina's men. There are many others who have remained at liberty who are in touch with other bosses whom we have in prison. This is why we have introduced special measures in the top security prisons to try to limit contact. It has brought controversy and criticism that the people confined under these rules are suffering too harshly, but we believe it was a necessity. Mobile phones have been abolished and dangerous prisoners are being kept in special prisons which are geographically isolated. But we know very well that we cannot completely stop their contact with associates outside.'

In view of Falcone's experience of seeing some of his most prized prisoners set free, I asked if he was sure that Michele Greco – freed on appeal four times before his present sentence – and Toto Riina himself will remain in prison. He cannot be certain because it is no longer within his domain: 'It is something that competent magistrates will have to work out for themselves.'

Thus it remains a chilling possibility that the most dangerous of Italy's Mafia bosses will not spend the bulk of their remaining lives inside. Even so, Mele, like Ferraro, remained hopeful that the spirit of collaboration and the basic premise of the law of the *pentiti* would continue:

> The atmosphere of collaboration has improved dramatically. Once, we could never get anyone to give evidence before a jury. But now we have the *pentiti*, others are coming forward. The law is controversial, and we have to continue to update it to ensure that the credibility of the *pentiti* is sustained. Of course, I have sympathy with the communities of Palermo and other parts of Sicily. It is true that on occasions it is like a city under siege. We have to appreciate, from this office in Rome, the feelings of those people who on the one hand want to collaborate with the State but on the other are still scared by what might happen to them. Let us not forget that many who have fought back have been killed.

It is a fact accepted by Dr Mele and the law enforcement groups that even though some of the biggest bosses are imprisoned the Mafia's influence remains as daunting as ever in these communities, where the Mafia thrives and as a criminal entity continues to grow, and is spreading its activity into every possible area. 'These days, they have no isolated field of operations. They will grab hold of anything that makes money, whether it is drugs or legitimate commerce, regardless of geographic location. They move with the market. Lately we have been dealing with the eastern bloc countries where after the fall of the Berlin Wall and communism, a difficult economic situation developed which is ripe for exploitation by the Mafia.

The Italian Mafia's links with the so-called Russian Mafia were already well established in 1994, but as Umberto Santino suggested to me in Palermo, the Sicilians through their connections in northern Italy had made a particular bee-line towards arms dealings in the wake of the collapse of the Soviet Union, and there was evidence of a particular Mafia interest in the most lucrative of all commodities available in Russia and its one-time satellite nations: nuclear materials.

In the summer of 1994, fears were expressed at the United

Nations Security Council that substantial quantities were being traded illegally and finding a home in countries where a nuclear presence could present a serious threat to world order. I put that question to Dr Mele. He was reluctant to go too deeply into the investigative operation, which was continuing, but confirmed that it was an aspect on which his own office was collaborating with Russian authorities. Only a few days before, he had sent one of his own investigators to Moscow for an exchange of information and to set up procedures for future liaison.

By then, the Russian Mafia was coming close to equalling the Italian Mafia in its global influence. The opening up of central and eastern Europe to capitalism had thrown open the last major frontier to organized crime. Data emanating from Russian authorities and passed to the Italians suggested that there were no fewer than 5,700 criminal groups operating within the former Soviet bloc, and the number was expanding.

Most worry of all to the authorities is the proliferation of arms dealing. In May 1994, for example, the prospect of the Russian Mafia, in cooperation with Italian chieftains, acquiring parts of the old Soviet nuclear inventory, once confined to the pages of thriller writers, became a chillingly real prospect.

In the town of Iazhevsk, 600 miles from Moscow, security forces intercepted a shipment of 100 kilos of uranium which was to have been smuggled into Italian hands through the Baltics and Poland. The incident was one of many which confirmed to the Russian, German and Italian authorities that the suspected trade in nuclear materials was already well established. The prospect of the allied criminal groups obtained access to nuclear weapons remained a distinct possibility.

Meanwhile, Germany's Federal police with whom the Italians are in constant touch, had made a detailed analysis of the threat of nuclear material falling into criminal hands and supplied the results of their survey. In 1992, there were 59 known attempts to purchase nuclear material within German territory, 99 cases of illegal trade in nuclear material and 18 cases where nuclear material was actually discovered in the hands of criminals and confiscated. In 1993, the cases of trafficking in nuclear material in Germany rose to 241 and in the first half of 1994, there were signs that the figure would be exceeded again. In 1993, German police identified 545 suspects thought to be involved in nuclear trafficking and under observation.

Dr Mele confirmed to me that there was evidence that the Italian Mafia had well-established trading connections with the former Soviet Union, and that weapons-grade plutonium was included on their shopping list.

> The investigation is still proceeding as we talk. At the moment we cannot be certain as to the source and nature of the deals, or even whether Italy is being used merely as a staging post for sensitive weaponry coming out of the former Soviet bloc, just as were were not sure some years ago whether Italy was a staging post for heroin or whether it was being manufactured here. Of course, it proved to be the latter. So we have now established a close contact with the Russian authorities, at two levels – from my office with contact through the magistrature and through the police and intelligence services. We remain alert to all these possibilities.

Meanwhile, the Italian Mafia's traditional 'industries' of extortion, blackmail, gambling, prostitution, anything from which they can earn money, continue to flourish. To those have been added other modern lucrative criminal trades, such illegal immigration which had become a new form of slave-trading with a burgeoning demand for women and children for forced labour and outright sex slavery. The illicit trade in children has become a colossal racket, stealing and selling children for adoption, as has the trafficking in human organs.

Under each heading, there is terrifying story to be told that would fill several books of this size. Meanwhile, in the less well-policed areas of international finance, incalcuable amounts of money are being laundered and cleaned up while the world's banks and global finance experts now speak of trillions of crime dollars floating through the system with remarkable ease and on top of the traditional Mafia money-laundering operations came those of the Russian criminals. Interior ministry officials estimated that 35 per cent of Russian

2,300 commercial banks had been infiltrated by criminal groups in 1994.

The links between the Russians and the Italian Mafia groups were quickly established, right down to notoriously ruthless Mafia families of remote 'Ndrangheta clans from Calabria in the deep south. In May 1993, it was discovered that an obscure finance company controlled by a 'Ndrangheta family was involved in buying and selling – laundering – billions of Russinan roubles and hundreds of millions of US dollars, despite having a minimal registered company capital. The Milan police discovered that 'Ndrangheta cells were being set up throughout Eastern Europe, and controlled from those mountainous regions of southern Italy, famous for its kidnappers. Soon, the Sicilian Cosa Nostra moved in behind them.

In the fight back, there are conferences and inter-country liaison groups, there are top-line police and intelligence organizations amassing their forces, there are dedicated men and women who put themselves at the highest risk, there are at local level in Sicily priests and school teachers trying to dismantle the cultural phenomenon. As yet, no one has a real answer. They keep on trying, and they keep on getting killed in the effort.

'I'm afraid it is true,' says Dr Mele, 'that the Mafia has incredible regenerative powers. It just goes on and on.' And so does the fight against them.

But although there is Mafia activity on a wide number of fronts, it is in the drugs operations that the Italian law enforcers believe that a new explosion is already underway, with the Italian Mafia in league with crime groups throughout Europe and the east, targeting what they see as a massive new trading area. It dawned upon them towards the end of the 1980s that, in comparison with the US, Europe was virgin territory for cocaine, and cheaper heroin.

Initially, cocaine from South America was shipped into Europe through Spanish ports, and the cities of Seville and Cadiz. While these remain major entry ports, the importation of cocaine, through the various criminal alliances, have simply exploded across Europe. The point of entry today can be anywhere; Finland or St Petersburg, the Netherlands or Poland and, in the east, through Turkey, Iran and the war-torn Balkans. Gangsters around the world have latched on to the booming

European market and the ease with which couriers may now pass through its borders.

With this prospect in sight, the Italian Mafia called its own international conference – much on the lines of the one Lucky Luciano called at a hotel in Palermo back in the 1950s. The meeting, staged in neutral territory in North Africa, was to establish elaborate agreements, principally between the Colombian Cali cartel and the Sicilian Mafia for wholesaling cocaine and laundering the proceeds. The agreements mirrored the franchising that the Sicilians set up with American distributors in the 1970s and the result is already apparent.

Cocaine and its associated products will be hitting the streets across the whole of Europe in such quantities that it will become a drugs epidemic. Of that there is no doubt. High targets for the Italians' own distribution network are Germany, France, Britain, the low countries and Scandinavia – the richest nations, in fact. The crime networks in the former Soviet bloc will buy in bulk for their own countries.

All routes, couriers, distribution and money laundering have been carefully planned by the Italians. Every arm of the Mafia is involved, the 'Ndrangheta, the Camorra but principally, as ever, the Cosa Nostra. The cocaine is being released in a controlled manner to get up the prices. From the law enforcement command centre in Rome, observing and tracking events, warnings are being sent out to comrade EC nations that the explosion is already under way, evidenced by a new round of drugs wars.

The killings in Sicily and elsewhere on the Italian mainland have started up again: three murders in Corleone on the very day these words are being written. These warnings from the Italian authorities have been treated with a certain ambivalence, especially in Britain where they are firing Customs officers and decreasing manning levels at key ports of entry. Dr Mele, meanwhile, goes on his travels, somewhat shamefaced that it is his countrymen who remain the stars of the global criminal network.

Another era is under way, and I left Dr Mele to continue his war. 'Where will I figure in your book?' he asked as I got up to leave.

'You are in the last chapter,' I replied.

'I hope it will not be that, for me, literally,' he laughs, and turns back into his eyrie, Falcone's old room, to resume the fight.

Epilogue

In Naples in November 1994 from all around the world people gathered for the United Nations World Transnational Conference on Organized Crime, with 187 countries sending representatives. Liliana Ferraro invited me to attend. The media arrived in force and the statisticians and ministry spokesman produced miles of figures, graphs and graphics to demonstrate the enormity of the challenge they are facing.

For Ferraro it was the realization of the dream and the project she inherited from Falcone and which, along with her fellow co-ordinator Judge Francesco Di Maggio, finally focused the minds of government leaders world-wide on the problems that Italy has been battling with like no other nation on earth for a century or more.

UN Secretary General Boutros Boutros-Ghali, taking time out from pressing international problems such as Bosnia, decided the conference was so important that he would preside over the opening himself, and the Italian Prime Minister Silvio Berlusconi chaired the whole three days.

Naples was chosen as the venue after it successfully hosted the G7 summit of world leaders in July 1993 and the massive clean-up of this desperate city was still evident. The former jewel of the Campania coast, this city was a fitting place for such a conference. It is among the worst cities in Italy for crime, worse than Palermo, and it also reflects the social problems confronting some of Italy's most deprived areas, one of the traditional key reasons why communities en bloc turn to the

Mafia. Apart from being the nerve-centre of the Camorra it has a shocking record of street crime.

Naples has an air of menace which seems strongest in the afternoons, and a young woman journalist from a local newspaper who sat next to me during the opening stages of the conference said she personally would not venture out into the streets alone after 2 p.m. But that is the point, said Ferraro, of choosing Naples. 'We are demonstrating the determination of the south of Italy to free itself from this evil curse.'

In doing so, the security forces drafted in 11,000 extra men: 8,000 police and 3,000 plain-clothes operatives, swarming the city and throwing a veritable ring of steel around the magnificent Royal Palace, built in the seventeenth century by the Spanish viceroys and which became the residence of the Bourbon kings. At the opening session, Boutros-Ghali and Berlusconi hosted a joint press conference and stressed the importance of this global initiative against crime. But soon it became evident that the interest of the questioners was not merely directed at the subject matter but at personalities, and the participation of political leaders of the host country in past events.

Berlusconi himself suddenly faced hostile probing and one close to me asked, 'Do you not think, Prime Minister, that in addition to the struggle against the illegal Mafias, there must also be a fight against the legal ones, the powerful people with institutional responsibilities who are guilty of collusion and cover-up?'

Berlusconi's face went taut. 'This conference will deal with all those who work against the very nature of democracy. The Mafia corrupts, the Mafia is able to insinuate itself into the institutions. It is an extremely grave phenomenon that exists not only in Italy but elsewhere. Our determination is to fight all such entities . . . The fact that I, the Prime Minister, have decided to remain in Naples for the three days demonstrates the importance which the Italian government attaches to this conference.'

Very soon, however, the Prime Minister was wishing he was somewhere else. The Milanese magistrates, in their wisdom, decided to make a dramatic announcement to coincide with the Naples meeting – that they wished to interview Berlusconi personally about allegations of bribery against him, alleging he may have been involved with his brother Paolo in illegal payments prior to his becoming Prime Minister. The conference exploded into controversy.

Berlusconi, looking drawn and hunched, arrived once again to meet the press and deny such implications, and rejected calls by his political enemies to resign immediately. High drama was reached as the Milan judges reacted angrily to suggestions that they were intent on bringing his government down, that theirs was a political and not a judicial intervention. Their only pursuit, they said, was that of seeking the truth.

Ferraro's conference was temporarily hijacked by the Milanese judges in their war on the establishment, and the eruptions which began there in the shadow of Vesuvius would go on exploding like mini-volcanos for many months.

I sat a few feet from Berlusconi as he attempted to brush aside the allegations emerging from Milan and re-focus the attention of the media to the importance of the subject matter of the Naples conference. He was a man under severe pressure and the writing was, on that day, being scrawled upon the wall. His days as Prime Minister were over, at least for the time being. He clung to office for a further nine weeks. Just before Christmas, the crisis deepened when the unpredictable leader of the separatist Northern League dropped out of the heterogeneous three-party coalition that had supported Berlusconi since his election in March, and in the process gave the prime minister a lambasting for alleged involvement in corruption and misuse of his media empire, although the true reason appeared to be the declining public support for Berlusconi's Forza Italia party.

That left Berlusconi without a majority in Parliament and he was unable to continue in office. President Oscar Luigi Scalfaro refused Berlusconi's demands for an immediate general election and appointed a new ministerial hierarchy to form the 54th administration of Italy since the war. The schemers and the plotters were out in force and the reconstructed Christian Democrats began moving back towards the hub of power to await a general election expected later in 1995.

And so, with Berlusconi's political miracle descending into farce after just nine months, Andreotti facing a multitude of accusations, and political and financial crises once again dominating public debate, the Mafia found itself presented with fertile ground for its own recuperation – just as Leoluca Orlando, Umberto Santino and Franco Nicastro predicted in their interviews recorded in earlier chapters.

Mafia boss Toto Riina was visibly smirking, arrogant and truculent (see last picture page) when he was hauled back before the courts in March 1995 – in the same week Andreotti was committed for trial. Riina, already serving several life sentences, faced a whole set of new charges against him, relating to murder and other crimes dating back to the 1980s. Two days before there had been a new outbreak of killings, a double murder in Corleone and another in Palermo. But Riina remains the boss, controlling a massive empire, expanding not declining, under the management of his aides on the outside. The need for international co-operation becomes increasingly vital.

The Naples conference was a step towards what Ferraro believes will ultimately be necessary, a centralised, cross-border fighting force – certainly in Europe and perhaps, eventually, under an international agency.

The conference was an undoubted success with positive decisions and recommendations being adopted. I chatted with Ferraro, who looked tired and on the point of exhaustion. She was still surrounded by her protective cordon. The fear of the security men that the Mafia may yet make an attempt on her life was no less prevalent than it had been before she stepped down from the directorate of Penal Affairs.

She talked, as ever, with commitment and dedication. Her mobile telephone rang intermittently and in between times, she chain-smoked the little cigars. She said:

> I think it has been one more very fitting memorial to Falcone. And it has become very evident that international cooperation, and perhaps ultimately an international force, is badly needed. It has been a great success. We have at last managed to bring government leaders together for the single purpose of discussing organized crime, uncomplicated by other issues – a specific focus on what is happening in the regions of global criminal activity.

It has presented us with the opportunity of discussing this issue not simply on the basis of policing the international effort, but also to talk about its effects on humanity, and on democracy itself because the criminal groups are now involved at a far higher level of activity than they were, say, five years ago, and they represent a threat to stablity of many nations, especially in the Third World.

We have achieved for the first time a very high level of participation, shown by the fact that we had among our delegates three heads of state, four prime ministers, five deputy prime ministers and more than sixty government ministers. It is the first time we have been able to speak clearly and specifically about the various characteristics of organized crime. We invited all the member states to take account of these characteristics when they make their individual laws and political decisions on matters of organized crime. So our objectives were as much about influencing the politics and socio-economic decision-making as about the actual police effort, and this was the original concept that Falcone had in mind.

'The fight must not begin and end with the police effort and the magistrates. The powers of the law enforcement agencies around the world must come down from the highest political levels. Only then can we begin to make more positive inroads into this particular war; to have legislation that is more closely focused on the problem. We have seen in Italy, to some considerable degree, what can be done when the politicians of the nation, backed up by a strong brigade of public servants, and driven by public opinion, actually take stringent measures which enable the law to take full effect.

There's no denying that we still have massive problems with the Mafia in Italy. But at last, the problem is no longer denied. It is being tackled. We have reached another milestone, and we must build again from there.

For Ferraro herself, the conference marked the end of a long journey, at least for the time being, but who knows where her destiny will lead her?

> The future is in the hands of God. I am a civil servant so I work for the State and my country. My personal attitude is that I will give all my efforts now to the Falcone Foundation and perhaps find time for some relaxation, though the extent of it will remain in the hands of the security people. The few of us who remain will work for and with Maria Falcone to defend the results of her brother's work and to foster his memory. I am moving to the Council of State to join a small group of judges charged with responsibility for the administrative position of the government.
>
> So perhaps, with my work for the Falcone Foundation, the Mafia will now become a hobby . . .

Some hobby. Outside, on the streets of Naples, silk-suited, black-spectacled mafiosi with bodyguards trailing a few paces behind paraded openly on the streets on the perimeter of the protected Royal Palace in a gesture aimed at taunting their enemies conferring inside the building. To those who fight them, there is always danger.

I shook hands with Ferraro as she prepared to leave for Rome, back once more to those protected environs. In the corridors of the palace, her *scorta* were waiting to accompany her down to her car, its engine running, ready to whisk her away at high speed, siren blaring. She can never know what might be around the next corner . . .

Sources and Select Bibliography

Prime Minister Silvio Berlusconi, *Report to the Parliamentary Committee for Inquiry in the Mafia,* Rome, October 21, 1994. And Press conferences attended by author, Naples, November 1996; Rome, December, 1994, and January, 1995.

Roberto Maroni, Minister of the Interior, statement and interviews, October/November, 1994.

Alfredo Biondi, Minister of Justice, *Report to the United Nations World Ministerial Conference,* November, 1994.

Giancarlo Caselli, Public Prosecutor, Palermo, *Statement on Use of Pentiti in the Fight against Organised Crime,* 1994.

Tiziana Parenti, President of the Parliamentary Committee for Inquiry into the Mafia, statement, 1994; Pino Arlacchi, Vice President of the Committee, interview, August, 1994.

Piero Arrighi and Luciano Galassi, *An Account of the Battle: Summary of Recent Successes of Italian Anti-Mafia forces,* 1990-94.

Luigi Federici, Commander in Chief of the Carabinieri, Summary of Operations to September, 1994.

Fernando Masone, Chief of Police, *Following Their Lead,* summary of intent, October, 1994.

By courtesy of the Italian Ministry of the Interior, publication entitled *Organised Crime in Italy*, November, 1994, sectioned as follows: Evolution of Crime Families; Law Enforcement Strategy; The System to Fight Organised Crime.

Ministry of Justice, *Report Italy, 1994: Definition and Characteristics of the Mafia Phenomenon.*

United Nations Commission special report: *Organised Crime In the Global Village*, 1994.

ANSA Dossier, *Organised Crime*, 1994, presented to the UN Conference at Naples, November 1994.

AGI, (Italian Journalist Agency), *CONTRO: Against Drug Trafficking, Smuggling, Secret Arms Dealing, Money Laundering, Illegal Immigration, etc*, Naples, 1994.

World Ministerial Conference on Organised Crime, Naples, 1994, Transcripts of speeches, debates and press releases.

Institute of Political Studies, Palermo, Sicily, Report: *Mafia in Politics*, 1992.

Umberto Santino, Palermo: *The Financial Mafia*, 1988. And, *Crime in Italy and Bank Counters*, Marinoli, Censis, 1985.

Justin Vitiello, *The New World Order*, Temple University, Philadelphia, 1992.

Financial Charts, DEA/FBI prepared for US Southern District, Manhattan, Pizza Connection Trial, 1985: USA v Michele Sindona, hearings (1978–79). And Gli Atti d'Accusa Giudici di Milano, Sindona, Italy, Editori R, 1986.

Umberto Santino, *The Sicilian Mafia and the Heroin Traffic*, for Pennsylvania State University, June 1, 1991.

Reports and conclusions, various, Judge Francesco Saverio Borelli, prosecutor heading financial and corruptions investigations, Milan, 1992–94.

Italian Parliamentary Anti-Mafia Commission, Report, 1976.

US Senate Permanent Sub-Committee on Investigations: *Organised Crime and Illicit Traffic in Narcotics*, hearings 1963, 1964 and final report 1965.

Derrière La Drogue, Umberto Santino and Giovanni La Fiura, Edizioni Gruppo Abele, September, 1993.

The Sicilian Connection: South-west Asian Heroin en route to the United States, report by Senator Joseph R Biden to US Senate Committee on Foreign Relations, 1980.

A Decade of Organised Crime, Pennsylvania Crime Commission, 1980.

Organised Crime Today, President's Commission, hearings, 1984–1986.

La Cosa Nostra In Canada, FBI Criminal Investigations Division, report, Washington, March, 1985.

Court documents and indictments in the trial of Gaetano Badalamenti, and others, 1984–85. Testimony of Tommaso Buscetta and Salvatore Contorno, to hearings in Palermo, 1984–86. And to Pizza Connection Trials, 1984.

Transcripts of evidence of both hearings, together with associated trials in Palermo and the US 1979–1988. Published testimony of major pentiti, Palermo, 1988–1994.

EEC Directives on vigilance and co-ordination of banking entities re money laundering: No. 73, June, 1973; No. 78, December, 1977; No. 349, June, 1983, and June, 1984.

USA: Senate Committee on Governmental Affairs: *Crime and Secrecy, Offshore Banks and Companies,* 1983.

US House of Representatives Foreign Affairs Committee: Task Force, 1984.

President's Commission on Organised Crime, Interim report: *The Cash Connection: Organised Crime, Financial Institutions and Money Laundering,* 1984.

CIA Memorandum, general issue, confidential, re: international financial services, complicity with money laundering activities, 1985.

And a second Re: Bahamas, 1985.

And a particular mention to the courageous editors and journalists of the *Giornale di Sicilia* whose daily reports provided a magnificent source on Mafia activity, and whose archives provide a wealth of historic material, much of it unpublished anywhere else in the world.

Books and Reports:

Alexander, Shana, *The Pizza Connection*, Weidenfeld and Nicolson, New York, 1988.

Arlacchi, Pino, *La Mafia Imprenditrice*, Societe Edittrice il Mulino, Bologna, 1983.

Arlacchi, Pino and Dalla Chiesa, Nando, *La Palude e la città* Arnoldo Mondadori, Milan, 1987.

Blumenthal, Ralph, *Last Days of the Sicilians*, Bloomsbury, London, 1989.

Cook, Fred J, *Mafia*, Coronet, London, 1973.

Dalla Chiesa, Nando, *Delitto Imperfetto*, Arnoldo Mondadori, Milan, 1984.

Chinnici, Giorgio, and Santino, Umberto, *La Violenza Programmata, Omicidi e guerre di mafia a Palermo dagli anni '60 ad oggi*, F. Angeli, Milan, 1989.

Falcone, Giovanni, with Padovani, Marcelle, *Men of Honour, The Truth about the Mafia*, Fourth Estate, London, 1992.

Lewis, Norman, *The Honoured Society*, Collins, London, 1964.

Madeo, Liliana, *Donne di Mafia*, Arnoldo Mondadori, Milan, 1990.

Nichols, Peter, *Italia, Italia*, Macmillan, London, 1973.

Leoluca, Fotia and Rocuzzo, *Leoluca Orlando*, Arnoldo Mondadori, Milan, 1990.

Puglisi, Anna, *Sole Contro la Mafia*, La Luna, Palermo, 1990.

Santino, Umberto, and La Fiura, Giovanni, *L'Impresa Mafiosa: Dall'Italia agli Stati Uniti*, F. Angeli, Milan, 1990.

Servadio, Gaia, *Mafioso, A History of the Mafia from Its Origins to the Present Day*, Secker and Warburg, London, 1976.

Shawcross, Tim and Young, Martin, *Men of Honour*, Collins, London, 1987.

Sterling, Claire, *The Mafia*, Hamish Hamilton, London, 1990.

Talese, Gay, *Honor Thy Father*, World Publishing, New York, 1987.

Tesera, Vincent, with Renner, Thomas C., *My Life in the Mafia*, Hart-Davis MacGibbon, London, 1983.

Yallop, David, *In God's Name*, Corgi, London, 1985.

Photographs:

From author's collection and taken for this book; others from: ANSA, Reuters and Popperfoto.

Index